Dickinson and the Boundaries
of Feminist Theory

Dickinson and the Boundaries
of Feminist Theory

MARY LOEFFELHOLZ

UNIVERSITY OF ILLINOIS PRESS
Urbana and Chicago

This book is printed on acid-free paper.

Library of Congress Cataloging-in-Publication Data

Loeffelholz, Mary, 1958-
    Dickinson and the boundaries of feminist theory / Mary
Loeffelholz.
        p.   cm.
    Includes bibliographical references.
    ISBN 0-252-01789-7 (cloth : alk. paper). — ISBN 0-252-06175-6 (paper :
alk. paper)
    1. Dickinson, Emily, 1830–1886—Criticism and interpretation.
2. Feminism and literature—United States—History—19th century.
I. Title.
PS1541.Z5L596   1991
811'.4—dc20   90-48721
                                                            CIP

Contents

Acknowledgments

Many friends and colleagues have generously given time to this project. I would like to thank Harriet Chessman, Joan Dayan, Margaret Ferguson, Elizabeth Gregory, Tamar Heller, Anne Herrmann, Harry Segal, and Byran Wolf for talking with me about Dickinson and feminist theory and for responding to my work. Susan Bianconi and Donna Heiland's tireless friendship and good advice have been sustaining through all the years of the book's writing. Diana Hume George read the entire manuscript with sympathetic alertness and saved me many an error or omission. Margaret Homans generously supported the project from its inception. Zohreh Sullivan, Robert Parker, Cary Nelson, Paula Treichler, and many other colleagues at the University of Illinois did much to make a newly fledged assistant professor's life easier in many ways, and more challenging in others; their kindness, intellectual community, and professional acumen made this work seem a manageable undertaking. I am also grateful to audiences at Yale and the University of Illinois for hearing out early versions of some of these arguments, and I would like to thank my colleagues at Northeastern University who have made me welcome. One of the pleasures of writing about Dickinson is that it has so often reminded me of Albert J. and Barbara Charlesworth Gelpi, with whom I first learned to read Dickinson seriously and from whose example I began to understand the life of teaching and writing.

I am very happy to have this chance to thank my parents, whose support for my work and continuing interest in it have made this book possible. Stephanie Hodal lived with the final stages of its composition; I thank her for her patience, and for what Dickinson once wrote of as "the sweet Adjacency that Exalts by humbling."

Dickinson and the Boundaries
of Feminist Theory

Introduction

At least two new approaches of major importance have entered criticism of Dickinson's poetry since the explosion of literary theory after the New Criticism: feminism and deconstruction. These two approaches have recently made productive alliances in Dickinson studies, beginning with Margaret Homans's *Women Writers and Poetic Identity* in 1981 and extending through several more recent books. Just to one side of the meeting between feminism and deconstruction, Joanne Feit Diehl's 1981 *Dickinson and the Romantic Imagination* read Dickinson's poetry through an original revision of Harold Bloom's notoriously Oedipal paradigm of male poetic careers. Like Homans, Feit Diehl put the problem of women's writing in terms of both the achievement and the questioning of a conventionalized, traditionally masculine identity or persona of authority. Like Homans, Feit Diehl found that Dickinson's negotiation of that problem issued in a kind of radical linguistic skepticism. For these feminist critics and others following their work, Dickinson's often-noted obliquities of language have assumed a newly gendered meaning in the context of feminist and deconstructive questions: her words are now credited with deconstructing binary gender oppositions and rewriting the conventionally gendered relationship between the poet and *his* muse, the poet and *his* literary tradition.[1]

A third event in post–New Critical Dickinson criticism is trying to happen: some critics representing the variously new historicisms and certain kinds of marxist and feminist thought are making an effort to bring their questions and methods to our understanding of a lyric poet who is notoriously difficult to attach to her social moment save, perhaps, through the category of gender. One approach to this problem is empirical: Barton Levi St. Armand's *Emily Dickinson and Her*

Culture: The Soul's Society assembles an exuberant variety of cultural materials—women's scrapbooks, journals, folk art, landscape paintings, funerary iconography—in an effort, as he puts it, to compile "not simply a cultural biography but a biography of American Victorian culture." Disavowing any particular theoretical agenda, St. Armand claims he comes "to the problem of the interaction between text and context with no set methodology, no ready-made rhetoric, and no monolithic ideological axe to grind." He aims at a reconstruction of contexts, at thick description rather than deconstruction: "modern scholarship needs a holistic approach to literary texts as much as modern medicine needs a holistic approach to the human body."[2]

The objections that may be raised against such an empiricism and its disavowals of theory are, of course, legion. Among other things, St. Armand's "holistic" or "organic" model of literary texts tacitly rules out systematic discussion, including feminist discussion, of how literary texts intersect with systems of literary and social power. St. Armand's analogies between text and human body, between cultural studies and individual biography, tend to wish wholeness upon divided and conflictual cultural systems. By an ironic reversal (about which the deconstruction St. Armand dismisses would find everything to say), critics who do not find organic *wholeness* in literary texts or their cultural contexts stand implicitly accused of bearing *monolithic* ideologies; critics who bring to their work a suspicion of the timeworn "organic" metaphor for texts and contexts stand implicitly accused of brandishing "ready-made rhetoric."

At the other end of the historicist spectrum from St. Armand's empiricism falls what Jonathan Arac calls " 'thin' or 'philosophical' history."[3] Often indebted to European marxisms and hermeneutics, "thin history" is by nature systematic (in the sense St. Armand damns); it analyzes cultural conflict and contradiction with conceptual building blocks on the scale of Enlightenment and Postmodernity. The most ambitious and self-searching attempt to bring something of this "thin history" to Dickinson studies, while rigorously questioning its assumptions, is Arac's essay "Walter Benjamin and Materialist Historiography," which concludes with an extended comparison of Baudelaire's and Dickinson's poetry. Guided in part by Benjamin's materialist anatomy of the relationship between Baudelaire's poetry and the experience of nineteenth-century urban capitalism, Arac finds imagistic and formal grounds on which to connect Baudelaire's "Spleen" poems with Dickinson's poetry of the " 'bandaged moments' of the soul."[4]

The problem for a materialist literary history, however, lies precisely in the excitement of this comparison. As Arac so frankly puts it: "I consider it embarrassing for the specificity of Benjamin's claims and damaging to their attractive materiality that it seems possible to transfer his insights about Baudelaire quite directly to the poetry of Emily Dickinson. For she lacked wholly the urban experience so fundamental to Benjamin's argument about Baudelaire" (199). Looking beyond the national boundaries that form the horizon of St. Armand's "biography" of a culture, Arac finds similarities between the two poets that do not fit readily into either the traditional categories of literary nationalism and period or the usual categories of materialist historiography. If we are to salvage the possibility of a "materialist historiography" from this comparison, Arac argues, it may be necessary to understand history in far more abstract, far "thinner" terms—yet without falling back upon a wholly unmaterialist history of ideas. Such "abstraction does not require that we abandon history for philosophy, but it changes the kind of history we practice" (210). Arac's conclusion suggestively coincides with the words of Helen McNeil, who reads Dickinson through feminism and deconstruction: reading Dickinson, she points out, "changes literary theory. To think about how Dickinson wrote is to experience gaps and silences in the existing models." [5]

My project in this book draws heavily on the conjunction of feminism and deconstruction, and if at some points it looks toward the new historicisms, it does so on the model of Arac's "thin history" rather than "thick description." The contexts through which I read Dickinson's poetry here are primarily literary and theoretical, intertextual rather than historical. Literary tradition and its conflicts to some degree thus stand in for larger cultural conflicts, [6] although I have also (along with other feminist critics interested in literary history) tried to insist that literary struggles over power are not, in themselves, ahistorical but part of larger historical struggles over access to power. In part, this project is an answer to the conclusion of Feit Diehl's *Dickinson and the Romantic Imagination,* which asks us to rethink Dickinson's work in the context of other women's writing, in the context of "a newly emerging tradition of women poets." I am indeed concerned to address Dickinson's fundamental contributions to our very idea of a "women's literary tradition," but I share Feit Diehl's sense that this tradition cannot be understood in isolation from male-dominated literary tradition. Tradition is a "compound frame" (to borrow a phrase from Dickinson), structured by differences as well as putative identities. My own methods thus favor theoretically dense close readings of texts and intertexts rather than a composite, "holistic" biography of a person/culture (to recall St. Armand's metaphor). I am interested in the production of identities out of differences—in the close linguistic texture of all such differential productions.

I therefore think it important to bring systematic theoretical ideas into contact with Dickinson's poetry for many reasons, but not least because Dickinson herself was in some respects a systematic writer—in the sense of an abstracting, allegorizing, and linguistically self-conscious writer. Granted, the systems of twentieth-century literary theory are presumably not identical with the patterns of Dickinson's own thoughts. But they need not be identical to pose important questions about, and to, Dickinson's writing; indeed, the notion of identity itself, in this context, begs compelling theoretical questions. The inevitable historical distances involved in reading theoretically, as Jerome McGann reminds us, can have their own value, provided we are self-conscious about them.[7] And deconstruction, along with psychoanalysis, would argue that Dickinson's thoughts were not identical to themselves: all reading and all thinking, not only theoretically self-conscious reading and thinking, score the traces of *différance.*

One of my aims in this book is to extend the conjunction of deconstruction and feminism in Dickinson studies to include varieties of psychoanalytic theory, particularly Lacanian psychoanalytic theory, that take language seriously into account. Until fairly recently, feminist critics of Dickinson's poetry have tended, for obvious reasons, to distrust psychoanalytic approaches. Sympathetic and nuanced in its own Freudian terms, John Cody's psychobiography of 1971, *After Great Pain: The Inner Life of Emily Dickinson,* nevertheless took for granted a closed psychic economy in which art and language are less-than-abundant recompense for psychic trauma and loss.[8] In Freudian theory, of course, this assumption would be true of men's language as much as women's. In practice, Freudian critics have tended to relate men's language to the generalized, culturally normative masculine trauma of castration, while women's language is seen rather as the result of specific, contingent individual suffering—as the artistic alternative to an individualized neurosis. Avoiding this particular Freudian trap, Albert J. Gelpi's Jungian approach in *The Tenth Muse* took the stigma of individual neurosis from Dickinson's work by generalizing Dickinson's struggles with poetic identity in terms of the Jungian model of women's engagement with the animus, the male principle within. The Jungian model, however, reified Dickinson's experience and representations of gender differences in the form of an eternal, quasi-Platonic opposition between masculine and feminine principles.[9]

For most early feminist critics of Dickinson, neither the Jungian model of eternal sexual dichotomies nor the unreflectively sexist (in application) Freudian doctrine of art as symptom-substitute was acceptable. But as feminist theoreticians such as Nancy Chodorow and Carol Gilligan began to engage with and revise Freudian thought from the perspective of object-relations theory, revisionary psychoanalytic theories—many of them centered upon the mother and the pre-Oedipal stage of psychic life—began to appear in feminist criticism of Dickinson's work. Rejecting the narrowly Freudian reading of Dickinson's art as an idiosyncratic, individual symptom, many of these critics successfully generalize Dickinson's themes and concerns in terms of the new theories of women's psychology. Leigh Gilmore, for instance, finds that in Dickinson's "I think I was enchanted" (poem 593), the poem's "fusion of precursor/lover/fellow poet . . . is consistent with feminist psychosocial readings of female development."[10] In light of the new psychoanalytic theories of women, Dickinson's art can be related in some ways to "typically" female development, rather than viewed as a symptom of developmental failure. So understood, Dickinson's poetry contributes to what many feminist critics now see as women's literary tradition—the ongoing presence of women's literary works to one another—a tradition now often theorized psychoanalytically in terms of mother-daughter relationships.

Object-relations psychoanalytic theory in feminist literary criticism runs into several difficulties, I think, when placed in relation to Dickinson's work. First, it has little to say about language specifically and how language enters the mother-daughter relationship, which it takes as primary. Second, it has little to say about the figure of the father, and about the Law of the Father, which can hardly be ignored in Dickinson's poetry. Finally, it risks idealizing and essentializing the mother-daughter relationship, along with any women's literary tradition modeled upon that relationship. Differences of all kinds, including sexual difference, are all too easily exiled to the "outside" of the mother-child dyad, and so to the outside of women's literary traditions. Problematic in its own right, this exiling of difference also contributes to the embarrassment of object-relations psychoanalysis before the problem of language, the system of differences through which all subjects speak and are spoken.

Against certain object-relations, feminist, psychoanalytic interpretations of women's development, therefore, I have found it useful to invoke some classically Freudian texts, along with the work of Jacques Lacan and feminists influenced by his work. I have done so not only because this work often seems more theoretically searching (particularly about questions of representation) than American object-relations psychoanalysis, but because it speaks to aspects of Dickinson's work and of women's literary tradition—that compound frame—that are at best inadequately addressed, at worst even actively repressed, by American object-relations psychoanalysis. The risks of engaging Lacanian theory will be obvious to many readers; I hope the risks of repressing aspects of Dickinson's work become obvious, too, in the course of this book's argument. I hope and know that, in any event, as Arac and McNeil so rightly insist, Dickinson's language speaks back to all the theories—deconstructive, feminist, materialist, psychoanalytic—that would address it.

NOTES

1. Margaret Homans, *Women Writers and Poetic Identity: Dorothy Wordsworth, Emily Brontë, and Emily Dickinson* (Princeton, N.J.: Princeton University Press, 1980) and Joanne Feit Diehl, *Dickinson and the Romantic Imagination* (Princeton, N.J.: Princeton University Press, 1981). Sharon Cameron anticipated the conjunction between Dickinson studies and deconstruction in *Lyric Time: Dickinson and the Limits of Genre* (Baltimore: Johns Hopkins Unversity Press, 1979), cautiously invoking Derrida's idea of *differance* in connection with Dickinson's poetics of loss (140–41). Christanne Miller's recent stylistic study, *Emily Dickinson: A Poet's Grammar* (Cambridge, Mass.: Harvard University Press, 1987), and Helen McNeil's *Emily Dickinson* (New York: Virago/Pantheon, 1986) both acknowledge and extend Homans's deconstructive and feminist approach to Dickinson's poems.

2. Barton Levi St. Armand, *Emily Dickinson and Her Culture: The Soul's Society* (Cambridge: Cambridge University Press, 1984), 2.

3. Jonathan Arac, *Critical Genealogies: Historical Situations for Postmodern Literary Studies* (New York: Columbia University Press, 1989), 285.

4. Arac, *Critical Genealogies*, 200. Arac cites Dickinson's poem 512.

5. McNeil, *Emily Dickinson*, 4.

6. See my essay "Dickinson Identified: Newer Criticisms and Feminist Classrooms," in Robin Riley Fast and Christine Mack Gordon, eds., *Approaches to Teaching Dickinson's Poetry* (New York: MLA, 1989), for some pedagogical instances of how literary history can stand in for other histories.

7. See Jerome J. McGann, *The Romantic Ideology: A Critical Investigation* (Chicago: University of Chicago Press, 1983).

8. John Cody, *After Great Pain: The Inner Life of Emily Dickinson* (Cambridge, Mass.: Harvard University Press, 1971).

9. Albert J. Gelpi, *The Tenth Muse* (Cambridge, Mass.: Harvard University Press, 1975).

10. Leigh Gilmore, "The Gaze of the Other Woman: Dickinson, Moore, Rich," in Temma F. Berg et al., eds., *Engendering the Word: Feminist Essays in Psychosexual Poetics* (Urbana: University of Illinois Press, 1989), 93.

1

My Father's Business: *Errands into Nature and Tales of the Caskets*

> As the proverb says, "He that would bring home the wealth of the Indies, must carry out the wealth of the Indies." There is then creative reading as well as creative writing.
> —Emerson, *The American Scholar*

Opening the possibility of "creative reading" in an essay devoted to the possibilities of American cultural originality, Emerson's imperial aphorism neatly collapses the difficulties of assigning creative origins. Creative reading and creative writing, in Emerson's description (the distinction between them moot, as is the distinction between nature, "the Indies," and prior texts), involve processes of exchange that turn out not to be exchanges at all. The questing merchant comes back with the very same wealth he set out with, and here the idealizing economic assumption that in markets (nature, texts, "the Indies") participants freely exchange perfect equivalents serves Emerson to deny the problematic possibility that readers, even creative readers, might gain more from a text than they bring to it—or, conversely, that a text might demand more from readers than it gives to them. Denying on the reader's behalf (and on the capitalist's) the possibility (the historical reality) of realizing surplus-value or profit in this transaction, Emerson gains for the possessor of this "wealth" the advantages of solipsistic self-reference, canceling the belated reader's potentially one-sided indebtedness. All origins refer back to the self, independently of any possible exchange of values; the Other (the Indies) is denied even as it is named; and the "wealth" itself slips, or rises, from its place in a chain of exchanges to a position of transcendental nontransferability or nonreferentiality. This "wealth" magically returns, unchanged, from any voyage it takes.

It is both within and against this Emersonian account of American poetic origins that I seek in this chapter to locate a group of Dickinson poems, for the most part relatively early works, in which Dickinson first of all undertakes versions and revisions of this idealist errand into nature. She then begins to connect this errand, the search for a language of nature, with the search for a language of female desire. Undertaking to specify "beginnings" in Dickinson's poetry, or thematic developments, is of course a risky venture, in the absence of a sure chronology dating the poems' composition, and it "involves the danger that the final product will have only a specious unity, a sort of grotesque resurrection."[1] Yet insofar as many of Dickinson's poems themselves seem to thematize problematic beginnings (while others thematize problematic endings, as we will see in chapter 2), entertaining origin stories is inseparable from constructing readings around them at all.

The poems discussed in this chapter form a configuration around one origin-plot out of many that have been discerned, or might be discerned, in Dickinson's relatively early work. These poems most often tell stories of blocked quests into nature, blocked initiations into erotic knowledge; mysterious dangers, uncertain and perhaps secret profits from their questers' ventures; they parody, fracture, condense, and diminish better-known romantic and transcendentalist precursor texts.[2] In this respect, some of these earlier poems might fairly be regarded as apprentice texts of Dickinson's *oeuvre*, texts in which she demonstrates to herself that she cannot write, or does not wish to write, poems that literally repeat male poets' encounters with nature. Yet these poems of blockage, failed language, and ambiguous quest objects, in their sometimes halting, often opaque way, repeat and critique the contradictions and liabilities of Emerson's account and other romantic accounts of natural poetic origins. These contradictions emerge most clearly around the gender of the romantic speaker, and so pertain to the woman poet particularly. But Dickinson's critique of course redounds on the contradictions of her culture more largely, especially her culture's contradictory association of women with idealism and quest objects (rather than subjects) of all kinds. These poems repeatedly socialize—render as an intersubjective contest for power— the kinds of poetic language that Emerson's metaphor of a creative economics without loss, consumption, or concrete exchange so ambiguously naturalizes.[3]

Emerson's economics of reading in his aphorism of origins locates him in the tradition of the romantic egotistical sublime as described by Thomas Weiskel and further elaborated with respect to Emerson by Julie Ellison.[4] To put the structure of sublimity with a reductive simplicity equal to that of the aphorism: the egotistical sublime, confronted with the apparent superior power of an other (nature or prior text), appropriates it for its own. And this gain leads to another: "The later consciousness, or ego, is aggrandized by the perceptual power of its former state" (Weiskel, 52). The creative reader, in Emerson's terms, appropriates the power of the creative writer (adds the power of the "Indies" to his own) but in the end comes out with a power greater than that of the writer. This power is greater by virtue of the reader's greater freedom and because it exists as sheer mental possibility rather than as concrete, realized, and therefore at least partly inert, linguistic production—Shelley's fading coal. The mind gladly acquaints or reacquaints itself ever-anew with this power it had "forgotten" it possessed. This "ethos of alienation," as Weiskel calls it, seems irresistibly drawn toward idealizing economic metaphors, both in Emerson's practice and Weiskel's critical reading of it. "Everything external or 'out there' is transmuted into the substance of the mind, which accumulates like a kind of capital" (Weiskel, 52). Or, in Marx's famous formula, M-C-M', whether M stands for money or mind: the creative mind cannot but gain its Indies (because, as Emerson argues, the mind really already has them) and only engrosses itself by relaying its substance through "nature." As Carolyn Porter puts it, "if one chooses to follow rigorously the course outlined in [Emerson's] *Nature*, one has only two choices: to be either an Emersonian poet or a capitalist entrepreneur. The poet retreats to a vantage point from which the world appears as a set of symbols to be used for imaginative transformation, making man 'whole again in thought,' while the capitalist sets about using the world, remaking it according to what he doubtless is capable of seeing as the 'pure idea' in his mind."[5]

Neither the Emersonian "whole man" of thought nor the capitalist entrepreneur was likely to seem an imitable model for nineteenth-century women aspiring to a poetic vocation. Women are symbolically debarred from the "wholeness" of humanistic thought—a wholeness that covertly presupposes lack, absence, fragmentation, castration, and therefore the desire to transform the multifarious world into the symbols that would image Man's wholeness (and repress its opposite). As Emerson sets it forward in *Nature*, nature exists not in its details (farms and trees, to be resisted), but in its horizon, the circle drawn by the poet's eye.[6] Women, as custodians of natural detail (gardeners, miniaturists, stereotypically given to numbering the streaks of the tulip) rather than sublime wholeness, are customarily denied this "use" of nature. Likewise nineteenth-century American women, at least those of Emily Dickinson's class, normatively "used" the world only derivatively and secondarily, as consumers rather than producers of the fruits of the capitalist entrepreneurial mind. The ways in which Emily Dickinson, in some of her beginnings as a poet, seizes upon Emerson's economical aphorism and its poetic ramifications suggest that Emerson's magically universal (like money, or capital) program for sublimity effaces or inscribes itself over sexual difference as well as over the other human relations abstracted in idealist economics. If Emerson's proverbial metaphor sublimates an economic vocabulary that is already repressively idealist (has already repressed the historical and material conditions of exchange), to what regions of "the Indies" does this metaphor exile sexual difference?

As Margaret Homans and Joanne Feit Diehl, among other critics, have argued, the familiar answer is that woman, the feminine, is consigned to nature and identified with the unspeaking material resources that are lifted into language by the poet but negated at the same time, as Emerson negates the actual externality and productivity of "the Indies" when he transforms them into the abstract "wealth" that is somehow always already his. "Where the masculine self dominates and internalizes otherness, that other is frequently identified as a woman, whether she is nature, the representation of a human woman, or some phantom of desire."[7] And therefore, in Feit Diehl's words, "gender blocks the identifications"—with the world, " 'the nature of things' "—that "Emerson so fluently assumes." If for male initiates of the sublime "external power is experienced as being related to the self, and so possession, in some hidden way, becomes a repossession of uncharted regions of the self," women poets lack confidence in this return of selfhood. "Thus the relation of sexual identity to the quest for the sublime reveals the woman poet's provisional status within the romantic literary tradition."[8] We might add the (middle-class) woman poet's provisional status within the romantic tradition's underlying bourgeois political identity as well, since women do not participate immediately or coherently either in bourgeois relations to capital or in bourgeois ideologies of individualism and universality. While "the woman poet" is provisional, however, she is at the same time always already implicated in romantic literary traditions (and class relations as well), since the sublime language of nature presupposes sexual difference as natural—while claiming at the same time to transcend that difference. Dickinson's poems offer a kind of parodic countersublime that challenges both the presupposition and the proposed transcendence, exploring romantic constructions (in popular as well as "high" culture) of both nature and sexual difference, while blocking or defamiliarizing conventional gestures toward their transcendence.

Dickinson begins very early in her poetic career to trace the fortunes of sexual difference in the American sublime's prototypical "errand into nature" by undertaking a desublimating or literalizing reading of Emerson's economic vocabulary of nature. In a poem dated by Johnson's chronology to 1858,[9] she asks, in effect, how an Emersonian reader of nature surprised in the act of coining aphorisms— or, as Weiskel puts it, accumulating mental capital—*looks* when the observer's eye belongs to a woman.

> I never told the buried gold
> Upon the hill—that lies—
> I saw the sun—his plunder done
> Crouch low to guard his prize.
>
> He stood as near
> As stood you here—
> A pace had been between—
> Did but a snake bisect the brake
> My life had forfeit been.
>
> That was a wondrous booty—
> I hope 'twas honest gained.
> Those were the fairest ingots
> That ever kissed the spade!
>
> Whether to keep the secret—
> Whether to reveal—
> Whether as I ponder
> Kidd will sudden sail—
>
> Could a shrewd advise me
> We might e'en divide—
> Should a shrewd betray me—
> Atropos decide!
>
> (poem 11)

"I never told the buried gold" is a perfect instance of how Dickinson's early poetry about poetic origins typically elides or fractures its own occasions and motivations, rendering origin stories themselves problematic. What kind of speaker is this; to whom does she (?) speak; what brought her out to see the sunset; what makes the sunset so threatening to her? The poem answers to Robert Weisbuch's contention that Dickinson's poetry is characteristically "sceneless," an allegory, or better, an "anti-allegory," minus secure grounding.[10] Beginning abruptly and without explanations, the narrative it tells is retrospective, the speaker's locations or mise-en-scène—both past and present—therefore all the more unsure. The final two stanzas seemingly belong to a suspended or undecided present ("as I ponder"), no more fixable than the initial stance of indeterminate retro-spection. "I never told the buried gold," the speaker begins (punning on telling as speaking, and telling as counting over, possession); but is the poem itself, then, a telling, a break with the policy of past secrecy? The answer to this undecidable question turns out to in-volve the reader too nearly, perhaps, for comfort: "Atropos decide!" whether the reader's compact with the speaker constitutes advice, coconspiracy, or betrayal. The reader, drawn into propinquity with the speaker ("He stood as near / As stood you here—"), enters a chain of imperiled witnesses to the poem's initial "event" of the gold's interment in the hill, the sun's literal grounding of his "wondrous booty." Yet this event itself implicates a mysterious prior event: how and where was this booty gained? What is the source of value and meaning in this landscape?

The poem calls the wished-for plenitude of Emersonian natural romantic beginnings (the hope that we always already "carry out" with us "the wealth of the Indies") into doubt. No unambiguous locus of wealth here, no innocent natural language: only an ever-lengthening chain of appropriations. As Cynthia Griffin Wolff argues, "Any American poet who wished to be 'Representative' was con-strained to address Emerson's optimistic assessment of the meaning a poet would discover in the landscape"; this is one of Dickinson's earli-est "anti-allegories" (again to borrow Weisbuch's term) to do so.[11] The poem restages and critiques what Myra Jehlen calls "America's primal scene, Columbus arriving on an unknown shore,"[12] the same primal scene revised in Emerson's staging of the creative reader as merchant arriving in the Indies.

Dickinson's restaging wholly denies and denaturalizes the kind of property and ownership that Emerson's readerly economics affirms despite its anxieties. In Dickinson's revision of the errand into nature, Emerson's readerly entrepreneur, his Columbus always claiming the Indies for his own discovery, is recast as a pirate. Dickinson's speaker ironically respects the Emersonian victory over literary and natural ori-gins by refusing to speculate openly upon the source of the "wondrous booty" and by, so she says, not telling the "buried gold" that its owner has no certain right to it, but her tactful refusal only underscores the sun's piracy. The speaker/observer comes upon the American roman-tic sun/son in a liminal moment—the aftermath, so to speak, of the American "primal scene"—as the sun is setting on the booty gained, the better it would seem to assert his possession, but also the better to hide it. Unlawful "booty" is in transition to natural property. Dickin-son playfully and skeptically materializes Emerson's metaphors of readerly accumulation. Like Wordsworth above Tintern Abbey, the

Emersonian piratical sun in a certain way immures in this burial site "life and food / For future years"—the sun endows the landscape with a stolen value; nature becomes a kind of bank in which the capital of sublimity will grow in the dark. In Dickinson's reading of it, however, this "natural" process is anything but. To describe a "natural" sunset through this speaker's elaborate, quasi-allegorical personifications is above all to stress the human eye's ever-present desires for and designs upon "nature." "Nature," in the language of this poem, punningly "lies" (like the hill in which the gold is buried); and its beauty is an elaborate, perhaps an illicit, construction, first by the "sun," then by the speaker.[13]

Emerson too, of course, like other romantics, empowers the human eye in nature. The first chapter of *Nature* famously credits the poet's eye with the power to create nature by abstracting its unruly plenitude and its traces of particular human labor into a smooth and total horizon. Dickinson's account of the human eye and its workings is distinctly different. She denies the eye's distance *from* nature and foregrounds its workings *on* nature; "I never told the buried gold" stresses a dangerous nearness—of sun to horizon, of speaker to sun, of reader to speaker. We are, deliberately and uncomfortably, too close for idealization. She also denies what Emerson claims to be the necessary isolation of the poet's eye ("if a man would be alone, let him look at the stars"). For Emerson, a landscape may contain other human beings as farmers but scarcely other seers; in any given horizon, the poet's "transparent eyeball" is singular. Dickinson's landscape, by contrast, is populated with two different seers of, two independent designs on, nature: the sun's and the speaker's. And our viewpoint is with the speaker, who feels threatened as the second comer in this landscape, a belated entrant upon the natural scene and an inadvertent witness to its prior appropriation by the sun.

The unspecified but vividly felt threat to the female observer in the scene would seem to be, metaphorically, that of entombment in the same grave with the gold—the treasure, feminized as "fairest ingots," that she sees "kissing" their pirate-captors's spade. The landscape is inhabited, in her telling, by symbolically sexual dangers that enforce her to silence: the egregiously phallic snake that may "bisect" the woody "brake" from which she spies on the sun and meditates upon her future disclosures. The speaker dramatizes the threat to a female speaking voice posed by conventional associations of nature as passive matter with the feminine. Were she to be detected by the piratical sun, she too might be buried and so be appropriated to the sun's landscape, as part of his female "booty."

Instead, she comes away from the scene she has witnessed with a kind of forbidden knowledge, which she obliquely proposes to share with her readers. She goes from innocence to experience without, however, succumbing to the sexual threat that emanates from the piratical sun and his landscape. The speaker's spying position, the snake that might have (but did not) "bisect the brake," curiously recall both Satan's and Eve's actions in *Paradise Lost:* Satan spying on Adam and Eve in the Garden, tempting Eve in the form of a serpent; Eve succumbing to the lure of forbidden knowledge. Dickinson's poem revises Milton's version of the female trajectory from innocence to experience, along with the more particularly American version of the myth of innocent Adam, alone in the Garden of the unspoiled United States. Dickinson's setting "sun" (setting in the west, but also like a hen on its golden egg) is a natural, but by no means an innocent, figure. The American garden in which the speaker locates herself is fallen and threatening, its glory stolen from elsewhere. Eluding the sexualized danger of the landscape, Dickinson's speaker comes away from the "primal scene" (to recall Jehlen's terms) of American romanticism with a different kind of knowledge and experience than the piratical sun would seemingly have intended for her.

The female speaker's allotted place in the male arche-plot that Dickinson's poem implicitly revises may become plainer by comparison to the fate of another female figure who encounters an American poet-quester, in Emerson's poem "The Sphinx." The Sphinx—half-female, half-animal—gives her name to the poem that Emerson insisted be placed at the head of every collection of poems he published in his lifetime, including the 1846 edition of the *Poems* that Dickinson received in 1850 from Benjamin Franklin Newton, her "preceptor" (as she called him) and friend. (Dickinson herself marked off "The Sphinx" in Newton's gift copy, presumably as an indication of special interest.)[14] "The Sphinx" is structured as a reported dialogue between the male Poet and the Sphinx, who blocks the poet's way into both nature and self-knowledge.[15] After informing the Poet that he, Man, is properly the riddle, to which only his own transcendence is the answer,

> Uprose the merry Sphinx,
>   And crouched no more in stone;
> She melted into purple cloud,
>   She silvered in the moon;
> She spired into a yellow flame;
>   She flowered in blossoms red;
> She flowed into a foaming wave:
>   She stood Monadnoc's head.

> Through a thousand voices
> Spoke the universal dame;
> "Who telleth one of my meanings
> Is master of all I am."
> (*CW* IX:24–25)

Once the poet speaks the unriddling words that name himself, the Sphinx metamorphoses into the gatekeeper, royal road, and beautiful doormat who assures ambitious male questers into nature, or into Emerson's book of poetry (and "The Sphinx" 's introductory position asserts that there is no difference between them), of their mastery over "her" meanings. As Emerson had written in *Nature*, "Every man's condition is a solution in hieroglyphic to those inquiries he would put" (*CW* I:4); the Sphinx, nature herself, is there to allow him to name himself. For most of the poem's first readers, however, the proffered mastery was less than self-evident, and after Emerson's death "The Sphinx" lost its pride of place in collections of Emerson's works. According to Emerson's editor, "The Sphinx" managed to "cut off, in the very portal, readers who would have found good and joyful words for themselves, had not her riddle been beyond their powers" (*CW* IX:403)—as good a negative (even a castrating) description of the poem's function as anyone could wish, and one that adds to the puzzlement over why contemporary readers found the poem so very opaque. This is not to deny the poem's difficulty, its more or less genuine need to set up a riddling nature, one that offers some resistance, as a precondition of attaining imaginative power. Emerson deliberately posed, through "The Sphinx," a trial of initiation for his volume's readers. As David Porter argues, one reason for the difficulty is the ambiguous location of the poem's speaker with respect to the Poet's dialogue with the Sphinx. "The poem's vexing ambiguity comes largely because it is unclear whether or not the Poet solves the Sphinx's riddle. . . . Yet encompassing the two-level structures of the supernatural riddler and the human riddle-solver, joyful nature and melancholy man, is a primary consciousness," an "all-seeing maker."[16] If the poem's final achievement (as opposed to its initiatory trial) of mastery is difficult to locate among its voices, what is plain are the sexual politics of this mastery. A half-human, half-"natural" speaking female subject offers her riddle and performs her metamorphoses at the male quester's word. She literally becomes the threshold of his power.

Dickinson's poem reverses not only the genders of Emerson's archetypal protagonists in "The Sphinx," but also the direction of Emerson's plot. Where Emerson's female Sphinx rises up, "crouched no more in stone," expanding to become a fertile nature for the male Poet, Dickinson's plundering sun "crouch[es] low to guard his prize," installing an already abstracted value within nature. Emerson's poem promises ever-renewed access to origins and natural language: whenever a man answers the riddle of his own transcendence, it implies, nature renews itself for him. Eden re-creates itself at the American Adam's self-naming word. No such renewal, no restoration seems to impend in Dickinson's poem, where the sun squats on his prize as if unnaturally to prevent the following sunrise, new daylight, or the expansiveness of natural fecundity. The falling/fallen sun hoards, rather than expends, value and meaning.[17] And in this sunset landscape, Dickinson's speaker looks not back for Eden but forward to last things, finally invoking as her muse the most inexorable of the Fates, Atropos, who is responsible for cutting the thread of life.

In light of the poem's ending, then, what kind of female voice issues from the speaker's witnessing to this "primal scene" of American romantic letters? That Dickinson's speaker has avoided the silencing fate of Emerson's Sphinx we know because her stance in "I never told the buried gold" is retrospective; she has, after all, gotten away with her voice, escaped being naturalized. Her retrospective irony distances her from the inanimate buried gold that she identifies as female: "Those were the fairest ingots / That ever kissed the spade!" Dickinson's speaker declines being identified with that sort of sleeping beauty. As an observer, however, Dickinson is implicated in the scene she has ironized. What is her relation to the forbidden knowledge she takes away? Can she or ought she to appropriate the gold whose entombment she has witnessed? Is there a language to be found in this scene that would not entail appropriating its feminized, "natural" signifiers of value and meaning?

To steal or not to steal; the poem's ending suspends itself between these alternatives. Margaret Homans has maintained that Dickinson's poetry in general testifies to "her recognition that nature is not to be possessed," whereas "Emerson, even though he shares some of Dickinson's knowledge of the vertiginous freedom of language, is disconcerted by nature's elusiveness, because his views of language include its powerful propriation of nature."[18] If nature is not to be possessed, it is also presumably not to be stolen. On the other hand, and on somewhat different grounds, Alicia Ostriker has called American women poets, after French theorist Claudine Herrmann's phrase, "thieves of language, female Prometheuses."[19] If property or possession is in any way available to Dickinson's speaker in this landscape, it is clearly necessary to ask what that property is in—nature or language?—and what relationship Dickinson's poem poses between nature and language.

If Dickinson in general thought that nature was not to be possessed immediately in language, nevertheless this early poem takes as its premise the sun's prior attempt (at the very least) to possess nature, an attempt to which Dickinson's speaker is willy-nilly a spectator and from which she brings away a forbidden knowledge. Because of this prior appropriation, what potentially stands to be possessed in this sunscape is not nature itself but its always already abstracted signification—the gold, the sun's symbol, a language—a condition from which the poem by itself does not rescue nature; its twilight account of beginnings is figuratively too belated to allow a resurrection of that kind. If, under the circumstances, the role of thief beckons to the speaker, it is one she does not definitively embrace, although she flirts with it in order to draw her audience into complicity with her. It seems almost too late in the day for the speaker to become even a Prometheus in any unambiguous way. The plundering sun has already perverted that role by burying the stolen fire instead of sharing it with humankind, and neither the falling sun nor speaker seem as close as Prometheus does to original mythic language, the fire of the gods.

If there is a language left, by the poem's end, to be "stolen," it is no longer quite Promethean, and no longer refers to a prior, given natural plenitude from which anything could be appropriated for the "first" time. The figurative grounds of possession and value, the relationship between language and nature, shift in the course of the poem under the gaze of Dickinson's skeptical observer. The iconic natural likeness between the sun and his golden plunder—figure of a nonarbitrary language guaranteed by real similarity—gives way to an arbitrary chain of contiguities (of buried gold to female observer, of observer to her imagined audience) and contingent possession by the last stanza. Emersonian "correspondence" language, in the poem's view, is not innocent or "natural" despite its claims to be; the sun's likeness to the gold he buries is no trustworthy sign of original ownership. The figure of possession is projected, in the optic of the female observer, from the axis of metaphor (possession as "natural" and hierarchical likeness) to the axis of metonymy (possession as accidental contiguity). By the poem's end, language is no longer a golden sign triumphantly invested in nature and natural likenesses, but a secret given or withheld from human ear to ear, like the gossip of "shrewds." A verbal thread of forbidden knowledge, its secrecy is guarded by a female spinner, "Atropos."[20]

Dickinson's parting invocation of "Atropos" (sometimes said to be the eldest of the Fates and wielder of the shears) in the poem's last line recalls still another of Emerson's poems. Dickinson's Atropos tropes on the dreadful balance of Emerson's Fates at the end of "Merlin," a poem sick with "Compensation" in which Emerson declares, "Balance-loving Nature / Made all things in pairs":

> Justice is the rhyme of things;
> Trade and counting use
> The self-same tuneful muse;

Poetry and commerce alike resound with the "rhyme" of universal justice; the language of correspondence is destiny; and truth dwells in the lineage of the Holy Family.

> Like the dancer's ordered band,
> Thoughts come also hand in hand;
> In equal couples mated,
> Or else alternated;
> Adding by their mutual gage,
> One to other, health and age.
> Solitary fancies go
> Short-lived wandering to and fro,
> Most like to bachelors,
> Or an ungiven maid,
> Not ancestors,
> With no posterity to make the lie afraid,
> Or keep truth undecayed.

Closed as Emerson's familial genealogy of truth seems, it is a conspicuously extrafamilial company, the Fates, who make "Merlin"'s final accounting:

> Subtle rhymes, with ruin rife,
> Murmur in the house of life,
> Sung by the Sisters as they spin;
> In perfect time and measure they
> Build and unbuild our echoing clay,
> As the two twilights of the day
> Fold us music-drunken in.[21]

Emerson's twilight vision of the Fates concedes more power to the singing Sisters than "The Sphinx" does to its female speaker. The mastery promised to the individual male Poet in "The Sphinx" is eventually located by "Merlin" in the universal rhyme itself rather than in the human subject. Dickinson's poem, on the other hand, invokes a slightly different, singular Fate as its muse, the third weird sister left out of Emerson's vision of perfect pairs. In Dickinson's poem, Atropos guarantees honor among thieves rather than ratifying Emerson's universal "perfect time and measure" and his willed faith in the rhyme of property. A spinster in every sense of the word, Dickinson's Atropos stands outside Emerson's familial, "natural" lineage of truth.

Although she does not stand guard over property, Dickinson's Fate, unlike Emerson's, is given her proper name: A-tropos, she who turns not or tropes not. We could think of her as Dickinson's antidote to the Sphinx, as a spectral, antithetical Mother Nature, as a "disfiguring figure"[22] for Dickinson's own poetic strategies. Atropos implicitly authorizes Dickinson's appearance on this very American "primal scene," while acting as a stay against the dangers it poses to the female speaker. Calling on her poem's Fate by her (im)proper name, Dickinson unbalances Emerson's sing-song "rhyme of things" and his sense of its "justice." And she effectively calls down a curse ("Atropos decide!") upon the reader who refuses to join her in this forbidden knowledge.[23] Atropos is one name, one way, of countering the silencing power of Emerson's Sphinx. By contrast, another early sunset poem sketches a female figure who might be called "Pantropos"—"all-troping":

> Blazing in Gold and quenching in Purple
> Leaping like Leopards to the Sky
> Then at the feet of the old Horizon
> Laying her spotted Face to die
> Stooping as low as the Otter's Window
> Touching the Roof and tinting the Barn
> Kissing her Bonnet to the Meadow
> And the Juggler of Day is gone
>
> (poem 228)

As the "Juggler of Day" here, this female figure—much more exuberantly than as "Atropos" of the earlier poem—this undoer of the Sphinx, is associated with the expenditure of language rather than its hoarding. Dickinson's "Juggler" tropes on herself with as much energy and fecundity as Emerson's metamorphosing Sphinx, but at her own will rather than at the behest of the male Poet.[24] Atropos or Pantropos, Dickinson's female muses in nature refuse to respect the anxious property of Emerson's poet-entrepreneurs.

Dickinson's early experiment with the American errand into nature, her characterization of the sun as a pirate, and her ambiguous appropriation of "his" language, testify to her early and much-reiterated realization that "Nature," as such, and the languages drawn from "her" are—to put it as generally as possible—the creations of human power-relations, or, as we now say, ideologically motivated constructions. In Christanne Miller's words: "For Dickinson, nature is not transparent and language is not an organic adjunct (or reflected image) of its processes. We 'consign' words to language instead of allegorically perceiving them in nature's great poem."[25] Not the least of these constructions or consignments, for Dickinson, is the traditional opposition between the male speaker, the subject of the languages of nature, and the feminized natural scene he bespeaks. "I never told the buried gold" allegorizes not the innocent perception of natural meanings, but rather Dickinson's felt sense of danger when faced with this ideologically specific construction of "natural" meaning, as well as her sense that there are no simple alternatives. For her, meaning is always already appropriated and inscribed within the natural landscape, and there is no obvious way of gaining a poetic voice without transgressing in this landscape.

In groups of slightly later poems, Dickinson experiments further —seriously, and in serious parody—with the sexual politics of the American "primal scene" as she had reworked them in "I never told the buried gold." In two poems copied out (according to Johnson's chronology) within a year of "I never told the buried gold," Dickinson herself assumes something very much like the role of the piratical Emersonian sun, robbing nature for the gain of her own poetic language. In the earlier of the two poems, Dickinson experiments with imaging nature as male, but as a relatively domesticated male peddler or shopkeeper rather than the threatening, acquisitive sun:

> I robbed the Woods—
> The trusting Woods.
> The unsuspecting Trees
> Brought out their Burs and Mosses
> My fantasy to please.
> I scanned their trinkets curious—
> I grasped—I bore away—
> What will the solemn Hemlock—
> What will the Oak tree say?
> (poem 41)[26]

The net effect is playfully deflating: where male romantics define themselves as the entrepreneurs of the Indies, Dickinson suggests, a woman appropriating nature is at most a petty shoplifter. Moreover, in a society in which middle-class women were increasingly defined as purchasers and consumers rather than producers of goods,

Dickinson alludes to, by transgressing, women's normative forms of extra-household exchange—in effect, she parodies one of middle-class women's few legitimate spheres of public "speech." In this sphere of speech, however, as in romantic nature, women as would-be subjects are all too nearly identified with the *objects* of exchange: Dickinson's adjective, "curious," in the poem's sixth line, applies equally to subject and inanimate object, the speaker and the Woods' trinket. Women are what they buy, or in the case of this speaker, what they steal. And the autonomy of the speaker's "fantasy," under these circumstances, seems questionable, like the autonomy of fantasy in consumer culture more generally: the speaker mock-anxiously refers the effect of her deed back to the judgment of "the solemn Hemlock" and the Oak. Far from an expansive nonhuman horizon of plenitude, "Nature" in this poem is a congeries of petit-bourgeois village patriarchs. Dickinson's playful irony cuts in two different historical and cultural directions: back to the high culture of romantic conquests of nature and the American "primal scene" of appropriation, and forward to the fast-growing new identities for women in consumer culture.[27] The speaking female subject, in this poem, transgresses against both romantic nature and village consumer culture.

In a companion poem of 1859, Dickinson inverts the sexual roles assigned to nature and the speaker in "I robbed the Woods—." Imagining nature as female and herself as a sexually ambiguous raptor, she again replays and parodies romantic errands into nature, this time in a way that distantly recalls Wordsworth's initiatory errand in "Nutting":

> So bashful when I spied her!
> So pretty—so ashamed!
> So hidden in her leaflets
> Lest anybody find—
>
> So breathless till I passed her—
> So helpless when I turned
> And bore her struggling, blushing,
> Her simple haunts beyond!
>
> For whom I robbed the Dingle—
> For whom betrayed the Dell—
> Many, will doubtless ask me,
> But I shall never tell!
>
> (poem 91)

In Wordsworth's "Nutting," the speaker recalls himself as a boy, "Forcing [his] way" into a "virgin scene," where he regards the bower's hazel-trees "with wise restraint / Voluptuous"—before ravaging their "quiet being." It is a ritual of initiation that returns the boy, sadder but wiser, to the female home he left behind him. He bears back with him not only the material booty, "rich beyond the wealth of kings," but more importantly, a knowledge to be transmitted into the present:

> Then, dearest Maiden, move along these shades
> In gentleness of heart; with gentle hand
> Touch—for there is a spirit in the woods.
>
> (ll. 54–56)

As Margaret Homans notes in her discussion of "Nutting"'s daunting effect on Dorothy Wordsworth's poetic voice, "the function of the encounter with nature is to return the boy to the human world, but with greater maturity, so that he may progress not just beyond nature but also beyond the frugal dame" (his mother, whom he leaves at the outset of his adventure) "to the dearest maiden" (whom he instructs at the poem's conclusion).[28] For the maiden, the speaker's transmitted knowledge or vicarious experience of this "virgin scene" is an ambiguous gift. It implicitly debars her from attempting the same errand into nature on her own behalf, since the scene is symbolically no longer virgin, after the boy's past ravages. Moreover, the Oedipal and heterosexual configuration of the episode renders her, the maiden, a potential quest object rather than subject of the story, allied to patient, quiet nature.

Dickinson's poem patently transgresses upon "Nutting"'s allotment of sexual roles. Her speaker dares exactly the aggression the young Wordsworth dares, violating a virginal bower of quiet— although Dickinson's bower is, wittily, already more conspicuously textualized than Wordsworth's, hidden in its *leaflets* (like a woman surprised reading a novel?). Dickinson's speaker neither starts out, as the boy in "Nutting" does, from the mother's house nor returns, as he does, to instruct a faithful female companion; those comforting familial props to the authority of Wordsworth's narrative don't furnish themselves to her. The venue and ultimate authority for the speaker's ritual of initiation in Dickinson's poem remain suspended in uncertainty, as do its sexual poetics. Does the reader "legitimize" the poem by imagining a male speaker, or accept the poem's diction ("bashful," "pretty") as more conventionally feminine—and so envision a quasi-lesbian rape? The poem suggests that an inverted, parodic assumption of male aggression does not give the female poet access to the kind of authoritative poetic voice that depends on the continuities of a male poet's imaginative autobiography, with its series of nurturing female auditors and muses. Instead, Dickinson's speaker is left pointing to her transgression, speaking her muteness rather than her acquired wisdom. She displays her forbidden, transgressive knowledge of feminized Nature almost in the manner of an hysterical symptom: she takes on, signifies in her own person the "hiddenness" and quasi-sexual resistance of the natural scene she violated. The speaker initiates herself into a pregnant silence rather than Wordsworthian authority.

Both "Nutting" and Emerson's "The Sphinx" could be described in Freudian terms as prototypically Oedipal initiations—with the important caveat, that the Oedipal father who issues forbidding prohibitions is elided or offstage in both poems, even if his threats are indirectly still registered.[29] In "Nutting," the very existence of a succession of female figures (frugal dame, Nature, maiden) marks a kind of Oedipal quest and its resolution, since the Oedipal crisis for the boy demands that he repress his first love for his mother and embark upon finding substitutions for her. According to Freud, and even more specifically for Lacan, then, this crisis enables the boy's entry into Symbolic language as such, the Law of the Father: repressing his attachment to the mother, entering upon a formalized language of substitutions and desire, his reward is to find—to *return* to in a sense, as Wordsworth does—a "dearest Maiden" who is the appropriate addressee of his desiring language.

Emerson's "The Sphinx" describes a similarly Oedipal crisis of initiation in less humane and domestic terms than "Nutting." Where Wordsworth's boy encounters a succession of human women before and after female nature, the quest of Emerson's Poet is resolved in the Sphinx, who incarnates an infinite (but nonhuman) series of metamorphoses in her own single (yet also, of course, irretrievably dual) person. Emerson's isolate Poet does not return from nature to the human world.[30] The Sphinx's change from immovable obstacle to welcoming nature, like the series of female figures in "Nutting," marks the male speaker's accession to the power of substitutions. " 'Who telleth one of my meanings,' " says the "universal dame," "Is master of all I am' "—because mastery inheres in, and refers to, substitution itself rather than any particular natural object. Indeed, as the more radically idealist romantics like Emerson and Percy Shelley thought, attachment to particular natural objects, including human objects, could only inhibit "universal" mastery. So Emerson's "Give All to Love" urges the initiate to keep himself "Free as an Arab / Of thy beloved," remembering that "when half-gods go, / The gods arrive" (CW IX:92).[31]

Describing Wordsworth's and Emerson's errands into nature as Oedipal trials of initiation is, of course, one more theoretical way of getting at the systemic obstacles they place in the path of a woman writer's accession to poetic voice. I would like to bracket, for the purposes of these readings, the feminist debate over whether this Oedipal paradigm is somehow inherent in language as such, or in language as acquired by human subjects under patriarchy, and if so, how extensive, historically speaking, patriarchy's sway might be.[32] I do want to claim, at a minimum, that this Oedipal paradigm informs the poets and poetry (but not only the poets and poetry) Dickinson read and thought about, and that it inscribes itself—creatively, and against many kinds of resistance—in her poetry. When Dickinson revises Wordsworth's and Emerson's adventures, moreover, it is not necessarily, or only, at the command of unconscious instances lodged in her own psyche in such a way as to be inaccessible to her own reflection. Such revisions can also be a recognition and an exploration of the social constitution of these romantic adventures. As I have suggested, Dickinson implicitly contends that romantic errands into nature and "Nature" herself are loci of human struggle and are ideological constructions.

Both poems 41 and 91, for example, suggest that simply assuming or inverting male and female roles within the romantic Oedipal quest leads to parodic nonresolutions for the female speaking subject, because the romantic errand into nature is neither gender-blind nor sexually symmetrical—any more than Oedipal dramas are symmetrical for girls and boys under the social arrangements of Dickinson's time and our own. In a series of later poems, Dickinson seems to experiment with still other ways of representing the position of a female speaking subject within this romantic and Oedipal paradigm. The problem of nature becomes an explicitly human problem. In a scenario to which she returns time and again, a female speaker tries to buy a favor from a denying father figure—tries and then fails to find the adequate language-token, the symbolic equivalent of exchange with which to enter his signifying economy. The language debated between the female speaker and denying father figure is typically one of "natural" and very often feminized tokens. These poems could be thought of as staging female Oedipal scenarios of "natural" language, or as asking under what circumstances a female speaker could be initiated into an authoritative language of nature, as the Poet is initiated in Emerson's "The Sphinx" and Wordsworth is in "Nutting." But Dickinson's poems once again underscore the lack of symmetry between the female speaker's situation and that of the male romantic in nature. The poems dramatize Dickinson's recognition that under the system of exchanges that constitutes patriarchy, her role is not to exchange tokens but to be exchanged as a token herself, not even to give herself away but to be given away—a function from which the speaker's "failure" with the Father ironically preserves her.

Dickinson's rendering of this feminine Oedipal romance continues her earlier theme of nature as always already commodified. Erotic relations, too, cast themselves in this language of abstract exchange. Compare poems 41 and 91 with this poem, assigned by Johnson's dating to 1861:

> I Came to buy a smile—today—
> But just a single smile—
> The smallest one upon your face
> Will suit me just as well—
> The one that no one else would miss
> It shone so very small—
> I'm pleading at the "counter"—sir—
> Could you afford to sell—
>
> I've *Diamonds*—on my fingers—
> You know what *Diamonds* are?
> I've Rubies—like the Evening Blood—
> And Topaz—like the star!
> 'Twould be "a Bargain" for a *Jew!*
> *Say*—may I have it—Sir?
>
> (poem 223)

"I robbed the Woods—," claimed the earlier poem; here Dickinson's speaker enters an even more explicitly eroticized conversation with a more powerful male figure.[33] She wants recognition; the linguistic tokens she offers in exchange for his sign of recognition mediate ambiguously between nature and culture. The gemstones she offers up are emblematic of nature ("Topaz—like the star!")—nature condensed into the smallest, most valuable, most negotiable units. "Rubies" are emblems of the sunset in the way that gold is the crouching sun's emblem in poem 11. But the gems are also emblematic of the speaker's own body. Dickinson connects "Rubies" to a natural sunset through a compressed double trope: first the simile of color likeness, then the allied but more disturbing metaphor of "Blood" for the ruddy sunset. The gemstones are both metaphors and metonyms of the speaker's body, connected both by likeness (through the rubies' blood color) and by contiguity (the female body that wears and displays the proffered gems). Therefore the speaker's enfigured body does not stand above and outside the poem's language of figurative substitutions: it is implicated in them, as a sexual and economic object, the circulating blood of the system. The speaker herself allusively implies that she is proposing a bargain in flesh. "Twould be 'a Bargain' for a Jew!"—Shylock's bargain, impossible for the speaker to conclude and remain alive to tell the tale.[34]

The bargain remains unclosed in almost all these poems. The female subject is unable to win recognition as a speaking subject in the father figure's medium of exchange:

> I asked no other thing—
> No other—was denied—
> I offered Being—for it—
> The Mighty Merchant sneered—
>
> Brazil? He twirled a Button—
> Without a glance my way—
> "But—Madam—is there nothing else—
> That We can show—Today?"
>
> (poem 621)

All of Dickinson's "Being" will not suffice for her to buy Brazil. Is there any productive way of asking what Brazil is to Dickinson, why this particular figuration of the unattainable romantic quest object? Rebecca Patterson connects this poem to Dickinson's pervasive imagery of diamonds and jewels, of which poem 223 is another, earlier instance. She finds the source of "Brazil" in a magazine article on "Diamonds and Pearls" that fascinated Dickinson: Brazil was the source of fabulous diamonds.[35] While the historical connection is surely suggestive, it does not mean that the poem is understood once the metonymy, Brazil for diamonds, finds historical authority. "Commonly [Dickinson's] diamond represents value," Patterson notes. "Throughout Emily's poetic career Brazil would be as reasonable a symbol of inestimable wealth as Golconda at an earlier period."[36] But the poem allows us to ask, Just how "reasonable" can symbols of inestimable wealth be? Why and how do they work, and for whom? In what structures of desire? Whatever desire and its languages may be in this poem, they are not reasonable. Source-searching itself, while necessary, only reiterates the question on a social/historical scale: Dickinson's diamonds have their source in the 1861 *Atlantic Monthly* article, which has its source in real diamonds, the source of which is Brazil, whose diamonds have become (how?) an agreed-on universal symbol of value. (Why was it worth the *Atlantic*'s while to publish such an article?) The real interpretive issue is the status of the metonymy itself, the substitution of the source for the object—and, therefore, how this figurative language itself sustains or undermines the ontology of value implicit in the idea of a "source" (a matter that concerned Dickinson well before 1861, as "I never told the buried gold" testifies).

In the *Atlantic Monthly* article (written by James T. Fields, editor and publisher of Emerson and other famous American authors), gem-stones function as the loci of narratives: each famous stone cited bears with it a fabulous history, always a history of rule and empire. Dia-monds change hands ever upward in the social hierarchy, from the slaves who unearth them, to the jewelers who polish them, to the kings who buy them and offer them to (or suffer their confiscation by) more powerful emperors. The article does not directly address the question of whether these narrative chains stem from the stones' in-trinsic "natural" value or whether those values are the product of the narratives themselves (to be more precise, the product of the social relations in which the narratives are embedded and retold). What is clear is that precious stones are in some ways mystifying synechdo-ches for history itself; stones, like the women who wear them, are normatively tokens in a never-ending rivalrous contest between men. Witness Fields's penultimate anecdote of "diamonds and pearls":

> There is a Rabbinical story which aptly shows the high estimate of pearls in early ages, only one object in Nature being held worthy to be placed above them:—
>
> "On approaching Egypt, Abraham locked Sarah in a chest, that none might behold her dangerous beauty. But when he was come to the place of paying custom, the collectors said, 'Pay us the custom': and he said, 'I will pay the custom.' They said to him, 'Thou carriest clothes': and he said, 'I will pay for clothes.' Then they said to him, 'Thou carriest gold': and he answered them, 'I will pay for my gold.' On this they further said to him, 'Surely thou bearest the finest silk': he replied, 'I will pay custom for the finest silk.' Then said they, 'Surely it must be pearls that thou takest with thee': and he only answered, 'I will pay for pearls.' Seeing that they could name nothing of value for which the patriarch was not willing to pay custom, they said, 'It cannot be but thou open the box, and let us see what is within.' So they opened the box, and the whole land of Egypt was illumined by the lustre of Sarah's beauty,—far exceeding even that of pearls."

As a tactic for ensuring his safety and his wife's, there is little to be said for Abraham's shift; as a game of linguistic rivalry between men, however, it is of course masterful. The revelation of Sarah's beauty at the end of the story renders the supposed essential worth of all the precious material goods named merely figurative. They become inade-quate metaphors for her body, the actual "referent" in the chest: like *The Merchant of Venice*, this tale is a variant on folk tradition's tale of the caskets.[37] The "patriarch"'s best property is the woman in the chest, the most "precious object in nature." The woman herself is Nature's immutable essence of value, a moral Fields seals with his final invocation of Shakespeare's description of Cordelia's tears, leaving her eyes *"As pearls from diamonds dropp'd."*[38] The argument's passage from history to sacred literature, from material gemstones to ideal women, is thereby complete.

If "Diamonds and Pearls" indeed represents part of the cultural context of Dickinson's poem, that context quite openly bears a heavy freight of historical meanings and sexual politics. Like the article, by the end of which material "diamonds and pearls" come to stand for ideal women, Dickinson's poem thoroughly evacuates the materiality of its historical referent, the diamonds of Brazil. But Dickinson puts nothing back in its place, least of all an idealized woman object. In no sense materially present as the poem's unproblematic historical "signified," "Brazil" is rather a place staked out within the contest of signifiers between Dickinson's speaker and the "Mighty Merchant"— in the way that diamonds and pearls become signifiers of male rivalry over, and possession of, women in Fields's story of Abraham and Sarah. Dickinson's "Brazil" literally belongs on the alliterative signifying chain that begins with "Being," the speaker's first move in the exchange, and ends so reductively with the "Button" twirled by the Merchant in refusal of her tokens. Alliteration—the arbitrary materiality of the signifier—is the only materiality available in the poem. The notion of a real, material "source" of absolute value, so far as this poem is concerned, stands exposed as a fiction: value is positional and differential, the function of a power-laden, unequal linguistic exchange between human beings.

This reading of the poem is not intended to deny the importance of historicity (the *real* Brazil) for Dickinson's poem, but to resituate history in a different way in the poem's language. The historical context is fully real for Dickinson's poem, but real via a terrific reduction to the signifier, "Brazil." This terrific reduction in the poem is analogous to the way gemstones in Fields's article bear a marvelously compressed burden of both history and capital, and Dickinson's poem seems conscious of that analogy.[39] The effect of Dickinson's reduction is to expose the fictionality, or linguistic basis, of what the article (intermittently) mystifies as unproblematic, essential, material absolute values. Dickinson thereby queries the basis of her own and the contemporary American reading public's historical fascination with an idealized "Brazil," this exotic, unknowable, yet utterly transparent (or, as Patterson puts it, perfectly "common") symbol of inestimable wealth.

The poem also extends her query, through this same evacuated symbol, into the related idealisms of literary history. As Joanne Feit Diehl notes, the poem makes yet another attack on Emerson's mercantile "doctrine of compensation."[40] Brazil comes out of the same cultural lexicon and the same sexual politics as Emerson's Indies, one of the topoi of inexhaustible natural wealth through which the male romantic (across many cultural fronts, not only that of poetry) alienates his power in order to reclaim it in larger, stranger style. The speaker's failure with the Merchant in this poem underscores again Dickinson's felt exclusion from a tradition in which such topoi of wealth are female and deny women's existence as speaking subjects by identifying them with materiality, that wealth which is "outside" language yet mastered by language.[41] She is, in a sense made transparently clear in Fields's article, supposed to *be* Brazil (guarantor of value-in-nature) for the merchant-poet, rather than speaking, naming, or desiring Brazil as a function of her own "Being." The merchant-interlocutor rejects her speaking subjectivity along with her offered sexuality, from which he turns aside to twirl his own button. His desire and hers share no common language.

"I asked no other thing—" dramatizes a would-be initiation into language, experience, or sexual knowledge, that is turned back by the denying father-merchant. If this poem and others like it draw in some measure upon a female Oedipal scenario of poetic voice, one of the difficulties besetting that voice would seem to be the uncompromisingly dyadic nature of the speaker's situation: pleading directly and only with the denying merchant, without intermediary or other possible addressees for her desiring language. According to Joanne Feit Diehl's pioneering analysis of Dickinson's transactions with male-dominated literary tradition, this restrictedly dyadic contest reflects the gendered assymmetry of poetic (but not only poetic) identity in our culture. Male poets invoke idealized female muses as props to their voices, and consequently "male poets retain the ability to separate their poetic fathers—mythic progenitors—from the muse." For women poets in this tradition, however, matters are different: in Feit Diehl's words, Dickinson's "dilemma of influence is at once complicated and radically simplified by her perception that the Composite Precursor and her muse are one and the same," in their symbolic genders at least. Her situation therefore is not to be relieved by splitting tradition into denying and fostering figures along gender lines, and it remains oppressively dyadic: speaking daughter against a composite male figure of denial. Dickinson's muse, whom Feit Diehl identifies with the male lover addressed in so many poems and in the notorious "Master" letters, tends to assume the same characteristics as the "Mighty Merchant." How can the two be differentiated? "Defending herself against the power of the one, she may lose the inspiration of the other."[42]

Feit Diehl's paradigm, proposed for women poets generally and not only Dickinson, has been criticized as reductively heterosexist as well as for its overt dependence on Harold Bloom's constitutively aggressive accounts of poetic influence.[43] Although its universality is open to question, her schema does propose a fresh way of thinking about the many poems of heterosexual romance that Dickinson did undeniably write, and about the "lover" himself, whose unknowable historicity has bedeviled Dickinson criticism since the poems first began to see publication.[44] In Feit Diehl's argument, it is because of the (in some ways oppressive) shape of literary tradition, not strictly because of any supposed innate heterosexuality on women poets' or Dickinson's part, that the "lover" becomes at minimum a kind of necessary fiction in Dickinson's poetic career. Feit Diehl's argument and others like it suspend the question, Who was the lover, and did she or didn't she? and raise others instead. How does the lover function for Dickinson's poetics? What would it mean, in Dickinson's cultural situation, for a woman to have (or to desire) an original desire? And how would her desire articulate itself with the masculine tradition's romance with (and of) originality? The debate over the lover's historical identity cannot be solved by such questions, obviously, but it can be reinterpreted as symptomatic of important issues in Dickinson's poetics (and indeed, for women poets more generally, as Feit Diehl claims). The question of the lover's reality—his material referent—lingers importantly, I would argue, in part because Dickinson invokes "him" in poems that explore the linkage between a transcendental poetics and signifiers evacuated of material referents. For the purposes of many of the poems, "he" has no essential identity, only a contested, differential identity-in-language. To extend and rewrite Feit Diehl's Bloomian insight, in language borrowed from deconstruction, "he," the Muse-lover, is the *différance* of the Composite Precursor, an unstable opening made into culturally male languages.

Poem 247, like "I asked no other thing—," dramatizes the speaker's attempt to win recognition for her desiring language from a denying father-merchant. Unlike "I asked no other thing—," however, this poem suggests an opening, however small, in the dyadic situation. Asking "you" for a glimpse of "his face," the poem names two addressees: the speaker's "Sovereign," the lover and indirect addressee, and "Shylock," the father-merchant, through whom her appeal must pass.

Are they two, or one? Their names connect them alliteratively, but Dickinson would seem to seek a split between them—a rift, to recall Feit Diehl's version of her poetic family romance, in the overbearingly united Composite Precursor of tradition.

> What would I give to see his face?
> I'd give—I'd give my life—of course—
> But *that* is not enough!
> Stop just a minute—let me think!
> I'd give my biggest Bobolink!
> That makes *two*—*Him*—and *Life!*
> You know who *"June"* is—
> I'd give *her*—
> Roses a day from Zanzibar—
> And Lily tubes—like Wells—
> Bees—by the furlong—
> Straits of Blue
> Navies of Butterflies—sailed thro'—
> And dappled Cowslip Dells—
>
> Then I have "shares" in Primrose "Banks"—
> Daffodil Dowries—spicy "Stocks"—
> Dominions—broad as Dew—
> Bags of Doubloons—adventurous Bees
> Brought me—from firmamental seas—
> And purple—from Peru—
>
> *Now* have I bought it—
> "Shylock"? Say!
> Sign me the Bond!
> "I vow to pay
> To Her—who pledges *this*—
> *One hour*—of her Sovereign's face"!
> *Ecstatic* contract!
> *Niggard* Grace!
> My *Kingdom's worth* of Bliss!

Here is another rivalrous contest in naming and possessing absolute value, another attempt by the female speaker to enter this contest on her own behalf. The first—but oddly, not the final—bid made in this war of words is the speaker's very life. The contract proposed to "Shylock," the poem's withholding merchant-interlocutor, would reward the speaker with an hour's glimpse of her "Sovereign's face." Dickinson's allusion to *The Merchant of Venice* invokes the Christian theology of redemption, as well as its most eloquent spokesperson in the play— Portia. Dickinson's speaker, like Portia, pleads with her "Shylock" for generosity; the representative of Old Testament law (and the jealous father) silently insists rather on sacrifice of life. Dickinson twists the Christian theology of redemption, however, by in effect proposing at the outset her own life to redeem her Sovereign's, her own life for Christ's, rather than the other way round. In the poem the speaker's life, however, unlike Christ's—the legitimate purchaser of human tenure in the Kingdom of Bliss—is seemingly not acceptable in ransom for her Sovereign's face. Human love is not enough for "Shylock"; so onto her scales the speaker also heaps up her wealth of natural capital, "Primrose 'Banks'— / Daffodil Dowries—spicy 'Stocks'—." And still she receives no sign of recognition from her merchant at the poem's close.

Dickinson's transactions with the Christian theology of redemption and Christian eschatology—the attempt to differentiate between Sovereign and father Shylock—will be the subject of the following chapter. What I want to focus on here, however, is the language of natural value in this poem, one more "tale of the caskets." As in the other poems we have looked at in this chapter, nature enters this poem in a belated or secondary way, as Dickinson's economic metaphors make plain. It is constituted in a human relation, between the speaker and her interlocutor, rather than existing either in an independent realm of its own or sheerly in the speaker's isolate mind and perception. It is a currency of power and desire but not one that Dickinson speaks with absolute assurance. "Shylock" can always deny her. In no case does Dickinson represent herself as possessed of the supple, expansive mastery over nature that Emerson's Poet gains at the end of "The Sphinx," or that Emerson expresses in a famous passage from the journals[45] (which Dickinson could not have read):

> The metamorphosis of Nature shows itself in nothing more than this, that there is no word in our language that cannot become typical to us of Nature by giving it emphasis. The world is a Dancer; it is a Rosary; it is a Torrent; it is a Boat; a Mist; a Spider's Snare; it is what you will; and the metaphor will hold, and it will give the imagination keen pleasure. Swifter than light the world converts itself into that thing you name, and all things find their right place under this new and capricious classification.

For Emerson, all words that can be applied to nature have power—become powerfully universal signifiers—for as the Sphinx says, it is only necessary to tell one of her meanings in order to be Master of all nature. It is only the principle of substitution itself that needs to be grasped, and once grasped, nature, like the accommodating Sphinx, metamorphoses itself infinitely at the command of the Poet's metaphorical substitutions. The only test of a metaphor's "holding" that makes sense in Emerson's context is the solitary imagination's pleasure, which for Emerson judges the entrancing effect of linguistic substitutions from a secure standpoint outside them. The male subject is not threatened (here, anyway) in his mastery by the play of signification; rather he rests his power in that free play, which is always the other side of Emerson's insistence on the unity of nature's horizon. For public consumption, Emerson put this capricious pleasure into more authoritarian terms. Once "caught up into the life of the Universe" (caught up, but not at the price of self-loss) the poet's "speech is thunder, his thought is law, and his words are universally intelligible as the plants and animals" ("The Poet"). Like Adam naming the beasts in Eden, he can do no wrong.

Dickinson's speaker also seeks pleasure in the deployment of natural signifiers in poem 247: "Bliss" and ecstasy hang in the balance of this contract for her, and perhaps for her interlocutor too, could she convince him of it. But the intelligible power of her nature-words is precisely what is in doubt. As the first bid in the game—her life—makes clear, the female speaker, unlike Emerson, is not herself outside and above the circle of nature's equivalents for exchange, substitution, metamorphosis. Her life is on the line in the exchanges sought. Her "Daffodil Dowries," like her own body, are normatively tokens of exchange between men. Assimilated to the natural capital she offers to "Shylock," the speaker apparently lacks the voice of power that could have made her heard, lacks the power to unriddle "Shylock" in the way that Emerson's Poet unriddles the Sphinx. Her very wealth of natural signifiers, her hyperbolic plenitude, only underlines her interlocutor's silence, as if to say: this is not a rivalry you can enter. The language of nature, which Dickinson wants to press into the service of a language of female desire, falls upon unresponsive ears.

A latter-day Portia, Dickinson pits her language of nature and desire against the language of the law but finally seeks redress from within the law: "Sign me the Bond!" In the final verse paragraph, the language of law eclipses the language of nature, the flesh it silently feeds on. What she seeks is not the abolition of law, but fulfillment within it—a New Testament over the old, the law of her "Sovereign" rather than her "Shylock." What she finds is that daughters do not speak their desires very successfully under the law. Shakespeare's Portia, despite the rules of her father's game, finds a way of communicating indirectly to her chosen Bassanio the casket he should choose in order to find and claim her. And of course Portia also works the language of the law wonderfully, afterward, in male disguise. Tracing Portia's path from loving plenitude to legalism, Dickinson's speaker adopts a more direct approach, but without necessarily being granted Portia's romantic resolution.

The paternal law structuring both Portia's and Dickinson's bids for experience, knowledge, and language—their trials of initiation—has stayed remarkably constant in some ways, historical variation notwithstanding. It is the constancy that leads Luce Irigaray and related feminist theorists to borrow from Lévi-Strauss's structuralist anthropology the notion that the exchange of women is the fundamental "law" of patriarchal culture. Inasmuch as "woman" is culturally an exchange-value as well as a use-value, Irigaray suggests, her bodily being is divided "into matter-body and an envelope that is precious but impenetrable, ungraspable, and not susceptible to appropriation by women themselves."[46] What it means for women to be culturally identified with matter or nature, if that is an ongoing concern for Dickinson and her poetic sisters, is therefore more complicated than a simple binary opposition between nature and spirit, or matter and idea, can convey. The notion of "woman" is split, distributed between poles of sheer materiality and ideal spiritual meaning. As "the highest object in Nature" (in James Fields's words) her "natural" value is utterly "metaphysical" (in Irigaray's philosophical translation),[47] a transubstantiation of the truly concrete. "Woman" under the law— like Portia, codified by her dead father's will into a beautiful image inside a leaden casket; like Sarah in James Fields's "Diamonds and Pearls," who is at once a material burden borne in Abraham's chest and the rather more compelling "precious envelope" of metaphorical words spun about her (with the contradictory aim of protecting and revealing her); more troublingly, like Cordelia, whose eyes are said to weep diamonds and pearls (in temporary amelioration of a catastrophe, a rent in the fabric of the universe, in which men's eyes are seen to be vile jellies)—bears with greater or lesser freedom and grace the social burdens of this bodily transubstantiation. Irigaray's abstract analysis of this "law" of exchange glosses the normative cultural production of woman's value (like James Fields's article), Shakespeare's romantic resolution of the law's splittings, and Dickinson's critical, parodic responses to both.

The theoretical problem, under this law of exchange, is to imagine how the "merchandise" could possibly experience and speak "her own" subjectivity. Teresa de Lauretis cautions that feminists working within such models must resist the implicit assumption that women's exchangeability is *founded* on nature, or "natural" sexual difference; rather, exchange or language *produces* nature (non-man, Emerson's

NOT ME) *and* sexual difference (also configured as man and non-man, man and the signifier of man, woman).[48] This is also the problem, and the caution, of Dickinson's poem. The poem does not take nature as a given; it is, I have contended, the speaker's desire, and her interlocutory situation with "Shylock," that produce "Nature" as the speaker's wished-for go-between, her "dowry" of language. Yet the speaker's production of nature, and her sacrifice of nature and herself to law, go unanswered in the poem. The law does not deign to recognize her speaking desire. For the female speaker, the language of absolute natural value verges all too nearly upon the law in which woman is the highest—and most silent—value in nature; the transparent "envelope" of value around her, in Irigaray's metaphor, prevents her voice from being heard.[49]

At times Dickinson imagined things differently, imagined her desire fully recognized through the very economistic and legalistic metaphors of exchange that hyperbolically fail her in "What would I give to see his face?"[50] Here she figures a relationship in which the female body's schism between concrete use-value and metaphysical exchange-value would be daily sublated in sexual consummation:

> I gave myself to Him—
> And took Himself, for Pay,
> The solemn contract of a Life
> Was ratified, this way—
>
> The Wealth might disappoint—
> Myself a poorer prove
> Than this great Purchaser suspect,
> The Daily Own—of Love
>
> Depreciate the Vision—
> But till the Merchant buy—
> Still Fable—in the Isles of Spice—
> The subtle Cargoes—lie—
>
> At least—'tis Mutual—Risk—
> Some—found it—Mutual Gain—
> Sweet Debt of Life—Each Night to owe—
> Insolvent—every Noon—
>
> (poem 580)

The contract she sought with Shylock in the earlier poem, if "ratified, this way—," would ceaselessly unriddle and expend the hoarded language of the female body. Poem 247's address to Shylock converted her self and nature into the language of a bond; this poem seeks to go in the opposite direction, converting the body's secret "Fable" into the concrete pleasure of "the Daily Own—of Love." Until so used, the "subtle Cargoes—," punningly, "lie—" as the "buried gold" punningly "lies" upon the hill, in poem 11. The "truth" of the body does not lie in its hoarding, in abstracted and inaccessible value, (that of the diamond secreted in a casket) but in use; the poem's seductive appeal relaxes the hypertrophic and suspect language of absolute (and useless, uncirculating) value associated with "Brazil"—its diamonds, its blocked erotic exchanges. And the speaker so offers herself without reservation and without recourse to an outside authority, father or law, to give her away.

This poem directly revises and, in a way, completes the blocked transaction of poem 247 and its sister poems. At a much greater distance, it also replies to the imperial solipsism of Emerson's aphorism "He that would bring home the wealth of the Indies, must carry out the wealth of the Indies," as well as to "The Sphinx"'s trial of male poetic initiation and to the Platonic idealism of "Give all to Love." Dickinson's speaker recognizes the Other, her Merchant, and seeks to draw him into a genuine exchange in hopes of realizing "the Isles of Spice" instead of into a transaction so abstracted as to deny the independent existence of the other, as Emerson's Indies are effectively denied. Likewise, Dickinson's wished-for version of erotic and poetic initiation is genuinely dual ("mutual") rather than one-sided, unlike the intiation in "The Sphinx," in which the female figure unfolds her wealth and metamorphoses her body at the male Poet's word and solely for his assurance of mastery. Dickinson's "Sweet Debt of Life" invokes the Puritan theology of marriage, in some respects egalitarian, which enjoined husbands to render the marriage debt of physical love unto their wives. The Merchant himself is potentially a body in her poem (she "took Himself, for Pay,") not solely a word-wielder, like Emerson's Poet; Dickinson's vision distributes body and word between the partners rather than polarizing their functions. Finally, Dickinson imagines locating the renewing powers of linguistic figuration and substitution within a concrete relationship rather than in the perpetual transcendence of such relationships that Emerson recommends to initiates in "Give All to Love." If Emerson feared that attachment to particular objects risked reifying the world into lumpish and untranscendable givens, Dickinson here announces an erotic creed in which "the Isles of Spice—" are realized, constituted, dissolved, and reborn in the dailiness of attachment—in which concrete commitment is the powerful antidote to reification.

While not so idealist, in the philosophical sense, as Emerson's Platonic transcendence of concrete human relations toward "the Gods,"

Dickinson's "I gave myself to Him" nevertheless idealizes heterosexual erotic relations as Dickinson herself—the most egregious biographical speculations aside—never actually experienced them.[51] This poem's insistent rhetoric of symmetry is subverted by her more typical scenarios of desire as economic exchange. Only rarely does Dickinson imagine herself so securely possessed of a language of desire and a willing interlocutor for it. More typically, as the poems discussed earlier suggest, her language hyperbolically flowers in defiance of her lack of authority and then cuts itself short for the same reason.

This chapter has traced, through some of Dickinson's relatively early poems, one direction—an important one—taken by Dickinson's exploration of the poetics of nature. Her "errand into nature" in most of these poems, leads her toward initiatory struggles for speech and erotic identity against the denying "Shylock," father-merchant, figure of the law. In certain poems, however, as Gilbert and Gubar were among the first to point out, Dickinson does invoke figures of Mother Nature as " 'Strong Madonnas,' . . . mothers who enabled (and empowered) this poet to escape her Nobodaddy's requirements, if only in secret."[52] "Atropos" (poem 11) and the "Juggler of Day" (poem 228), in their respectively shadowy and spectacular ways, defend Dickinson against the notion of Nature as male poetic property.

By way of a coda, then, to the father-merchant's dominance in this chapter and in much of Dickinson's early poetry, we conclude with an autumnal poem written much later in her career, in which Dickinson explicitly takes cognizance of the trope of Mother Nature. We might see this poem as posed between two kinds of romantic precursor texts: the generously sensual autumnal poem of warmth and ripeness caught in suspension, of which Keats's ode "To Autumn" is the apotheosis, and on the other hand Emerson's bare winter epiphany on the Boston Common in the famous "transparent eyeball" passage from the first chapter of *Nature*. Here Dickinson pays tribute to the antithetical generosity of the "Typic Mother" who seasonally authors and unveils herself:

> The murmuring of Bees, has ceased
> But murmuring of some
> Posterior, prophetic,
> Has simultaneous come.
> The lower metres of the Year
> When Nature's laugh is done
> The Revelations of the Book
> Whose Genesis was June.
> Appropriate Creatures to her change

The Typic Mother sends
As Accent fades to interval
With separating Friends
Till what we speculate, has been
And thoughts we will not show
More intimate with us become
Than persons, that we know.

(poem 1115)

Like the "Juggler of Day," the Typic Mother affords an "alternative to the grim patriarchal deity" of Dickinson's childhood,[53] a counter-scripture, but not without a certain severity all her own. Her "Revelations"—the shedding of leaves, the silencing of the bees—allow the skeleton and ground-note of existence to be seen and heard. Nature abstracts herself; the bare outlines of thought emerge.

Dickinson's autumnal scene resembles Emerson's crossing of the Common in her emphasis on Autumn's power to make bare, separate, and reveal. But her Autumn progresses elusively yet inexorably, unlike Emerson's sudden elevations—which grasp him, "glad to the brink of fear" and "uplifted" (*CW* I:9–10)—and more akin to Keats's gradual "soft-dying day," which like Dickinson's (albeit far more concretely) is attended with "appropriate creatures." Dickinson's speaker stays in the same place, yet everything recedes from her: the bodily inflected presence of another's voice ("accent") yields to the abstractions of distance, space, and sight ("interval," a term on the border between sound and sight). Nor does this scene enforce the hammering I-I-I of Emerson's famous epiphany ("I am nothing; I see all; . . . I am part or parcel of God"). Dickinson's first-person plural implies a haunting collectivity even in this distancing of one consciousness from the next: a widening and a stillness, to be sure, but not quite an erasure of other existences.[54] The final verb remains in the present tense, not the past tense (persons that we *know*), even while the Typic Mother and the human mind collude in an intimacy of speculative power that outdistances the nearness of immediately lived experience. The Typic Mother's revealing changes, and the poet's experience of them, distinguish themselves from Emerson's Sphinx and her metamorphoses at the male Poet's command by the elusively shared power of the relationship between them. Mother Nature authors the Scripture, but in seeming collaboration with "what we speculate." The power of the poet's mind, however, is not immediately experienced in an Emersonian present tense of mastery; it falls instead in an interval between anticipated futurity and the traces of a past tense: "Till what we speculate, *has been*"—the autumnal interval of what Dickinson elsewhere

calls nature's "Druidic Difference" (poem 1068). This interval, difference, or trace, rather than nature's contested properties—the "buried
gold" of poem 11's piratical sun, the diamonds of "Brazil," Emerson's
"wealth of the Indies,"—typifies Dickinson's surest poetic language
of nature, as we will see it again in chapter 4.

NOTES

1. David Porter, *The Art of Emily Dickinson's Early Poetry* (Cambridge, Mass.:
Harvard University Press, 1966), x. This work helpfully canvasses some of the
earlier disagreements about the shape of Dickinson's career (1–20), as does
Greg Johnson's *Emily Dickinson: Perception and the Poet's Quest* (University:
University of Alabama Press, 1985).

2. Karl Keller has also seen Dickinson's work as characteristically parodic
of Emerson's: "The parallels with Emerson could easily be judged parodies
because for the most part they diverge so far from the sources—and criti-
cally, even mockingly." *The Only Kangaroo among the Beauty: Emily Dickinson
and America* (Baltimore: Johns Hopkins University Press, 1979), 159. Keller's
fascinating chapter on Dickinson and Emerson discusses as well Dickinson's
attraction to Emerson's aphoristic style, speculating that Dickinson saw the
aphorism as "a thing *men* make," alienated yet useful in certain moods (182).

3. This reading of Dickinson's relation to Emerson's imagination thus draws
on, but departs from, Joanne Feit Diehl's important chapter on Emerson in
Dickinson and the Romantic Imagination. What Feit Diehl regards as a perhaps
inevitable, but still constricting, move on Dickinson's part to "polarize" Emerson's fluid consciousness into a sexualized dyad (173) that nevertheless remains confined to her isolate consciousness, my argument instead takes to be
an adversarial but constructive act of immanently social analysis. The same
shift of evaluation applies to Feit Diehl's later discussion of Dickinson's "internalization of the conflict between the Emersonian me and the not me,"
in which Dickinson, according to Feit Diehl, "does not differentiate, as had
Emerson, between persons and things." See Feit Diehl, "In the Twilight of
the Gods: Women Poets and the American Sublime," in Mary Arensberg, ed.,
The American Sublime (Albany: State University of New York Press, 1986), 183,
184. The possibility of being identified with "things" is a matter of concern
for Dickinson in the poems under discussion here. For a related critique of
Feit Diehl on Dickinson, Emerson, and "the abyss," see Margaret Homans's
review in *Studies in Romanticism* 22 (1983): 445–51.

4. Thomas Weiskel, *The Romantic Sublime: Studies in the Structure and Psychology of Transcendence* (Baltimore: Johns Hopkins University Press, 1976) (hereafter cited in the text as Weiskel); and Julie Ellison, *Emerson's Romantic Style*
(Princeton, N.J.: Princeton University Press, 1984). See also an interesting
parallel in Barbara Johnson's essay, "Poetry and Its Double: Two *Invitations au
voyage*," in *The Critical Difference: Essays in the Contemporary Rhetoric of Reading*
(Baltimore: Johns Hopkins University Press, 1980). Johnson notes the conver-

gence of "shopkeeper language" and Baudelaire's naturalized erotic quest, the terms of which surprisingly echo Emerson's: "These enormous ships . . . loaded with *riches* . . . are my thoughts. . . . You lead them gently toward the sea which is the Infinite . . . and when, fatigued by the swell and *stuffed with products from the Orient,* they come back to their native port, they are still my thoughts, grown *richer,* which come back from the Infinite to you" (*L'Invitation au voyage,* 34; translation and emphasis Johnson's). As Johnson suggests, "the aesthetic notion of correspondences takes on an *economic* meaning" (35). Johnson, like Weiskel, invokes the analogy to Marx's analysis of capital (36–37).

5. Carolyn Porter, *Seeing and Being: The Plight of the Participant Observer in Emerson, James, Adams, and Faulkner* (Middletown, Conn.: Wesleyan University Press, 1981), 118. But Porter's marxist-inflected reading also stresses the Emerson whose habits of thought are opposed to reification, who takes objection to finding that "things are in the saddle, and ride mankind." Richard Grusin argues that Emerson's economistic thinking defies the logic of capitalism, or of a marxist analysis of production and exchange, and participates instead in a quasi-sacrificial extravagance that is a vehicle of rivalry, an insight that will illuminate Dickinson's economistic language as well. " 'Put God in Your Debt': Emerson's Economy of Expenditure," *PMLA* 103, no. 1 (January 1988): 35–44. It could be concluded from these divergent readings that Emerson's economistic thought is (quite typically) inconsistent and at best intermittent and inconclusive in its resistance to governing capitalist thought; Porter reminds us of "the power of the dominant culture over even the most critical and resilient minds among the ranks of the disaffected" (94), and Emerson was, if surely resilient, not necessarily among the very most disaffected of his generation.

6. *Nature,* chapter 1. Naomi Schor points out that in Western aesthetics, the notion of the detail is highly charged, and denigration of the detail goes hand in hand with devaluation of the feminine. See *Reading in Detail: Aesthetics and the Feminine* (New York: Methuen, 1987), 3–22.

7. Margaret Homans, *Women Writers and Poetic Identity.*

8. Feit Diehl, "In the Twilight of the Gods," 173–75.

9. John Evangelist Walsh contends that the poem was actually composed in 1853, on the grounds that "several of its phrases are anticipated or reflected in letters 91, 102 and 120." *The Hidden Life of Emily Dickinson* (New York: Simon and Schuster, 1971), 255. Save for letter 120's mention of " 'Atropos,' " however, the verbal parallels seem slight or trite.

10. Robert Weisbuch, *Emily Dickinson's Poetry* (Chicago: University of Chicago Press, 1975), chapters 2 and 3, passim.

11. Cynthia Griffin Wolff, *Emily Dickinson* (New York: Alfred A. Knopf, 1986), 282.

12. Myra Jehlen, *American Incarnation: The Individual, the Nation, and the Continent* (Cambridge, Mass.: Harvard University Press, 1986), 2.

13. This is where Barton Levi St. Armand's discussion of this and related "sunset" poems goes astray. He too finds that as "a witness to this covert

act" of the sun's, the poet "had then to decide her own poetic strategy" in response: "The problem of whether to keep the secret of the treasure of sunset or whether to reveal it was the problem of art itself." "The Art of Peace: Dickinson, Sunsets, and the Sublime," in *Emily Dickinson and Her Culture*, 266–67. But it hardly seems sufficient to say that Dickinson's goal in this and other poems was to capture "the ghost or likeness of the sunset by an imaginative fidelity to the exact conditions of what was before her, in the open air, aided by a long attentiveness and obedience to the ways of natural phenomena and an informed understanding of their physical processes" (267), as the American Luminist painters of her time did. Dickinson's poem scarcely makes any effort to render a natural plenitude of phenomena "faithfully"; phenomena are always already abstracted or "plundered" into language and allegory in this poem. For a reading of Dickinson's sunset poems that attends to their contests between visual representations and the conditions of figurative language, see Margaret Homans, " 'Syllables of Velvet': Dickinson, Rossetti, and the Rhetorics of Sexuality," *Feminist Studies* 11, no. 3 (Fall 1985): 569–93.

14. See Keller, *The Only Kangaroo among the Beauty*, 150 n. 2.

15. "The Sphinx," in *The Complete Works of Ralph Waldo Emerson* (Boston: Hougton Mifflin, 1876–1903), IX:20–25 (hereafter cited as *CW*).

16. David Porter, *Emerson and Literary Change* (Cambridge, Mass.: Harvard University Press, 1978), 80.

17. Dickinson's fallen sunset landscape, with its phallic snake guarding access to the falling sun's forbidden knowledge, may be connected to more general nineteenth-century notions about the fall of natural language. John Irwin has intriguingly speculated that in nineteenth-century conceptions of language and its origins, the phallus came to stand for a fallen human language in which natural and necessary links between signifier and signified are broken: "the phallic tree of knowledge links entities by an arbitrary imposition, by the interpolations of the discontinuous, fecundating spoken word between mind and object." *American Hieroglyphics: The Symbol of the Egyptian Hieroglyphics in the American Renaissance* (New Haven, Conn.: Yale University Press, 1980), 34.

18. Homans, *Women Writers and Poetic Identity*, 192–93.

19. Alicia Suskin Ostriker, *Stealing the Language: The Emergence of Women's Poetry in America* (Boston: Beacon Press, 1986), 211.

20. Poem 11's Atropos is perhaps the first instance of a spinster-artist in Dickinson's poetic career, but of course not the last. As Sandra Gilbert and Susan Gubar point out, Dickinson's later spider poems also exploit "the strength of the longstanding mythic tradition which associates virgin women—women who spin, or spin/sters—with spinning spiders," and with women artists. See *The Madwoman in the Attic: The Woman Writer and the Nineteenth-Century Literary Imagination* (New Haven, Conn.: Yale University Press, 1979), 632. Adalaide Morris has noted that poem 11 was among those sent over the fence to Sue Gilbert Dickinson, and so the audience implied for Dickinson's pirated "secret" was perhaps first of all literally another woman (and a "shrewd") with whom Dickinson exchanged secrets, and poetry. See

" 'The Love of Thee—a Prism Be': Men and Women in the Love Poetry of Emily Dickinson," in Suzanne Juhasz, ed., *Feminist Critics Read Emily Dickinson* (Bloomington: Indiana University Press, 1983), 106. Morris underscores the equality of the relationship with Sue; I would also stress Dickinson's playful threat and her sense of drawing the other into shared danger.

21. "Merlin," ll. 115–17, 101–13, 124–30, in *CW* IX:123–24. Dickinson's earliest known poem, the valentine of 1850 (poem 1, written shortly after she had received the gift of Emerson's poems from Newton), pokes fun at the vision of an ontologically coupled world.

22. Barbara Johnson's phrase; see *Defigurations: du language poétique* (Paris: Fammarion, 1979).

23. The implicit curse-ending of this poem might be compared with that of poem 23, which playfully reproaches a "missing friend," foretelling that "he no consolation / Beneath the sun may find." The "curse" strategy, especially uttered in the childlike persona of poem 23, makes a rather passive-aggressive case for the power of the poet's language.

24. Dickinson herself vacillated in her pronouns for the "Juggler," in some copies writing "it's" [*sic*] for "her." The version published anonymously in the *Springfield Daily Republican*, March 30, 1864, read "her." She never made the Juggler certifiably male.

25. Christanne Miller, *Emily Dickinson: A Poet's Grammar*, 152–53.

26. The poem exists also in another copy, made a few years later in 1861, which begins "who robbed the woods"—and ascribes the theft to a male figure: "His fantasy to please—." This version normalizes, in some respects, the sexual politics of the romantic errand into nature, bringing it in line with poem 11, "I never told the buried gold," but it still deflates that errand.

27. For an interesting sociological account analyzing the articulation between romanticism and consumer culture drawn on in Dickinson's poem, see Colin Campbell's *The Romantic Ethic and the Spirit of Modern Consumerism* (Oxford: Basil Blackwell, 1987), especially part 2. The historical reconstruction of women's roles in the age of consumer capitalism is an immense and still growing field. For an earlier, specifically Americanist account (far more unsympathetic than Campbell's) of women's sentimentalist fictional subjectivity as constituted through consumption, see Ann Douglas, *The Feminization of American Culture* (New York: Alfred A. Knopf, 1977), esp. 60–68.

28. Homans, *Women Writers and Poetic Identity*, 53.

29. Thomas Weiskel notes the absence of a threatening father's authority as a characteristic feature of the expansive "egotistical sublime." *The Romantic Sublime*, 162.

30. "The Sphinx" does, before the entrance of the Poet, feature a human madonna with child: "The babe by its mother / Lies bathed in joy," as the Sphinx observes. But like Yeats's similar tableau of the "youthful mother" with "a shape upon her lap / Honey of generation had betrayed" ("Among School Children"), this attractive picture is delusive and would entrap the Poet, did he succumb to its lure, in mere human immanence—would "drug" him, in the Platonic metaphor "The Sphinx" shares with "Among School Children."

31. As Feit Diehl notes, Emerson's romanticism thus displaces the Words-worthian epithalamion as emblem of the relationship between mind and nature and "erase[s] the possibility of any explicitly human mutuality that can survive the incursion of the acquisitive imagination." "In the Twilight of the Gods," 182.

32. For representative summaries of this debate and bibliographical guides to it, see Nelly Furman, "The Politics of Language: Beyond the Gender Principle?" and Ann Rosalind Jones, "Inscribing Femininity: French Theories of the Feminine," both in Gayle Greene and Coppelia Kahn, eds., *Making a Difference: Feminist Literary Criticism* (London: Methuen, 1985), 59–79, 80–112.

33. Ruth Miller, noting that the poem, along with others like it, was sent to Samuel Bowles, reads it as a demand that he recognize Dickinson by publishing her poetry (as well as acknowledging her erotically). *The Poetry of Emily Dickinson* (Middletown, Conn.: Wesleyan University Press, 1968), 114ff. Her later, bitter "Publication—is the Auction / Of the Mind of Man—" (poem 709) seemingly rejects her earlier submission of her own desire "To Disgrace of Price—."

34. Greg Johnson's study of Dickinson's pearl imagery also reminds us not to "overlook the extent to which Dickinson made of herself, of her own literal body, an image of the exalted quester whose progress she narrates in her poems." *Emily Dickinson: Perception and the Poet's Quest*, 127.

35. James T. Fields wrote the article, "Diamonds and Pearls," which appeared in the *Atlantic Monthly*, March 1861, 361–71. See Rebecca Patterson, *Emily Dickinson's Imagery* (Amherst: University of Massachusetts Press, 1979), 84. J. A. Lavin also ventures that "Brazil" stood for a kind of cloth sold at the time. "Emily Dickinson and Brazil," *Notes and Queries*, n.s., 7, no. 7 (July 1960): 270–71.

36. Patterson, *Emily Dickinson's Imagery*, 84, 144.

37. In this variation on the story, the casket itself is not literally plural, but the precious contents ascribed to it are. Fields's chain of associations in his essay—from this anecdote of Abraham and the casket, to *King Lear*—astonishingly anticipates the movement of Freud's well-known essay, "The Theme of the Three Caskets," which begins with *The Merchant of Venice* and moves on to discuss *Lear* as still another tale of the caskets, a tale of male choice between three women. *The Standard Edition of the Complete Psychological Works of Sigmund Freud*, trans. and ed. James Strachey (London: Hogarth Press, 1911–13, repr. 1958), XII:291–301. Moreover, Freud then concludes that the three women represent, for men, what mythology figures as the Fates: "The sisters are known to us. They are the Fates . . . the third of whom is called Atropos, the inexorable" (296)—bringing us back to Dickinson's poem 11, with its closure upon Atropos. This early cluster of Dickinson poems seems to turn a perennial theme of the male imagination, the male life cycle, inside-out from the daughter's standpoint. In Freud's haunting words, *Lear*'s death-goddess, Cordelia, "bids the old man renounce love, choose death and make friends with the necessity of dying" (301).

38. Fields, "Diamonds and Pearls," 371. This story, and the article's con-

44   *Dickinson and the Boundaries of Feminist Theory*

cluding reference to Shakespeare's *King Lear* (the gentleman's report of Cordelia's tears, IV.iii), contrast with a preceding, and much more threatening, long anecdote about Queen Elizabeth's shifts to steal the pearls of Mary, Queen of Scots. Good women *as* jewels—Sarah and Cordelia—mend the ideological breach made by Elizabeth's self-seeking covetousness and her exercise of regal power in her own desire to *have* jewels. Elizabeth is the only woman in the article whose relation to the gemstones is active.

39. Fields notes: "A very large amount of the world's capital is represented in precious stones, and ninety per cent of that capital so invested is in diamonds. This was not always the case." "Diamonds and Pearls," 368.

40. Feit Diehl, *Dickinson and the Romantic Imagination*, 167. Feit Diehl maintains that "Brazil—the ultimate exotic—remains an adequate symbol for the unifying quest of her poems" (167). It seems to me that the poem instead undermines the linguistic possibility of such a symbol, and also the powers that would go with it.

41. See Homans, *Bearing the Word: Language and Female Experience in Nineteenth-Century Women's Writing* (Chicago: University of Chicago Press, 1986), chapter 1, "Representation, Reproduction, and Women's Place in Language," for an extended theoretical critique of the male tradition identifying women with materiality and literal rather than figurative meaning in language.

42. Feit Diehl, *Dickinson and the Romantic Imagination*, 18–19.

43. See, for instance, the exchange that followed the publication of Feit Diehl's "'Come Slowly—Eden': An Exploration of Women Poets and Their Muse" (drawn from the first chapter of *Dickinson and the Romantic Imagination*), in *Signs* 3, no. 3 (1978): 572–87. Homans's review (see note 3 above) defends Feit Diehl on this score at eloquent length.

44. The footnote of biographical disclaimer or speculation is by now a recognizable subgenre of Dickinson criticism. The usual format followed lists all the historical candidates (male and sometimes female) advanced for "the" lover's position and then either chooses among them or excoriates the folly of choosing among them on insufficient evidence. Rather than summarize this scholarship, my argument in this chapter will briefly address the significance of the debate itself. It is worth noting that some recent feminist critics, following the lead of Sewell's splendid biographical saga of the Dickinson family (and looking in some cases to rescue Dickinson from critical practices they dislike), recognize that the biographical significance of *all* the important parties to Dickinson's life is up for discussion. Richard B. Sewall, *The Life of Emily Dickinson* (New York: Farrar, Straus and Giroux, 1974; repr. 1980). See, for instance, Cynthia Griffin Wolff's *Emily Dickinson* and Barbara Antonina Clarke Mossberg's *Emily Dickinson: When a Writer Is a Daughter* (Bloomington: Indiana University Press, 1982) for illuminating feminist readings of Dickinson's relationship to her brother Austin and her mother, two rather neglected biographical figures. More recently and tendentiously, Vivian R. Pollak takes as one of her central topics "Dickinson's ambivalence toward her precursors (I refer, of course, to her parents)" in *Dickinson: The Anxiety of Gender* (Ithaca, N.Y.: Cornell University Press, 1984), 30. I would not repudiate Pollak's identifica-

tion of precursors with parents, only question its exclusivity, the "of course" (of course, polemically ironic) of it. Dickinson's Mother Nature and father-merchant are mother and father as well as revisionary figures out of poetic tradition—but mother and father culturally generalized and available to a criticism not solely focused on the reported incidents of Dickinson's family life, pertinent as those are. Nor do I think this tendency to generalize or abstract such figures peculiar in any way to the psychic life of poets. If psychoanalysis means anything in any cultural context whatever, Oedipus is everyone's myth in a way not directly contingent upon specific life events.

45. Entry of Summer 1841, in *Selections from Ralph Waldo Emerson*, ed. Stephen E. Whicher (Boston: Houghton Mifflin, 1957), 185.

46. Luce Irigaray, "Women on the Market," in *This Sex Which Is Not One*, trans. Catherine Porter (Ithaca, N.Y.: Cornell University Press, 1985), 176. For a suggestive feminist reading of *The Merchant of Venice* that addresses the question of how women can find room to speak under this "law," see Karen Newman's "Portia's Ring: Unruly Women and Structures of Exchange in *The Merchant of Venice*," *Shakespeare Quarterly* 38, no. 1 (Spring 1987): 19–33.

47. *"In order to become equivalent, a commodity changes bodies.* A super-natural, metaphysical origin is substituted for its material origin. . . . *a commodity—a woman—is divided into two irreconcilable "bodies":* her 'natural' body and her socially valued, exchangeable body, which is a particularly mimetic expression of masculine values" ("Women on the Market," 180; emphasis Irigaray's).

48. See Teresa de Lauretis, *Alice Doesn't: Feminism, Semiotics, Cinema* (Bloomington: Indiana University Press, 1984), 18–20ff.

49. Abstract as it sounds, this schism in woman operated as a concrete social prohibition against women's public speech in the nineteenth century, as many feminist historians have noted: public speech, it was contended, would depreciate the hyperbolic value placed on women's pure *being* in the sphere of the home.

50. For a survey of Dickinson's economic poems of desire that connects them to specific nineteenth-century bourgeois mores of sexual behavior, see Joan Burbick's "Emily Dickinson and the Economics of Desire," *American Literature* 58 (1986): 361–78. Burbick finds that "Dickinson's writings delineate the cultural language of desire for the Victorian woman in an age that attempted to 'rob' the female body of delight."

51. William Shurr's *The Marriage of Emily Dickinson* (Lexington: University of Kentucky Press, 1983) recently makes the most extreme (and necessarily inconsistent) case for taking *all* of Dickinson's erotic metaphors, including her metaphors of consummated marriage, as the literal record of experience. The case is inconsistent because the stories the metaphors "tell" are in some instances incompatible with each other, if each is literally true to experience. Some of them have to be figurative, if others are to be literally true—and how is one to tell the difference?

52. Gilbert and Gubar, *The Madwoman in the Attic*, 647.

53. St. Armand, *Emily Dickinson and Her Culture*, 266.

54. In response to Feit Diehl and other critics who stress the absolute-

ness of Dickinson's skepticism, Christopher Benfey has beautifully written that what Dickinson's skepticism typically asks us to renounce "is not the world, or other people, or our bodies. She asks us to renounce our demands for proof, for certainty, for possession." *Emily Dickinson and the Problem of Others* (Amherst: University of Massachusetts Press, 1984), 110. And the "Typic Mother" in this poem indeed pauses short of casting human consciousness into a wholly solitary abyss of mind: intimacy is yet the native of her bleak trees.

2

Love after Death:
Dickinson's Higher Criticism and the Law of the Father

"I thought that nature was enough," Dickinson writes in a poem dated around 1873, "till Human nature came":

> But that the other did absorb
> As Parallax a Flame—
>
> Of Human nature just aware
> There added the Divine
> Brief struggle for capacity
> The power to contain
>
> Is always as the contents
> But give a Giant room
> And you will lodge a Giant
> And not a smaller man
> (poem 1286)

This poem is not to be taken exactly as literal fact about Dickinson's career; she wrote poems "about" nature before, during, and after the writing of this poem. Nevertheless it talks about a process that may, for Dickinson, parallel Wordsworth's initiation into a humanized nature out of an unreflective innocence. Dickinson's initiation into "Human nature," however, almost instantly overleaps Wordsworth's middle realm of humanized nature to join a struggle with "the Divine" itself. Dickinson often favored optical metaphors for the experience of heaven or the afterlife, and in this poem a technical term from optics, "Parallax" (the apparent displacement of an object seen from two different vantage points), conquers the natural substance of "Flame" (presumably a distant object occulted by the speaker's shift of viewpoint?). As in Emerson's essay "Circles," where a larger circle can always be drawn around a smaller's circumference, displacement follows displacement. Having absorbed nature, human nature confronts the Divine. Who won? Dickinson leaves that third point of the dialectic tantalizingly in doubt.

In this retrospective, schematic account of her poetic career, Dickinson presents as "Brief," finished, abstract, and absolute a struggle that would seem in fact to have been represented over and over in the poems: the translation of her own experience and her own early poetic "errands into nature" into a realm out of nature, the translation of her Oedipal romance with/in nature into the more gigantic realm of a struggle with the Divine. Most often and most famously for Dickinson, especially in the early-to-mid-1860s, the preferred realm of her "struggle for capacity" is the realm of eschatology: the life after death, the Last Judgment. Her poetic romance takes the form of a love that, whether consummated or not in any sense on earth (usually not), derives its essence from its defiance of heavenly law. As became true of many of her "nature" poems, these poems are about abstract law, about power rather than humanly individualized passion—about "parallax," in Dickinson's own metaphor, rather than flame, and one of their chief actors is the forbidding Father of the Law.

As we have already seen, Dickinson early on in her career turns encounters with "nature" into encounters with Shylock, the Merchant, the lover who is also the denying Father of the Law. The problem for Dickinson (or any woman poet in this Romantic family romance), according to Joanne Feit Diehl, is that any male lover/muse—inspirer of speech, conferrer of vocation—threatens to collapse into the overpowering, silencing Father. Unlike women muses for male poets, Fathers do not exist only to serve the poet's voice. In Feit Diehl's paradigm, the woman poet is in a situation analogous to that Freud ascribes to women generally who have "successfully" entered upon the Oedipus complex: such daughters run the risk of never resolving the complex in the way sons do, never absolutely distinguishing father from lover. They cannot quite learn the language of the law's differences (between family and nonfamily, between generations). Why not?

According to Freud, women's relationship to the Law of the Father is notoriously one of deficiency and doubled lack. Women are lacking, first, because "already" castrated; second, because in the nature of things they cannot submit to the threat of castration:

> In girls the motive for the demolition of the Oedipus complex is lacking. Castration has already had its effect, which was to force the child into the situation of the Oedipus complex. Thus the Oedipus complex escapes the fate which it meets with in boys: it may be slowly abandoned or dealt with by repression, or its effects may persist far into

women's normal mental life. I cannot evade the notion (though I hesitate to give it expression) that for women the level of what is ethically normal is different from what it is in men. Characteristics which critics of every epoch have brought up against women—that they show less sense of justice than men, that they are less ready to submit to the great exigencies of life, that they are more often influenced in their judgments by feelings of affection or hostility—all these would be amply accounted for by the modification in the formation of their super-ego which we have inferred above.

That is, the girl "normally" persists in desiring the father rather than internalizing his law and seldom wholly succeeds in transferring her desire to a male—a son—who under the Law of the Father (which the son has internalized by virtue of his identification with the father), differs from the father only in being available to her.[1] The Law of the Father insists that she take as an object a man different, yet truly the same, which fulfills the law's requirement of "inexorable" rightness, of submission to life's exigencies. The difference between her father and the son to whom she is given is not the same as the difference to the boy between his mother (first object of his desire) and the wife he eventually takes, since in the latter difference castration intervenes, while in the former it does not; and this lack in the difference between her allotted male objects (generated by the lack in her) disqualifies the girl from a capacity for making judgments. She in whom "castration has already had its effect" (on whom it can have no effect), who has in the place of the missing organ "nothing to see," cannot administer justice that is "ethically normal" to male thinking.

As the little-boy/Freud's dismissal of the female genitals declares, the judgment here deemed normative—to which the girl lacks access —privileges sight. The male gaze, marking presence or absence of the phallus, becomes the little boy's point of entry into the law. Seeing that "nothing to see" impresses him with castration anxiety, in recompense for which he will internalize the father's law, and at the end of a long road, reap the social rewards of so doing. The popular iconographic representation of Justice—a blind woman, holding the scales—informs us of this story, by reversal and condensation. Her blinded face recalls to the male viewer the threatened punishment, for fear of which he internalized the Law of the Father; at the same time, her blindness perhaps allays fears of women's power, independently exercised.

The gaze of the little girl informs her once and for all of her own deficiencies. "She sees and makes her decision in a flash."[2] The daughter's place as an object of exchange under the Law of the Father henceforth is to be judged, not to judge; to be seen (even while she has nothing that signifies to be seen, her whole body is fetishized) and not to see. According to Freud, she possesses in a radically diminished way the psychic agency that is felt by the ego as an *overseeing*. As recent feminist film theory has put it, women are not (in normative cultural productions at least) positioned to possess the gaze.[3] In terms of her Oedipal romance, lacking the gaze means that she must, in her double bind, substitute the son for the father in her desire *while not being able to discriminate between them*, without access to the means of seeing and representing their differences, since the phallic signifier (the threat of castration) privileged in the order of vision only draws its line for the boy, between woman as forbidden mother and woman as available object of desire. Lest this psychoanalytic description seem entirely abstract, we may note that on the practical level—the level of social organization both described and prescribed by psychoanalytic theory—women in mid-nineteenth-century American and English society were, despite real and important inroads into public action in the women's movement, still largely debarred from the places in the institutions that distributed power along the law's lines of internalization and identification: the places Dickinson's father held, for instance, as a lawyer, member of Congress, and treasurer of Amherst College. What would later be Freud's formulations of the superego were actually embodied in social practice and political rhetoric.

Theoretically speaking, then, the nineteenth-century woman poet was barred, in the cultural myth of which Freud was only one later redactor, from what Thomas Weiskel describes as the essential structure of the "sublime moment," its recapitulations of the "positive resolution" of the *boy's* (as Weiskel omits to note) Oedipus complex. In the "sublime moment," the individual ego conquers an awesome external threat by identifying with a transcendent faculty that it at once contains, introjects, and is contained by.[4] The difficulty with this moment for women poets, Feit Diehl suggests, is that "if authority is associated with the patriarch, then the woman poet cannot so easily experience the identity between self and all-powerful other; instead, his presence may seem so 'ravishing' (a term long associated with the workings of the sublime), that she is vanquished. As avatar of the patriarch, his power remains external to hers, for she is not the son who joins that male company of descendental poets known as poetic tradition."[5] "Already castrated," as Freud would put it, she has no direct access to the initiatory agon through which a male poet may assume his identification with patriarchal tradition.

The question, then, is where places of cultural contradiction exist for Dickinson in which the story of the Law of the Father can be questioned. For Dickinson and many of her contemporaries, both male and female, one such mid-nineteeth-century locus of contradiction and conflict centered around Christianity, the decline of Calvinism, and the questioning of Scripture's revealed authority. A general cultural problem of authority, here, seems to intersect both with the particular issues of Emily Dickinson's familial biography and with her poetic quest after an initiatory romance that would make sense for a woman poet. Christian eschatology and Christian theology of the redemption set a scene—supernatural or transcendent or sublime—in which Dickinson plays out the overdetermined questions: Can the son be different from the father, and in terms of what vision could his difference be represented? Can a woman's gaze disrupt the compact of Father and Son that sustains patriarchal Law?

Christian Trinitarian theology (under fire in many quarters in the nineteenth century, but orthodox at Dickinson's Amherst) proposes that the Son is, and is not, different from the Father. A religious vocabulary that, as Homans argues, triggered Dickinson's awareness that language is figurative, also sets the terms for Dickinson's exploration of the family romance as a struggle for poetic power. If, as Feit Diehl suggests, Dickinson characteristically modifies the various "compensatory gestures" of the Romantic poets into conformity with her own more absolutely skeptical vision, she also parodies Christianity's grand compensatory gesture, the redemption. Her undercover rhetorical analyses dismantle the Father's claims to self-identity with his Son and absolute control over Logos. If the Father needs a mediator, if he sends to us human language, his language can be appropriated to ends other than his own:

> God is a distant—stately Lover—
> Woos, as He states us—by His Son—
> Verily, a Vicarious Courtship—
> "Miles," and "Priscilla," were such an One—
>
> But, lest the Soul—like fair "Priscilla"—
> Choose the Envoy—and spurn the Groom—
> Vouches, with hyperbolic archness—
> "Miles," and "John Alden" were Synonyme—
>   (poem 357)

Dickinson's Puritan forebears paid homage to "a *figurative*, a *metaphorical* God*,*" in John Donne's words; but the Father of poem 357 is, as Dickinson mimics him, an unsuccessful user of rhetoric by Puritan standards. For Puritan theorists of rhetoric, Ann Kibbey points out, the separation of sound from sense undermined what would ideally be "some intrinsic meaning to be discovered in the relation between the audible figure and the referent"; in successful Puritan plain style, "the sound design of . . . words becomes the primary sensory evidence that [their] referents—Father, Son, and child of God—actually exist."[6] The Father's rhetoric of incarnation in Dickinson's poem, however, punningly entangles itself in undermining reference from sound to sense, Son to God. God's distance, in the poem's first line, is inseparable from his stateliness: his kingly presence, his "state," can never be present in this life to us. Its absence defines the difference between here and hereafter. Yet it is God the Father who offers to send language across the gap between here and transcendence. God "states us," that is, tells us something authoritatively in the voice connected to his (absent) presence, his "state"—but this locus of authoritative voice is precisely what we as yet lack, and its lack is the occasion of redemption (which will "state us," taking the pronoun as direct object) as well as the occasion of the poem. The repetition of "state" and the pun on it only draw attention to the insecurity of what is to be established, the link between God's state and his incarnate statement, the Son. God—or the poem's unspecified speaker, treacherously standing in as God's rhetorical representative—compounds his rhetorical error in the third line by alliterating "Verily" and "Vicarious." Correspondence in sound, according to Puritan understanding of homiletic rhetoric (and according to any theory of language as presence), should indicate correspondence in meaning. "Verily," however, aligns itself with authoritative truth-in-presence—"Verily, I say unto you . . ."— which is anything but vicarious. "Verily" is exactly what cannot be pronounced vicariously.

Linking the Christian drama of redemption to the American founding myth of the Puritan's City on the Hill, Dickinson playfully tries American national identity along with God the Father's identity. (A few years earlier, Longfellow had published his long, romantic version of *The Courtship of Miles Standish*). In her vision, Miles Standish, Priscilla, and John Alden enacted a historical type of God's courtship—an enactment, however, that goes significantly awry. The historical Priscilla's desire misread Miles's vicarious language of courtship. She responded to John Alden's presence by passing a judgment unforeseen by either of the male participants in the triangle, preferring the envoy over the groom, the signifier over the presumptive but absent signified. Priscilla and Miles Standish were never pronounced one flesh, and the vows were never said, just as "One" in the poem's fourth line is literally unpronounceable when preceded by "an." Dickinson's graphic insertion, *an* for a, impedes sacramental speech. The silent *n* does not speak, but it does not hold its peace, either; it stands for the separability of Standish and Alden, signifier and signified. Here, as throughout her career, Dickinson subverts the authority of voice with the constitutive absence of the letter, speech with writing.[7] Dickinson as mock-faithful transcriber of God's message forestalls in the same graphic gesture both the union of God and the human soul and the union of men and women in marriage.

The identity of Father and Son is, for Dickinson's speaker, a matter of hyperbolic assertion, not mystical essence; Christianity's arithmetic of redemption is a punning joke of "hyperbolic archness" (a joke that elsewhere, for Dickinson, threatened to look "too expensive"). What God the Father, or any rhetoric of authoritative presence, strives to make one in language—sound and sense, message and messenger, Father and Son, man and wife—can always be divided again. The soul escapes in the company of its John Alden, a son not synonymous with his Father, wooed away from him by Dickinson's irony.

Dickinson's subversion of Christianity's redemptive family romance touches on areas of theology that also attracted Emerson's interest, but to different ends. From his own standpoint, in Unitarianism, idealism, and the problematics of influence and authority, Emerson had come to find Christ's mediation between God and humanity an intellectual embarrassment: "Christianity is rightly dear to the best of mankind; yet was there never a young philosopher whose breeding had fallen into the Christian church by whom that brave text of Paul's was not specially prized: 'Then shall also the Son be subject unto Him who put all things under him, that God may be all in all.' Let the claims and virtues of persons be never so great and welcome, the instinct of man presses eagerly onward to the impersonal and illimitable, and gladly arms itself against the dogmatism of bigots with this generous word out of the book itself."[8] Interestingly, Emerson uses the same language to describe Christianity that Freud uses to describe the female superego: it is not "impersonal" enough, not abstract enough. Historically, Emerson's complaint may well be related to the feminization and domestication of theology in the nineteenth-century United States, with its emphasis on Jesus as comforter. In this liberalizing Protestant theological climate, Ann Douglas notes, God in the Incarnation "has ceased to be an 'abstract excellence' and become a 'person,'" almost a literary character in a domestic novel.[9] Emerson's adversary is probably not only the old Calvinist doctrine of the redemption, which he defensively labels "the dogmatism of bigots," but the perhaps excessively generous and personal Jesus of domestic Christianity.[10] Getting stalled on Christianity's compensatory, earthbound gestures (that is, on its central doctrine of redemption, whether Calvinist or sentimental), Emerson thinks, interferes with the philosopher's direct relation to the Godhead. When dogmatically interpreted as timelessly present truth, once and for all revealed, the teachings of Jesus are the potential enemy of Emerson's own originary ambitions.[11]

Dickinson's poetry steers a different course through the theology of redemption and apocalypse. Unlike Emerson, as Albert J. Gelpi has said, Dickinson did not shed the idea of "the God of the Old Testament and Calvinist Christianity . . . nor could she doubt Jehovah's fatherhood, however inexplicable that might be."[12] Like some of her female contemporaries, Dickinson retains and elaborates upon Christian theology as a family romance in which father, son, and female speaker are in certain respects personalized. No doubt her attraction to older notions of "Jehovah's fatherhood" was biographically overdetermined by Edward Dickinson's looming presence in the Homestead, but it has more abstract and culturally general references as well, and above all it is a poetic choice made with poetic consequences.

Dickinson's differences from her more sentimental women contemporaries must be noted here. Sentimental or feminized theology was often connected to forms of religious revivalism that Dickinson herself consistently resisted, both in her youth at Mount Holyoke and after. In retaining a personalized theological family romance, Dickinson is not interested in exalting an essential "women's sphere" or promoting a complementary "woman's language" of feeling that would supplement or ameliorate—without displacing—male languages of authority. Instead she seeks out the differences within male language itself, the contradictions within the Law of the Father, and plays them out through skeptical quotation, punning reference, and self-deconstructing figures.

Like some contemporary women writers of domestic fiction, Dickinson frequently represents herself as a speaker from the afterlife, but not with the intention of domesticating heaven or staging a family reunion in the hereafter. Instead, as Cynthia Griffin Wolff argues,[13] she offers a "corrective for this 'liberalized' religion" and its "vogue for posthumous comfort":

> Do people moulder equally,
> They bury, in the Grave?
> I do believe a Species
> As positively live

As I, who testify it
Deny that I—am dead—
And fill my Lungs, for Witness—
From Tanks—above my Head—

I say to you, said Jesus—
That there be standing here—
A Sort, that shall not taste of Death
If Jesus was sincere—

I need no further Argue—
That statement of the Lord
Is not a controvertible—
He told me, Death was dead—

(poem 432)

Anything but a consoling or domesticated and conventionally feminized version of Christology, the poem undermines oppositions between life and death and undermines connections among voice,
breath, spirit, and presence. Along with the Higher Criticism, which
had by this time made its way into Bostonian discussion circles (and
points farther west), the poem draws attention to the problematic distance between the actual promises of the present Christ and their
historical reception. Not only does God the Father need Jesus to represent him on earth, John Alden to his Miles Standish, but the words of
Jesus need to be repeated in circumstances that challenge belief. What
language can be trusted? "The Bible is an antique Volume," Dickinson
later would write, "Written by faded Men / At the suggestion of Holy
Spectres" (poem 1545).[14] "Holy Spectres" at best confer only dubious
authority upon Scripture, but in this radical earlier poem the divine
afflatus comes in even more grotesque form, "From Tanks—above
my Head—." The speaker's anti-natural respiration apes life just as
Dickinson's rhetoric mimics the authoritative narrative of the Gospels:

I breathed enough to take the Trick—
And now, removed from Air—
I simulate the Breath, so well—
That One, to be quite sure—

The Lungs are stirless—must descend
Among the Cunning Cells—
And touch the Pantomime—Himself,
How numb, the Bellows feels!

(poem 272)

The "positive" testimony of these speakers to the afterlife takes, in
effect, the form of a double negative reinforced by alliteration: re-

peating Christ's promise that "death was dead," she *denies* that she is *dead*, she *simulates* so well that to be *sure* (of what? Her life—or her death?) her listeners would have to dare her very insides to know the truth. Doubting Thomases in reverse, they could then be sure that this speaker was truly dead. Dickinson's testimony (her diction invokes both the law and a religious profession of faith) hollows out and inverts, rather than embraces and feminizes, the figure of Christ and the language of redemption.

Whatever Dickinson's knowledge of the Higher Criticism, poem 432 shrewdly seizes upon exactly the one of all Jesus' reported utterances that caused the early church the most consternation and gave a starting point to much later biblical criticism—the promise, as Jesus' early audience interpreted it, that the second coming was due within a lifetime of Christ's death. This utterance was interpreted literally at first, but had to be reinterpreted figuratively by the time the Gospels were compiled and the sacred canon established in the second century after the death of Christ. The early church transformed itself from a group of apocalyptic sects into a centralized body resigned to living in history by resolving this hermeneutical crisis, but by Dickinson's time this resolution was under siege from textual scholarship. Dickinson puts her finger on the instability. "If Jesus was sincere—," he may nevertheless have lacked authority speaking as man, not God; if he was not sincere (a doubt the poem fosters), he is comprehended in Dickinson's arraignment of the "Heavenly Father" for his own "Duplicity" (poem 1461). If he was sincere but spoke figuratively, interpretations of his words cannot be checked or rendered final. Any repetition of Christ's promises by another speaker, like the dead/undead speaker of poem 432, only lengthens the distance between the words' repetition and their original authority. Iterability itself—figured by the transformation of divine afflatus into canned air—is both the necessary precondition of sacred texts and the inevitable erosion of their originary authority.

Little indicates the speaker's gender in either of these poems. A male gender is ascribed to a body part, the "Bellows," in poem 272, but not to the speaker as a whole.[15] The speaker's voice seems in fact to depend on her/his/its alienation from the body for its authority; the detached voice points out the abstracted details of its own bodily mechanism for inspection. Yet Dickinson's concern with the relationship between bodily presence and authoritative voice, her concern therefore with the Christian theology of the Incarnation, contrasts suggestively with Emerson's confident (and perhaps culturally masculine) dismissal of "persons," his leap toward "the impersonal and illimitable," his hostility toward any mediator between individual and the "all in all." For Emerson, the relationship between body and speech would ideally be transparent (like his famous eyeball). Dickinson in these poems insists on the intractably mediated nature of speech: if her speakers quest after the illimitable Divinity, they do so encumbered by tanks and bellows. Incarnate truth in the spoken word—what Jesus was supposed to bring—cannot be transparent or immediate. Jesus does not transparently reveal his divinity or his identity with the Father, nor can the poet herself be immediately at one with her speech, body transparent to its spiritual afflatus. But Dickinson will take this loss, if she can bring home her deconstruction of the Father/Son's claims on language as presence and self-identity.

Dickinson's interrogation of religious language and Christology is one with her interrogation of the Law of the Father, of the family romance and women's possible places in it. The structure of this interrogation, for Dickinson, is almost always triangular—unlike Emerson, who desires the unmediated relationship with the all-in-all. Faced with the orthodox scheme of God the Father and Christ the Son, Dickinson time and again usurps the Son's place of mediator between humankind and the Father and asserts her own power in a separate romance with the Son. Her favorite setting for this drama is apocalyptic rather than natural: she speaks from an afterlife that is a scene of final judgment. She asserts the power of judgment and, relatedly, the power of her gaze—the two powers denied women in the cultural myth of sexual difference, as Freud magisterially codified it. At the same time, however, this assertion is necessarily mediated to some degree by the triangle in which it is embedded (the triangle of the Symbolic Order, as Lacanian theory would have it), and her desire inevitably is mediated by the gaze of the Other.

The outlines of Dickinson's autobiographical myth of life and love after death are familiar to all her readers. On earth, Dickinson and her lover are separated, the love affair never consummated as part of the order of nature. In heaven, they meet again.

'Twas a long Parting—but the time
For Interview—had Come—
Before the Judgment Seat of God—
The last—and second time

These Fleshless Lovers met—
A Heaven in a Gaze—
A Heaven of Heavens—the Privilege
Of one another's Eyes—

No Lifetime set—on Them—
Appareled as the new
Unborn—except They had beheld—
Born infiniter—now—

Was Bridal—e'er like This?
A Paradise—the Host—
And Cherubim—and Seraphim—
The unobtrusive Guest—

(poem 625)

Dickinson exultantly refuses to regard the unmediated sight of the Father—every believer's goal—as the goal of life and afterlife. Cynthia Griffin Wolff observes that "every important element of the poem turns upon the use of the "eye/I," and fulfillment for the lovers comes, punningly, as the last and eternal "interview." The participants in this marriage "brazenly" usurp "the right of Christ to claim His bride." [16] The poem celebrates the entire presence of the lovers, each to the other, mirrored in a face-to-face encounter.

As one of the most persistent imaginative scenarios in Dickinson's repertory, this poem and others like it inevitably court the theoretical templates of psychoanalytic reading. But which psychoanalysis? Wolff's biographical reading draws on feminist interest in object-relations psychoanalysis and its privileging of the pre-Oedipal relationship to the mother. According to Wolff, Dickinson's recurrent imaging of the afterlife as a face-to-face encounter stems from a basic situation of early infancy and the lasting desire to which that situation gives rise: the mother-child dyad, "the preverbal stage of life, when communication is achieved *visually* and *silently* through a complex interaction of eye contact and face-to-face play." If this stage proceeds happily, an infant emerges with a secure sense of self, and her succeeding acquisition of language only adds another power to the security of the first mother-child presence. If mirroring and mothering are not quite sufficient, the infant may emerge from this preverbal state with her "initial attitude to language" ominously "distorted": viewing language as an inadequate substitute for the flawed initial mirroring, and at the same time overvaluing—through her unmet desire—both the powers of language *and* the powers of immediate, face-to-face communicative presence. [17]

Wolff's object-relations framework gives compelling testimony to the pervasiveness and the ambivalence of Dickinson's desire for face-to-face encounter. From the other psychoanalytic perspectives, however, especially those inflected by encounters with deconstruction, there are reasons to call it into question. For example, the object-relations framework has little to say about the persistent thematics of the father in most (but not all) of these poems. Why are they mostly about male objects (when a gender can be read out from them)? Where does gender enter the object-relations account of the acquisition of language; how do women learn to substitute male objects for the first, female object of the gaze? Nor does the object-relations framework account for the persistence of the triangle even in poems that insist, as poem 625 does, on the primacy of the face-to-face dyad. How important are the "Cherubim—and Seraphim—" in such a poem? The gaze of the others may be vital even if it exists in part as a pressure to be resisted or conquered by the lovers' own "Interview." Nor does the object-relations framework by itself, in its focus on the pre-Oedipal dyad of mother and child, have a way of explaining the persistent gendering of the gaze, in Western culture, as male.

Finally, the attitude toward language that Wolff describes as a "distorted" outcome of the pre-Oedipal process—experiencing language as an inadequate substitute for an original "presence" that itself is always already lost—is, from other psychoanalytical perspectives, the condition of acquiring language at all. The path of language acquisition Wolff holds up as normal—experiencing language as a happy supplement to maternal presence—can be seen as a screen for, or repression of, the trauma of loss or castration through which language is learned. Observing his nephew play with a spool, Freud noted that he attached language to his mother's absence and played out the scenario of her departure and return with a verbal game: "fort/da," the spool went out with a word and was reeled in again with a word. The "fort/da" game is everybody's heritage, not the unhappy secret of a "distorted" few (but everybody's differently). Performing a deconstructive reversal of Wolff's story, one could say that "distortion" always comes first, and the happy success story of mother and child is a distorted (re)construction of another origin.

Locating the place of the father in Dickinson's autobiographical myth of the face-to-face encounter, then, invokes basic debates in feminist theory over allegiances to object-relations versus Oedipal and poststructuralist versions of psychoanalysis—and to the differing accounts of language fostered by each theory. British theorists Juliet Mitchell and Jacqueline Rose have represented Lacanian psychoanalysis and its (deliberately) outrageous insistence on the primacy of the phallus and the Oedipal or Symbolic Order; American feminist critics have more often preferred the school of feminist psychoanalytic theory derived from object relations, pioneered by Nancy Chodorow and taken up by Carol Gilligan.[18] Margaret Homans has recently intervened in this debate by tracing out a half-hidden narrative of aggression against the mother, or the idea of her presence, in classical Freudian and Lacanian theory. The mother is not absent in this body of psychoanalytic theory by fiat of nature or the very structure of language, Homans suggests; rather, she is actively disappeared, in a move that links psychoanalysis to other founding myths of Western culture.[19]

Yet even if the mother's absence is contingent upon androcentric culture rather than the structure of language as such, Homans finds that Lacanian theory does help describe much of the experience of nineteenth-century women writers vis-à-vis language, exactly because "androcentric myth has, in effect, shaped female experience."[20] And challenging it, Dickinson's career suggests, entails engaging it. As we have already seen, the questions left unanswered by Wolff's object-relations account of Dickinson's face-to-face scenario of desire are precisely those taken up—albeit through a lens of androcentrism—in the classical Freudian scenario of the daughter's (inevitably defective, to him) maturation. The cultural gendering of the gaze as male; women's "deficient" relationship to the gaze; the close association between themes of the visible, castration and sexual difference, and ideas of justice and morality: all these themes appear in Dickinson's eschatological romance of the face-to-face encounter. Moreover, the tension in these poems between the face-to-face encounter and the dyad's "outside" looking in suggests a comparison to Lacanian theory's distinction between the Imaginary psychic order (the register of visual likeness, identity, recognition, and the gaze of the mother) and the Symbolic (the register of structure, language and exchange, the Law of the Father).[21] In suggesting the pertinence of classical Freudian and Lacanian categories of thought, I am by no means arguing that Dickinson simply accepted the cultural position spelled out for women in psychoanalytic thought; rather that she carried her brief before the Law of the Father out of a sense that there the kingdom, the power, and the glory (words she was deeply invested in appropriating) lay.[22]

Freudian and Lacanian theory can help us take seriously the presence of the third—the father, God, the triangle embedded in the poems' very structure of address—in those poems exalting the afterlife's dyadic face-to-face communion with the lover. In poem 625, Dickinson's rendition of this dyadic meeting in the third person of the poem's narrative itself calls into question the all-sufficiency of the lovers' dyad and the possibility of rendering it into language without the mediation of a third gaze. The poem places its readers in the place of the witnessing third, even in the place of God the Father. In a sense God, and readers, are asked to experience desire through the mediation of the lovers' gaze. Another poem in this vein makes this structure of address explicit. Written this time in the first person, this poem addresses a judging God or a reader rather than the lover himself. The speaker modulates the scene of Last Judgment into a scene of instruction, an apocalyptic lesson in human love:

> Of all the Souls that stand create—
> I have elected—One—
> When Sense from Spirit—files away—
> And Subterfuge—is done—
> When that which is—and that which was—
> Apart—intrinsic—stand—
> And this brief Tragedy of flesh—
> Is shifted—like a Sand—
> When Figures show their royal Front—
> And Mists—are carved away,
> Behold the Atom—I preferred—
> To all the lists of Clay!
>
> (poem 664)

Like poem 625, this poem turns on the relationship between "I" and the gaze: Last Judgment reveals all to the sight, and the speaker invites God and her readers to "behold" where her own gaze has fallen. Where Emerson found Christ's mediation an embarrassment and obstacle in his, man's, pursuit of the "impersonal and illimitable," Dickinson turns aside from the Father's unmediated presence, in the last instance, to be a defiant respecter of persons. In her own revision of the figure of the Christian soul as the "Bride of Christ," she chooses her own envoy and spurns the groom.

Yet this lover is anything but an individual, naturalistic person. The Atom she prefers has no biographical referent for the purposes of this poem, and Dickinson flaunts the absence of any particular referent. The Atom is a mathematical originary point of no extent in itself and no characteristics save for the poet's willful, mysterious preference. It is an atom of pure difference, generated along a signifying chain, a list of substitutions. Its way of existing calls into question the very possibility of filing away "Sense from Spirit," of filing away the signifier in order to reveal a transcendent signified of individual identity. Charles Anderson points out "the verbal play [of alliteration and rhyme] that meshes spirit and flesh" even as they are supposed to emerge " 'Apart—intrinsic' "; the signifier hangs on, and the speaker deploys it. Literally speaking, the Atom has no gender; punningly, as Christanne Miller points out, it is male, Adam.[23] *Ecce homo!* Once upon a time, Adam, with God the Father's authority, put names to every beast and thing in "all the lists of Clay"; now Dickinson's speaker apocalyptically unnames them, and Adam too. Adam as a disabling male precursor, with God, in the production of "literal language in which words are synonymous with meaning," dies to this poetry and is resurrected as the Atom: a necessary third term, a deconstructive muse, the nothing and everything left over when the figurative "Mists—are carved away." Refusing Christ the Son, the Father's "second Adam," substituting her own, mysterious Atom, she elects herself out of the Father's bargain of redemption.

This poem does not fit an object-relations account of the lover's dyad as a reenactment of the mother-child bond's mutual presence. An atom virtually presents no visible face; still less does it seem capable of mirroring its partner's desire. Nor does this poem seem particularly aberrant within Dickinson's canon of apocalyptic love poems. In almost every case, Dickinson inserts a vision of an Imaginary dyad, two lovers mirrored in their reciprocal gaze, within a counter-language of Symbolic outside gazes. In the law of the Symbolic, what matters is not visual likeness, identity, or mirroring, but place in a structure of exchange: the relationship of atom to atom, not the atom's seemingly natural or intrinsic properties. For Lacanian psychoanalysis, the arbiter of such exchanges is the phallus, symbol of the rule of the Father. Disrupting God the Father's redemptive bargain, the marriage of soul to Christ the Son, Dickinson in a sense usurps the phallic place of the gaze, of judgment, of choice; the place of author of creation and revelation, alpha and omega.

Dickinson's eschatological love poems again and again rewrite a heretical Book of Revelation. Her revision of the apocalypse and the Last Judgment also, necessarily, projects itself backward into her understanding of earlier biblical texts, texts understood to be types or prefigurations of the New Testament's events. For orthodox believers who trusted typological readings, the Bible's coherence of type and antitype, prophecy and fulfillment, testified to its divine inspiration. By Dickinson's day, the Higher Criticism had learned to regard this coherence as an effect of the process of canonization, in which those Christian texts that came to be regarded as orthodox were collated with earlier texts of which they had to be seen as the fulfillment. Dickinson's skepticism (perhaps tutored by the Higher Criticism) about the authority of Jesus' utterances in the New Testament extended to the Old Testament as well, but that did not prevent her from commenting on the continuity of God the Father's vengeful character. Here Dickinson projects her role as alternative mediator or judge in the Last Judgment back into one of the Old Testament's most punitive scenes of vision, a scene that thematizes delay or denial of vision's fulfillment:

> It always felt to me—a wrong
> To that Old Moses—done—
> To let him see—the Canaan—
> Without the entering—
>
> And tho' in soberer moments—
> No Moses there can be
> I'm satisfied—the Romance
> In point of injury—
>
> Surpasses sharper stated—
> Of Stephen—or of Paul—
> For these—were only put to death—
> While God's adroiter will
>
> On Moses—seemed to fasten
> With tantalizing Play
> As Boy—should deal with lesser Boy—
> To prove ability.
>
> The fault—was doubtless Israel's—
> Myself—had banned the Tribes—
> And ushered Grand Old Moses
> In Pentateuchal Robes
>
> Upon the Broad Possession
> 'Twas little—He should see—
> Old Man on Nebo! Late as this—
> My justice bleeds—for Thee!
>
> (poem 597)

The Law of the Father does not even do justice by its own representatives. From Dickinson's perspective it looks more like a bullying scheme of male rivalry, with the Father at the top of the heap. Dickinson's private court of literature (in which Scripture is seen for what it is—"Romance") would deal out better justice. Trading on the orthodox reading of Moses as a type or prefiguration of Christ, in that he was punished for the sins of Israel, Dickinson again marks her dissent from God the Father's substitutive plan of redemption. She would apportion credit and blame where they are due. Moreover, the poem implicitly criticizes the orthodox Christian interpretive tradition that brings the Old Testament into coherence with the New by treating the Old Testament as the prefiguration of the New, justifying Moses' fate by its prefiguration of Christ's. Dickinson defends Moses' rights not as Christ figure, but as a fellow author. His own book, the Pentateuch, entitles him to his "Possession" of Canaan, and that is the right Dickinson would enforce. *Her* justice "bleeds" for him: Dickinson herself, by the poem's end, becomes the alternative Christ figure, redeeming the writers of books in defiance of the Law of the Father.

Dickinson does not have to believe in orthodox Christianity in order to believe in the Law of the Father—not only as her own father represented it, but as very nearly the transcendental principle of culture that Freudian and Lacanian psychoanalysis understand it to be. Authored and defended by the Law of the Father, the Bible exists for her as a book to be written over repeatedly, from beginning to end. Such a rewriting does not erase the Law or the sacred text but rather supplements it, in something like the Derridean sense of the word. Belated, secondary, small in scale, human rather than divine, lyric rather than epic, authored by a woman, Dickinson's poems nevertheless challenge the hierarchical ordering of all those binary oppositions. Type and antitype, Moses and Christ, Christ and Dickinson, Moses and Dickinson, change places and exchange powers. So, in this poem, Dickinson's visionary apocalypse of fidelity obliterates ordained boundaries between life and death, heaven and hell, beginnings and endings, Genesis and Revelation:

> They put Us far apart—
> As separate as Sea
> And her unsown Peninsula—
> We signified "These see"—
>
> They took away our Eyes—
> They thwarted Us with Guns—
> "I see Thee" each responded straight
> Through Telegraphic Signs—
>
> With Dungeons—They devised—
> But through their thickest skill—
> And their opaquest Adamant—
> Our Souls saw—just as well—
>
> They summoned Us to die—
> With sweet alacrity
> We stood upon our stapled feet—
> Condemned—but just—to see—
>
> Permission to recant—
> Permission to forget—
> We turned our backs upon the Sun
> For perjury of that—

Not Either—noticed Death—
Of Paradise—aware—
Each other Face—was all the Disc—
Each other's setting—saw—
(poem 474)

The poem's first stanza writes an alternative book of Genesis: the separation of the two lovers recalls the dividing of the waters from the dry land, the "Sea" from "her unsown Peninsula." "And God called the dry land Earth; and the gathering together of the waters called he Seas: and God saw that it was good" (Genesis 1:10, KJV). Against "their" power to separate, the lovers (if that is the right word for them) pose their own powers of seeing and saying; separation gives rise to signification. After this creation-by-separation (the way also of Blake's oppressive Urizen[24]), the heavenly and punitive judges *decreate* their subjects, taking away their eyes, but not their language, and threatening them with phallic "Guns." To a language already founded upon an original separation, however, these further losses—and their implied castration threat—are no insuperable obstacle. "I see Thee": the lovers' language evolves, under these further threats and separations, from designating themselves in a collective third person ("These see") to the use of personal pronouns.

A Lacanian psychoanalysis would see Dickinson's revision of Genesis in psychological terms as a concise account of how the human subject enters the Symbolic Order, or how that order enters him. The subject learns to designate his place in the order of language and human relationships by the shifting counters of personal pronouns. Under the threat of castration, he learns to place himself and other human beings with respect to their places in a system organized by having or not having the phallus—the phallus linked, in psychoanalytic theory as in Dickinson's poem, with the privilege of the visual. Lacanian theory complicates Freud's account of sexual difference (the fear of castration on the boy's part, due to the "fact" of castration on the girl's) by insisting that castration is everybody's "fact," the phallus nobo(dad)dy's possession in fact. The place of the phallus is the place of the Other: the phallic mother first of all, in the infant's Imaginary, and later the place of the symbolic Father, not identical to any one of its actual, biological occupants.

Jane Gallop, summing up the Lacanian distinction, writes that "the penis is what men have and women do not; the phallus is the attribute of power which neither men nor women have." In Dickinson's poem, whatever gender the two lovers may have, they share their castrated position. Only the third term in the triangle, the mysterious powers above, wield the gun and the vision that deprives the lovers of vision. But, Gallop adds, "As long as the attribute of power is a phallus which refers to and can be confused (in the imaginary register?) with a penis, this confusion will support a structure in which it seems reasonable that men have power and women do not."[25] Lacanian theory's perversely comfortable assurance that everyone is castrated (a kind of decaying humanism) can be an alibi for separating psychoanalysis from engaging a discussion of sexual difference as practical inequality. Does Dickinson's poem engage sexual difference?

Perhaps it does so, but not as a fixed entity. Sexual difference is somehow natural and created or prescribed at the same time, like the rather mysterious difference or distance between the Sea and "her unsown Peninsula." Assuming the convention or biographical fact (shared by other similar Dickinson poems) of a heterosexual love affair, and following the muted phallic symbolism of the Peninsula, we could decide that the lover's sexual difference has been ordained by the punitive powers above as part of their division and organization of the world, in their Urizenic mode of creation. But Dickinson's metaphor for the relationship between Sea and Peninsula pulls in other directions if closely considered. How separate in fact are Sea and her unsown Peninsula? "Unsown" suggests, among other possibilities, a peninsula as yet held within the sea itself, not yet separate at all, not yet born. Moreover, it seems to ascribe to the Sea herself a phallic power of sowing her own peninsula. The metaphor for separation, distance and (sexual) difference includes within it other possibilities that confound separation and (sexual) difference.

Summoned initially by and into a symbolic order of language (structured by personal pronouns, distance and lack), the lovers are then summoned into a punitive, castrating Crucifixion scene at the Last Judgment. Like Paolo and Francesca in Dante's *Inferno*, they are "condemned" to endure to infinity the love they lived: not, in their case, an adulterous embrace, but the sight without the embrace. Heaven or Hell? Dickinson's speaker scorns their judges' power to distinguish between them. Turning their backs upon the law of the "Sun," upon the symbolic order of their separation, the lovers reconstitute what in Lacanian terms would be described as an Imaginary couple. Each mirrors the other, as the repetitive, alliterative language of the last two stanzas underscores. Without difference between them or lack, with their earlier pronominal separation ("I see Thee") now dissolved into "Each other" and the language of "Telegraphic Signs" abandoned for their mutual "Disc" of presence, the lovers know all they need to know of Paradise. Their apocalyptic fidelity replaces God's Sun/ Son-centered theology with a splendidly decentered astronomy that recalls—albeit on a much smaller scale—Blake's antiheliocentric engravings, or the spectacular and confusing cosmic ending of Shelley's *Prometheus Unbound,* in which another father-god is triumphantly replaced.

I have so far argued that a classically Oedipal psychoanalytic theory, even Lacanian terminology of the Imaginary and the Symbolic orders, resonates more fully with Dickinson's body of apocalyptic love poetry than does most current revisionary, mother-centered object-relations psychoanalysis, even as informed by feminist thinking. This position is worth rethinking, however, through comparison to the poetry of Dickinson's much-loved Elizabeth Barrett Browning. Barrett Browning "was Emily Dickinson's central heroine, the woman poet whose youth most closely resembled Dickinson's own" (especially in her overbearing father) and whose *Aurora Leigh* "Dickinson seems virtually to have known by heart."[26] Despite her own powerful father, however, Barrett Browning's most famous poem is saturated with figures for the mother. Her dealings with this potent Victorian image (potent on both sides of the Atlantic) are fascinating in their own right and throw into higher relief Dickinson's in some ways remarkable refusal of mother figures. Moreover, Barrett Browning shares—indeed, is perhaps one of the sources for—Dickinson's will to revise and revise again scenes of apocalypse and last judgment in her own poetic terms. Power over the gaze in the scene of last judgment, for Barrett Browning as for Dickinson, is the woman poet's Imaginary vehicle for claiming poetic vocation. In Barrett Browning's *Aurora Leigh,*[27] unlike Dickinson's poems, the contest for the apocalyptic gaze is narratively connected to a thematics of the lost mother's face. What mother-centered visionary alternatives to the Law of the Father might Dickinson have encountered in Barrett Browning's exuberant chronicle of the growth of the woman poet's mind?

Unlike Dickinson's lyric persona, Barrett Browning's heroine Aurora has to grapple with an external, social interlocutor for rhetorical possession of the judgment-hour gaze. Her adversary is her would-be suitor, cousin Romney. The rhetoric of last judgment enters (sometimes egregiously) from the very first moments of their acquaintance. Romney comes into Aurora's life carrying a book which Aurora dismisses as

> mere statistics (if
> I chanced to lift the cover), count of all

> The goats whose beards grow sprouting down toward hell
> Against God's separative judgment-hour.
>
> (1.525–28)

Romney's political vocation strikes young Aurora as energy misspent trying to look after the goats rather than the saved, his book of statistics a poor second to Holy Scripture and holy poetry. Their conflict and their courtship come to center upon the rival claims of their two vocations, claims expressed through just this rhetoric of last judgment. Each tries to occupy the same rhetorical turf and the same set of metaphors for power. Upon her childhood discovery of the power of language, Aurora says,

> my soul,
> At poetry's divine first finger-touch,
> Let go conventions and sprang up surprised,
> Convicted of the great eternities
> Before two worlds.
>
> (1.850–54)

When Romney, come to propose to her, finds Aurora instead crowning herself with ivy as witness to her poetic vocation, she defends her choice against his amused censure:

> I would rather take my part
> With God's Dead, who afford to walk in white
> Yet spread His glory, than keep quiet here
> And gather up my feet from even a step
> For fear to soil my gown in so much dust.
> I choose to walk at all risks.
>
> (2.101–6)

Better dead and in the company of the saints, Aurora claims, than feminine in middle-class Victorian terms; her vocation lifts her into the ranks of the saved, while Romney keeps statistics on God's goats. Romney objects that her vocation is a trite expression of personal feeling, echoing standard Victorian praise/blame of women writers. In the face of widespread social suffering, he complains, women "generalise / Oh, nothing,—not even grief!" (2.183–84)—a complaint that anticipates Freud's derogation of women's lack of a sufficiently abstract, impersonal superego. Yet Romney wants desperately to conscript Aurora's sentimental (as he thinks) particularity of mind to his own abstract and general vision of social reform. He proposes a bargain, couched in apocalyptic language. He sees the world as a "heap of headless bodies, shapeless, indistinct" where "The Judgment-Angel scarce would find his way / . . . To the individual man with lips and eyes" (2.381–84). Come with me, he invites Aurora,

> And hand in hand we'll go where yours shall touch
> These victims, one by one! till, one by one,
> The formless, nameless trunk of every man
> Shall seem to wear a head with hair you know,
> And every woman catch your mother's face
> To melt you into passion.
>
> (2.386–91)

Guided by Romney's firmer vision, Aurora will cloak his general compassion with a power of individual love sufficient to raise the dead in body and soul.

To Aurora's ears, however, Romney's reimagination of apocalypse as a family romance expanded to include all humankind blasphemes her own, particular, earliest romance. Her retort reminds Romney both of her sexual difference and her own mother's early death:

> "I am a girl,"
> I answered slowly; "you do well to name
> My mother's face. Though far too early, alas,
> God's hand did interpose 'twixt it and me,
> I know so much of love as used to shine
> In that face and another.
>
> (2.392–97)

In language recalling Jane Eyre's dismissal of St. John Rivers's suit, Aurora tells Romney that he desires "a helpmate, not a mistress." [28] Recollection of her own mother's gaze, briefly as she knew it, enables Aurora to resist being coopted by Romney's vision and to defend her own work—work, she says, that "The heavens and earth have set me since I changed / My father's face for theirs" (2.456–57).

As this exchange makes clear, Aurora's and Romney's competing rhetorics of last judgment are intertwined in Aurora's mind with the family romance of her own parents and the thematics of the maternal gaze. This pattern structures the entire poem in ways too elaborate to recount here. Dolores Rosenblum, however, has persuasively mapped the importance of the mother's face for the narrative of *Aurora Leigh*. In an argument that exactly parallels Cynthia Griffin Wolff's reading of Dickinson's face-to-face poems, drawing also on feminist object-relations theory, Rosenblum traces in *Aurora Leigh* a story of recovering the maternal gaze. Marian Earle—who on the verge of marrying Romney is abandoned, raped, and rediscovered in Italy with her infant son by Aurora—assumes the place of the mirroring mother for Aurora. In Rosenblum's reading, Aurora's encounter with Marian's mother-face is the precondition for her eventual reconciliation with Romney, blind at the poem's end from the (literally) burning collapse of his house of dreams: "Looking into the mirror face of a mother-sister marks Aurora's discovery of an integrated self and a poetics."[29]

Unlike most of Dickinson's apocalyptic love poetry, then, Barrett Browning's novel-epic does explicitly counterpose a male eschatological discourse—generalizing, abstract, distrustful of merely individual sentiment—against a vision of the mother's face. Where Rosenblum sees the thematics of the mother's gaze as issuing in reciprocity and the daughter's "integrated self," a different psychoanalytic reading, or a deconstructive reading, might press upon remaining inequalities in the relationship of figurative mother and daughter, Marian and Aurora; upon the instability of integrated selfhood; upon the always already existing contamination of the mother/child dyad by the Oedipal triangle in Aurora's experience. These problems raised by competing psychoanalytic theories in turn bear on how we evaluate a poetics issuing not from the mother's gaze alone but from the clash of gazes, maternal and male, in *Aurora Leigh*.

For Lacanian theory, the achievement of integrated selfhood under the gaze of the (m)Other is the mark of the "mirror stage" and the Imaginary register of apperception. Lacanian theory, however, departs from object-relations theory in its emphasis on the misrecognition entailed in the Imaginary exchange of gazes, the *mesconnaissance* inseparable from every act of mirroring, the alienation entailed by any "integrated" identity.[30] The mother's gaze does not, for Lacan, mirror the infant as she or he actually is in the present; rather the mother's gaze directs the child toward an image of itself (which need not be in a literal mirror). That image—stable, bounded, coherent, tantalizingly complete—becomes an ego ideal, not a representation of the child's present bodily identity or experience. The image inaugurates the subject's ego as a necessary fiction of wholeness.

In Lacan's account of the mirror stage, then, the mother-infant dyad is not the reciprocal closed circuit of mutually enforcing egos, as it tends to be in object-relations theory. Internal difference is necessarily at the heart of the subject's quest after coherence; the moment there are two egos and two gazes present in the "dyad," there is (at the very least) also a triangle for each subject.[31] Nor is the mirror stage, the register of the Imaginary, or the mother-infant relationship securely closed off from the symbolic order of the Law of the Father. The child's desire to be mirrored in the gaze of the Other is a desire for recognition, a desire to be the desire of the Other; insofar as the (m)Other's desire has already been ordered by the Law of the Father, the mirroring dyad of mother and child anticipates the child's entry into the Symbolic Order.

If Aurora's discovery of Marian in Italy is, as Rosenblum puts it, "a liberating recovery of the truth," of "the mother and the mothered child in herself,"[32] it is also the scene of a startling, indeed rather ludicrous, *mesconnaissance*. Aurora accuses Marian not of sexually producing an illegitimate child, but of having *stolen* him (6.631ff). When Aurora eventually lets slip her suspicion that Marian fled her engagement to Romney in order "to take / The hand of a seducer" (6.747–48), Marian indignantly but obliquely tells Aurora the unspeakable truth: that she was raped and abandoned: "I was not ever, as you say, seduced, / But simply, murdered." (6.770–71). Aurora has learned that she is speaking to a dead woman, dead like her own mother. The discovery of Marian in this sense repeats without fundamentally revising the lesson of Aurora's own family romance: motherhood is death. Or as Marian instructs Aurora, who might be tempted to argue her back into belief in her own existence: I may breathe for my child's sake, but "I'm not the less dead for that: I'm nothing more / But just a mother" (6.823–24).

As a "symbol for the birth of self" and provider of "a myth of [Aurora's] own origins," then, the rediscovered Marian is a more ambivalent figure than Rosenblum's object-relations psychology accounts for.[33] If Aurora's and Marian's reunion enacts a pre-Oedipal or, in Lacanian terms, an Imaginary reunion between mother and child, the reunion is with an absence as much as a presence.[34] It is haunted both by the daughter's misrecognition and by an unspeakable, originary violation—the absent father's rape of the mother. Moreover, object-relations psychology, by virtue of its near-exclusive focus on the early dyadic mother-child relationship, in a certain way replicates Barrett Browning's and Victorian culture's conflation of women's (permissible) sexuality with motherhood. Exiling the problem or phallic threat of fatherhood to the "outside" of the mother-child relationship, *Aurora Leigh*—and in certain ways, object relations too—offers up a "mythic" or Imaginary idealization of that relationship and its language of the mirroring gaze. Yet *Aurora Leigh*, more ambivalently, also insists that the mirroring mother is a dead woman, the gaze in some way fundamentally unreciprocated.[35]

Certainly the gaze is fundamentally unreciprocal, and thoroughly implicated in the Law of the Father rather than a maternal poetics, when Romney arrives to be reconciled with Aurora. In the poem's concluding lines, Aurora re-presents the ordered vision of the City of God to blinded Romney's internal vision. Taking up Christ's position as mediator between God and man, she tempers Romney's punishment with mercy and love (she is his "compensation," 9.907). Aurora keeps her vocation, and Romney his vision of social transformation, albeit in chastened form. Vocation and transformation, however, are reconceived in a Neoplatonic Christian mold. Art will open the door between the world of "sensuous form / And form insensuous" (9.920–21), while social reform will work in humble paths, doing what it can in patience toward the time when "HE shall make all new" (949) and the earthly city will mirror the City of God. In this mission love and work, poetry and social reform, male and female, will be reconciled.[36]

And this is exactly the vision Emily Dickinson subverts, despite her shared fascination with appropriating eschatological Christian rhetoric for the woman poet's vocation. Gilbert and Gubar label Barrett Browning "Dickinson's spiritual mother" but find that Dickinson "rejected [Barrett Browning's] compromises," the compromises that make up the fabric of *Aurora Leigh*'s concluding apocalyptic vision. What Dickinson rejected may have been not only the particular social thematics of Barrett Browning's "aesthetic of service," but the general sort of dualistic thinking that sustains Barrett Browning's compromises. Aurora Leigh believes in, and defends herself in terms of, oppositions between real and ideal, language and the ineffable, body and soul—and man and woman. The poem's concluding Platonic vision depends upon the reality of such oppositions, and the necessity of their resolution in heaven before their reconciliation on earth. The earthly complement of Aurora's heavenly vision, for women and men, is the Victorian ideology of complementarity: the belief that men and women are fundamentally different beings whose different natures, capacities, and duties render them mutually necessary to one another. While Aurora struggles throughout the poem against Romney's initial hope that she will complement him (by humanizing his vision of social reform), their final relationship preserves much of the ideological framework of complementarity, albeit within an altered balance of power. She will complement his humbled inward sight with her outward vision; Romney asks her to "shine out for two, Aurora, and fulfil [*sic*] / My falling-short that must be! work for two, / As I, though thus restrained, shall love!" (9.910–12). Rejecting the usual Victorian version of complementarity, in which women were for love and men for work, Barrett Browning still exalts marriage as the union of dualities and the "mystic counterpart" of God's love, which (like the Rose of Sharon, its symbol) draws different human relations into a unity "sweetened from one central Heart" (9.883–90).

Dickinson's eschatological love poetry thwarts such mystic unions at almost every turn. On the simplest level of plot, obviously, marriage very often does not take place in these poems or cannot be consummated. But more than that, Dickinson seems to question the very idea of marriage as the resolution of oppositions and as an earthly mirror of heaven. Often the "lovers" of the poems are simply not specified in terms of oppositions. Shorn of particular vocations or social locations in Dickinson's lyrics (a move not possible in Barrett Browning's verse novel), they may even lack determinate gender. Their relationship, whatever the word for it, is hard to describe in terms of Victorian sexual complementarity. Nor is the lovers' marriage the complement of a greater bliss in heaven. The human lovers rather compete with heaven; instead of Barrett Browning's mirrored type and antitype, human marriage and divine love, Dickinson renders a rhetorical struggle. Heaven is not the fulfillment of earth, but a continuation of her battle with the Law of the Father. Speaking again in terms of Lacanian psychoanalysis, Dickinson's poems tend to conclude with Symbolic lack, rather than the wholeness and coherence of Imaginary mirroring.

Dickinson's eschatological poems foreground God the punitive Father, the figure suppressed in *Aurora Leigh*'s conclusion in favor of a Christ-centered vision. For Dickinson, Barrett Browning's compensatory Christ who gave "the life, too, with the law" (9.873) would be the too-obedient Son of his Father, mitigating the harshness of his Law without challenging it. Her own revisions of theology as family romance, as we have seen, detach her Son/lover from loyalty to the father, or they revise the romantic triangle of Father/Son/female believer by placing the female speaker in Christ's role as mediator between the silent lover and the Father. When Dickinson's speakers assume this Christlike position, they do so not with Aurora Leigh's splendid obedience, but in defiance, setting their own vision of human love against the splendor of the City of God as Aurora mediates it to Romney.

Thus far, Dickinson's rejection of Barrett Browning's unifying apocalyptic "compromises" is fairly clear in its outlines. More mysterious, perhaps, is Dickinson's seeming lack of interest in Barrett Browning's figure of the mother as she intersects with Barrett Browning's favored eschatological rhetoric of the woman poet's vocation. Why was this not more attractive to Dickinson? In nineteenth-century

American "feminized" theology, the merciful Christ and mothers were frequently cultural allies against the punitive Father of Calvinism. Both mothers and Christ offered compensations for the rigors of the Law of the Father, as the home and church would also become refuges from the harsher world of industrial capitalism. Not content with any simple division between a domesticated and religious feminine sphere and a male world of work, competition, and suffering, Barrett Browning's *Aurora Leigh*—like later American feminists—struggles toward bringing together love and work, love and social reform. Resisting notions of private motherhood as after-the-fact compensation for social injustice, American feminists advanced the ideal of Social Motherhood: women's reforming work in the public sphere as modeled upon, and justified by, women's traditional caretaking roles in the private family. Rather awkwardly, but with a certain symbolic acuity, Barrett Browning splits her own vision of Christlike Social Motherhood in two in the conclusion of *Aurora Leigh*. Marian "dies" and lives again only for the sake of giving life to her son; she conflates the powers of the Virgin Mary and of Christ dying for the sins of mankind.[37] Aurora learns a more general social vision (as Romney had earlier said she needed) in order to mediate, Christlike, between Romney and heaven. Marian bears and cares for the male Word (her infant son) in her body; Aurora bears the male Word (the text of Revelation) in her language, from heaven to Romney's waiting ears.

What Dickinson may have seen and mistrusted in mother figures as they appeared both in nineteenth-century American "feminized" theology and *Aurora Leigh* is their tendency to bear, and offer compensation for, the Word of the Father—whether they are Christlike themselves, or carriers of Christ, or both (as in Marian's case).[38] Social motherhood bears within it a dualism—female values of compassion versus the father's world of severity—that comports well with the complementary resolution of *Aurora Leigh*'s ending but not with Dickinson's seemingly profound distrust of such resolutions. Dickinson's Christology, then, runs parallel to, but does not quite intersect, that of many of her female (and avowedly feminist) contemporaries. It is critical, not complementary. She desires a Christ, a Son different from the Father, but not the better to submit herself to the Father's sternly redemptive bargain. Rather than superadding feminine compassion to the uncertain mercies of the Father's Law, rather than enfleshing and softening the Father's Word, Dickinson struggles within the very confines of that Word's violence:

> Proud of my broken heart, since thou didst break it,
> Proud of the pain I did not feel till thee,

Proud of my night, since thou with moons dost slake it,
Not to partake thy passion, *my* humility.

Thou can'st not boast, like Jesus, drunken without companion
Was the strong cup of anguish brewed for the Nazarene

Thou can'st not pierce tradition with the peerless puncture,
See! I usurped *thy* crucifix to honor mine!

(poem 1736)

In this strange love poem, an ever-stronger, presumably female speaker addresses an ever-weaker man who seems both a secular betrayer and a type of Christ.[39] The speaker who does finally usurp her interlocutor's crucifix is neither motherly (like Barrett Browning's Marian) nor a faithful bearer of Christian words. In the startling line that reverses her initial masochistic attitude into sadistic aggression, she claims instead to "pierce tradition with the peerless puncture." She has companioned him in drinking the "cup of anguish"—not only Christ's cup in the garden of Gethsemane, but the visionary draught through which so many Romantic questers inaugurate their initiatory trials.[40] Putting her body and her passion in place of his, refusing to let him offer up his body for her redemption, she assumes both castration and phallic power for both of them.

If there is a literary antecedent for this speaker's pointed usurpation of her Christ/lover's crucifix, perhaps it is to be found in Charlotte Brontë's *Jane Eyre* rather than among the self-sacrificial mother figures of *Aurora Leigh*—although *Jane Eyre* is also a precursor text, perhaps *the* precursor text, for *Aurora Leigh*.[41] Again, like so many of Dickinson's eschatological poems, and like Freud's account of sexual difference, this poem centers around a contest over the gaze. The speaker demands that her interlocutor *see* her. Setting aside for the moment the Christian reference of Dickinson's crucifix, what kind of specter does her interlocutor "see" in this poem? He sees a being in whose company he is gradually drained of strength; whose thirst is slaked by night; who punctures; against whom his own crucifix is no defense. He sees something rather like a vampire, whose passion strangely recalls Bertha Rochester's characterization in *Jane Eyre*. Recounting her memories of Bertha's visit to her chamber the night before her expected wedding day, Jane Eyre tells Rochester that the visitor reminded her "of the foul German Spectre—the Vampyre."[42] The "ebon crucifix" and "dying Christ" that hang in the outer room of the chamber in which Bertha is imprisoned (*Jane Eyre*, chapter 20) are likewise ineffectual against her nocturnal depredations. Bertha is both mother (a bad one) and, to Jane's eyes, almost virile (tall in stature, "swelled and dark" with blood in all her features, chapter 25)—

a phallic (m)Other from a place outside England's racial and sexual order. She both stands in the way of Jane's and Rochester's marriage (as Rochester's living wife) and makes it possible by at last sacrificing her own body to the blaze that takes away Rochester's sight, giving Jane a terribly gained equality with her eventual husband.

Aurora Leigh exorcises this terrifying mother figure;[43] Dickinson, in this difficult poem, explores the possibility of identifying with her passion and her power, against (but at the same time, within) the Law of the Father. If, for Freud and Lacan, woman is twice lacking in relation to the Law, twice castrated (because unable to be castrated in the first place), Dickinson's speaker is twice crucified. Face to face with her Christ/lover, she mirrors back to him not his fullness, but his wounds. No wholeness comes from this mirroring, nothing like the City of God that concludes *Aurora Leigh*. Yet her doubled wound strips the Son—the Logos, the Father's truthful representative—of his authority, claiming the gaze and language for her own.

NOTES

1. Sigmund Freud, "Some Psychical Consequences of the Anatomical Distinction Between the Sexes," 1925; repr. in Philip Rieff, ed., *Sexuality and the Psychology of Love* (New York: MacMillan, 1963), 192.

2. Freud, "Some Psychical Consequences," 187–88.

3. Laura Mulvey inaugurated this line of feminist theory in her article "Visual Pleasure and Narrative Cinema," *Screen* 16:3; Jacqueline Rose explores the current state of the debate in *Sexuality in the Field of Vision* (London: Verso, 1986). For a fine general discussion of the psychoanalytic paradigm's implications for reading women's poetry, see Leigh Gilmore, "The Gaze of the Other Woman," 81–104.

4. Thomas Weiskel, *The Romantic Sublime*, 94.

5. Joanne Feit Diehl, "In the Twilight of the Gods," 177.

6. Ann Kibbey, *The Interpretation of Material Shapes in Puritanism: A Study of Rhetoric, Prejudice, and Violence* (Cambridge: Cambridge University Press, 1986), 19, 13.

7. For an excellent general discussion of Dickinson's preference for writing over speech, see Helen McNeil's *Emily Dickinson*, 63–91.

8. "Circles," repr. in *Selections from Ralph Waldo Emerson*, ed. Stephen E. Whicher (Boston: Houghton Mifflin, 1957), 174.

9. Ann Douglas, *The Feminization of American Culture*, 127. For an ample account of feminized literary Christianity as it relates to Dickinson, see Barton Levi St. Armand, *Emily Dickinson and Her Culture*, chapter 4, "Paradise Deferred: Dickinson, Phelps, and the Image of Heaven," 117–51.

10. In his private life, Emerson may not have been immune to the consoling possibilities of domestic Christianity. He seems privately to have cast his first

wife, Ellen Tucker, as the third person of a sentimental Trinity after her death, writing in his diary five days later that "Ellen went to heaven to see, to know, to worship, to love, to intercede" (cited in Julie Ellison, *Emerson's Romantic Style*, 57). This closeted sentimental piety, Ellison argues, only aggrandized the more Emerson's public persona of the Unitarian orator.

11. Emerson's view of Jesus' authority, and of the Higher Criticism's related problem of oral versus written language, underwent several changes in the course of his career. See Barbara Packer, "Origin and Authority: Emerson and the Higher Criticism," in Sacvan Bercovitch, ed., *Reconstructing American Literary History* (Cambridge, Mass.: Harvard University Press, 1986), 67–92.

12. Albert J. Gelpi, *Emily Dickinson: The Mind of the Poet* (Cambridge, Mass.: Harvard University Press, 1966), 37.

13. Cynthia Griffin Wolff, *Emily Dickinson*, 261.

14. For Gelpi, these lines indicate that Dickinson was "aware—in general terms, if not in argumentative detail—of the questions raised by . . . the Higher Criticism." *Emily Dickinson: The Mind of the Poet*, 48. See also Barton Levi St. Armand, *Emily Dickinson and Her Culture*, 176–77.

15. Dickinson may consistently have gendered breathing as masculine; see the suggestive remarks on other such poems in Joanne Feit Diehl, "Dickinson, the Father, and the Text," in Lynda E. Boose and Betty S. Flowers, eds., *Daughters and Fathers* (Baltimore: Johns Hopkins University Press, 1989), 335.

16. Wolff, *Emily Dickinson*, 380.

17. Ibid., 53–54.

18. See the introductions by Juliet Mitchell and Jacqueline Rose, eds., in *Feminine Sexuality, Jacques Lacan and the école freudienne* (New York: W. W. Norton, 1983; repr. 1985), and Nancy Chodorow, *The Reproduction of Mothering: Psychoanalysis and the Sociology of Gender* (Berkeley: University of California Press, 1978), and Carol Gilligan, *In a Different Voice: Psychological Theory and Women's Development* (Cambridge, Mass.: Harvard University Press, 1982). Gilligan directly addresses Freud's notion that women lack an abstract moral sense, the internalized superego. For an excellent survey of the debate and the interpretive possibilities opened by it, see Shirley Nelson Garner, Claire Kahane, and Madelon Sprengnether, eds., *The (M)other Tongue: Essays in Feminist Psychoanalytic Interpretation* (Ithaca, N.Y.: Cornell University Press, 1985); and Jane Gallop's essay, "Reading the Mother Tongue: Psychoanalytic Feminist Criticism," in Françoise Meltzer, ed., *The Trial(s) of Psychoanalysis* (Chicago: University of Chicago Press, 1987), 125–40.

19. Margaret Homans, *Bearing the Word*, chapter 1. See also Christine Froula, "The Daughter's Seduction: Sexual Violence and Literary History," in Boose and Flowers, eds., *Daughters and Fathers*, pp. 111–35. Women's silence in literary history and psychoanalytic theory is "the effect of repression, not of absence" (112).

20. Homans, 14.

21. Here and throughout, "Imaginary" with a capital "I" will refer specifically to the word's technical meaning in Lacanian theory.

22. See Wolff's *Emily Dickinson*, 131, on Dickinson's exaltation of "power"

(one of her father's favorite words, and also one of Emerson's) in the trio from the Lord's Prayer.

23. Charles R. Anderson, *Emily Dickinson's Poetry: Stairway of Surprise* (1963; repr. Westport, Conn.: Greenwood Press, 1982), 172; Christanne Miller, "How 'Low Feet' Stagger: Disruptions of Language in Dickinson's Poetry," in Juhasz, ed., *Feminist Critics Read Emily Dickinson*, 140.

24. In *The Book of Urizen*, Blake writes his own alternative to Genesis. A "dark power" who works in brooding secrecy, Urizen creates by separating and laying down law in his "Book of brass": "Times on times he divided, & measur'd / Space by space in his ninefold darkness." Blake's illuminated title page shows a bearded patriarch squatting on a book and writing with both hands. Behind him, a set of Mosaic tablets—the written law—repeats the oppressively closed symmetry of his posture. For *The Book of Urizen* and a reproduction of the title page, see Mary Lynn Johnson and John E. Grant, eds., *Blake's Poetry and Designs* (New York: W. W. Norton, 1979), 142–59.

25. Jane Gallop, *The Daughter's Seduction: Feminism and Psychoanalysis* (Ithaca, N.Y.: Cornell University Press, 1982), 97. See also Gallop's *Reading Lacan* (Ithaca, N.Y.: Cornell University Press, 1985), chapter 6, "Reading the Phallus," for an excellent reading of the dispute over the status of the Lacanian phallus.

26. Helen McNeil, *Emily Dickinson*, 151, 153. Ellen Moers was the first feminist critic to draw attention to Dickinson's fascination with Barrett Browning and *Aurora Leigh*, in *Literary Women* (Garden City, N.Y: Doubleday, 1976). Many other feminist critics have commented recently on Dickinson's admiration for Barrett Browning, although most center their discussion on the elegiac poems Dickinson wrote specifically for Barrett Browning (poems 312 and 593). See the assessments by Vivian R. Pollak in *Dickinson: The Anxiety of Gender* and Christanne Miller in *Emily Dickinson: A Poet's Grammar*. Pollak finds Dickinson's elegiac tributes fraught with repressed competition, and denies any influence from the other poet on Dickinson's style (240–44); Miller takes Dickinson's admiration as sincere, but also sees Barrett Browning as "no major stylistic model" for Dickinson (165). Dorothy Mermin, on the other hand, declares that Dickinson was "minutely influenced" by passages in *Aurora Leigh*. *Elizabeth Barrett Browning: The Origins of a New Poetry* (Chicago: University of Chicago Press, 1989), 207.

27. Elizabeth Barrett Browning, *Aurora Leigh and Other Poems* (London: The Women's Press, 1978). All further references to *Aurora Leigh* (hereafter *AL*) cited in the text.

28. See Sandra Gilbert and Susan Gubar's remarks on *Aurora Leigh's* revisions of *Jane Eyre* in *The Madwoman in the Attic*, 575–76. Barrett Browning disclaimed *Jane Eyre's* influence (see Mermin, *Elizabeth Barrett Browning*, 184–85), a gesture congruent with the ambivalence surrounding mothers in the poem, and with the absence in the poem of a viable women's literary tradition for the poem's heroine.

29. Dolores Rosenblum, "Face to Face: Elizabeth Barrett Browning's *Aurora*

Leigh and Nineteenth-Century Poetry," *Victorian Studies* 26, no. 3 (Spring 1983): 335.

30. See Lacan's early essays, "The mirror stage as formative of the function of the I," and "Aggressivity in psychoanalysis," in *Ecrits*, trans. Alan Sheridan (New York and London: W. W. Norton, 1977), 1–29, for his exposition of the mirror stage. For an interpretation of Lacan's quarrel in these years with ego psychology (which overlaps with object relations), see Gallop, *Reading Lacan*, chapter 2: "The American other."

31. See Ellie Ragland-Sullivan's *Jacques Lacan and the Philosophy of Psychoanalysis* (Urbana: University of Illinois Press, 1986), chapter 1, "What is 'I'? Lacan's Theory of the Human Subject."

32. Rosenblum, "*Aurora Leigh* and Nineteenth-Century Poetry," 332–33.

33. Ibid., 333.

34. Similarly, Barrett Browning's famous maternal metaphor for the muse of Victorian poetry, "The full-veined, heaving, doubled-breasted age," is not, in fact, a metaphor of presence. If the poet catches her "Upon the burning lava of a song" (a violent metaphor indeed), what will be left to the touch of "men" afterward is not the maternal flesh itself, but the "impress" or negative trace it leaves behind (*AL* 5.213–19).

35. The class privilege Aurora enjoys with respect to Marian of course extends this lack of reciprocity. Invoking Althusser's marxist revision of Lacan, we could say that the mirroring of the two women's reunion creates an Imaginary "whole" identity—Woman as ideological construction—that glosses over the women's actual inequalities.

36. Gilbert and Gubar try to separate "Barrett Browning's compromise aesthetic of service" from "Aurora Leigh's revolutionary impulses," suggesting that the first operates as a protective cover for the second (*The Madwoman in the Attic*, 579). But the *kind* of revolution anticipated in the poem's concluding lines—Neoplatonic and Christian—seems metaphysically at one with its supposed cover story, and inseparable from it as the poem stands.

37. On Marian as virgin mother, see Rosenblum, "*Aurora Leigh* and Nineteenth-Century Poetry," 333–34.

38. Margaret Homans sees this situation as constitutive of nineteenth-century British women writers' relation to language; see *Bearing the Word*, chapter 1.

39. The poem exists only in a transcript made by Mabel Loomis Todd. It may be tempting to hazard that the original was destroyed because it was addressed to, or in some way revealed the identity of, a biographical addressee, but other poems existing only in transcripts are cooler and in no way incriminating, insofar as we can now judge, so this hypothesis is suspect.

40. Compare Keats in "The Fall of Hyperion," who drinks his draught at the behest of a female muse, Moneta.

41. When queried by her readers, Barrett Browning denied that she had *Jane Eyre* in mind as a model for Romney's blinding. For most readers, however, the echoes have been too patent to ignore. See Gilbert and Gubar, *The*

Madwoman in the Attic, 570–74; and Cora Kaplan's introduction to the poem, *AL*, 23–24.

42. Charlotte Brontë, *Jane Eyre* (New York: W.W. Norton, 1971), chapter 25, 250. Hereafter citations in the text will refer to chapter numbers, for the convenience of readers using other editions.

43. The exorcism is complicated indeed. Barrett Browning first splits some of Bertha's plot functions—as the heroine's rival and eventual maker of the marriage—between Marian and the Lady Waldemar, the "good" mother and the "bad" mother. (This splitting is a consistent strategy in *Aurora Leigh*— see Rosenblum, "*Aurora Leigh* and Nineteenth-Century Poetry," 328–29, and Dorothy Mermin, *Elizabeth Barrett Browning*, 192.) Then it is Marian who comes to the fore as the "good," self-sacrificing mother, who gives up her claims on Romney for the sake of her child; yet Marian's father directly causes the injury in which Romney loses his sight.

3

Violence and the Other(s) of Identity: *Dickinson and the Imaginary of Women's Literary Tradition*

> What defines psychical trauma is not any general quality of the psyche, but the fact that the psychical trauma comes from within. A kind of *internal-external* instance had been formed: a "spine in the flesh" or, we might say, a veritable spine in the *protective wall of the ego*.
>
> —Jean Laplanche, *Life and Death in Psychoanalysis*

> Out back of this old house
> *datura* tangles with a gentler weed
>
> its spiked pods smelling
> of bad dreams and death
>
> I reach through the dark, groping
> past spines of nightmare
>
> to brush the leaves of sensuality
> A dream of tenderness
>
> wrestles with all I know of history
>
> —Adrienne Rich,
> "From an Old House in America"

Rich's "spines of nightmare"[1] metaphorically grasp a central problem for the conjunction of feminism and psychoanalysis, a problem that bears crucially on how feminism and psychoanalysis together may struggle to make sense of the violence patent and latent in so much of Emily Dickinson's poetry. Feminism (along with marxism) has historically come to grief with psychoanalysis over the issue of whether to understand the internal dynamics of human psychic life as determining the external structures of human social life, or vice versa. The attempt to politicize psychoanalysis—or, on the contrary, to exclude its relevance for politics—has typically, in Jacqueline Rose's words, "polarised into a crude opposition between inside and outside," in which some kind of primary, monolithic agency is attributed to either the social realm or the unconscious—or even both at once.[2]

Against this tendency, Rose argues that feminism must attend to division and contradiction both in the human subject and in the social world, rather than work within a rigid dichotomy of the internal and the external. Feminism, she suggests, "is in a privileged position to challenge the dualities (inside/outside, victim/aggressor, real event/ fantasy, and even good/evil) upon which so much traditional political analysis has so often relied."[3] Classical psychoanalysis, with its confounding of the categories of real/fantasy, its delineations of an "other" within the self's "inside," ought to be feminism's ally in this challenge. Yet this very challenge to reigning dualities of political analysis is not without perceived political dangers. For "as feminism turns to questions of censorship, violence and sadomasochism, psychoanalysis hands back to it a fundamental violence of the psychic realm— hands back to it, therefore, nothing less than the difficulty of sexuality itself." Patriarchy or violence against women cannot simply be demonized as Other; "there can be no analysis for women which sees violence solely as accident, imposition or external event."[4]

In Rich's metaphor, the "spines of nightmare" convey exactly the problem of a violence whose source cannot be finally determined as internal or external, nor easily disentangled from the roots of sexual difference and pleasure. The hope of disentangling the place where "*datura* tangl[es] with a simpler herb" is apocalyptic, like the biblical parable of Last Judgment upon which the poet draws. Someday the wheat may be separated from the tares. For now, "the line dividing / lucidity from darkness / is yet to be marked out," and the attempt to live out such lucidity in the present is marked by violence. To separate oneself from all the violence "outside" is to dream of "Isolation" along with "the frontier woman / leveling her rifle along the homestead fence." The incipient violence of such lucidity—the isolating and purifying light—turns into "a suicidal leaf / laid under the burningglass / in the sun's eye." For now, violence burns on both sides of the so lucidly defended boundary between inside and outside, self and other.

Intertextual allusions in Rich's poem underscore the uncertain, contested boundaries between inside and outside. Rich's "Old House" is inhabited by other poems which in turn are inhabited by other poems. The ending of "From an Old House in America" invokes an earlier poem by Rich, "Face to Face," in which Rich's confrontation with what she then (in 1965) knew of history yields only generically male figures of the early American settlers. Yet her ambivalent nostalgia for their "old plain words" forced out of loneliness concludes with Rich's appropriation of another woman's words for the pioneers' hoarded secrets: "behind dry lips / a loaded gun." Effaced from this poem's self-consciously didactic, textbook vision of American history, Emily Dickinson nevertheless haunts the poem through an irresistibly violent metaphor for speech. Not quite inside or outside the American tradition Rich invokes in "Face to Face," not certainly inside or outside Rich's poem itself, Dickinson's faceless gun guards, but at the same time renders unstable or breachable, the always potentially violent boundary between self and other.

The Dickinson poem that Rich so presciently invoked in 1965, "My Life had stood—a Loaded Gun" (poem 754), has since then attracted diverse interpretations, especially feminist interpretations. It has become the locus of discussion for feminist critics concerned about accounting in some way for the aggression of Dickinson's poetry, beginning with Rich herself. In her 1975 essay "Vesuvius at Home," Rich names "My Life had stood—a Loaded Gun—" as the " 'onlie begetter' " of her vision of Dickinson, the poem Rich had "taken into myself over many years."[5] The language of Rich's critical essay suggestively echoes the issues of the poems Dickinson had already haunted and would later haunt for Rich. While not explicitly violent in the way of Dickinson's loaded gun, Rich's metaphor of incorporating, *eating* Dickinson's poem establishes, but only to transgress, the boundary between inside and outside. Invoking the dedication to the "onlie begetter" of Shakespeare's sonnets identifies Dickinson's poem with a male literary tradition (although the overriding aim of Rich's essay is to link Dickinson to other women writers) and identifies Dickinson herself with a phallic power (the loaded gun's power) of inseminating Rich's thoughts. It is hardly necessary to add that Rich's language is intimately, evocatively complicit in these respects with the language of Dickinson's poem itself. What it means to be inside or outside another identity; what it means to "take in" or possess; the very meaning of a boundary—are put into question by "My Life had stood—a Loaded Gun—." In this and other poems, Dickinson's often violent transactions with what is "outside" her reflect a situation for women poets of the dominant Anglo-American tradition in which, according to Joanne Feit Diehl, "the 'Other' is particularly dangerous . . . because he recognizes no boundaries, extending his presence into and through herself, where the self's physical processes, such as breath and pain, may assume a male identity."[6] The male Other who occasions her speech may also commandeer her very bodily identity,

leaving no refuge of interiority that is her own. Adrienne Rich's reading of "My Life had stood—" internalizes Dickinson's struggle with
the problem of boundary and violence, rendering Dickinson both as
the Other male ravisher and as an aspect of Rich's own interior.

Following the traces of Dickinson's insistence in Rich's poetry and
criticism, in this chapter I will explore instances of violence as it is
linked to boundaries between inside and out in Dickinson's poetry,
and I will look at how this violence connects Dickinson's poetry to
recurrent themes in other nineteenth-century poetry by women. The
connection between violence and problems of boundary often operates, in these poems, through a specific rhetorical figure: chiasmus,
a rhetorical crossing or inversion of elements. As in "My Life had
stood—a Loaded Gun," or "Proud of my broken heart, since thou
didst break it" (poem 1736), the assignment of passivity to one member of a pair and activity to the other may invert itself over the course
of a poem. The loaded gun gains in power, autonomy, and consciousness while its Master falls asleep; the speaker of poem 1736 reneges on
her initial vow *not* to partake of her Christ/lover's passion and usurps
both their crucifixes by the poem's end. Aggression turned inwards,
as masochism, becomes aggression turned outwards (and vice versa),
in a crossing that Dickinson figures as the piercing of a boundary:
"Thou canst not pierce tradition with the peerless puncture" (poem
1736). Self and other exchange places around this rhetorical violence
of the chiasmus, Dickinson's linguistic Way of the Cross.

As Jacqueline Rose's and Jean Laplanche's psychoanalytic speculations suggest, the rhetorical violence of Dickinson's poetry may participate in some intrinsic (for all we know to the contrary) violence of
identity (always already divided, in Freudian and Lacanian thought)
and sexual difference (always assumed under a psychic threat, castration). Feminist readings of Dickinson's violence, however, point also
to the specificity of women writers' experience within the "tradition"
that Dickinson's speaker so strangely offers to "pierce," a tradition
that historically has done violence to women's literary productivity.
Within this tradition, Joanne Feit Diehl suggests, it may be necessary
for Dickinson to kill in order to live—to be killed in such a way that
"she becomes agent rather than victim, even if the end be the same."[7]
Aggression is not a matter solely of Dickinson's isolated psyche or
even her biographical family; to think so would be to fall into the
very trap of reifying an inside/outside opposition that, as Rose argues,
psychoanalysis and feminism rightly collaborate to subvert.

Among the Others of tradition for Dickinson's aggressive poems are
the writings of other women, especially Emily and Charlotte Brontë,

and to a lesser extent, Elizabeth Barrett Browning.[8] Instances of violence, imprisonment, and bodily violation in the Brontës' and Barrett Browning's poetry and fiction bear comparison, at the very least, to Dickinson's poems. To put it more strongly still, the Brontës' writing may have served as a kind of collective female muse to Dickinson's poetry, in something of the way that Dickinson's "My Life had stood— a Loaded Gun—" has been a muse to Adrienne Rich's poetry and critical writing. The complexity of Rich's relationship to Dickinson's poem, however, suggests that matters of boundary and identification are not automatically simplified or idealized when influence and inspiration become properties of relations between women writers. "Taking in" (as she put it) Dickinson's "My Life had stood—," Rich became host to a haunting guest who was not a self-identical, coherent, unified mother-image but part of a fierce contest over the boundaries of power and identity.

Dickinson's relation to the Brontës and other women writers may be no less complicated. Her "literary daughteronomy," in Sandra Gilbert's telling pun,[9] is not so much the "empty pack" (poem 650) of an utterly absent mother, as it is the inheritance of a painful internal/external division in the women writers with whom she most identified, writers who themselves had painfully difficult transactions with male literary tradition. Rather than the ideally untroubled mother-mirror of object-relations psychoanalysis, a female literary tradition— the Imaginary ego ideal of so much recent feminist criticism—may be fractured or inverted, a chiasmatic upside-down reflection, in its very conditions of possibility.[10] In Jane Gallop's words, " 'the other' is already inscribed *in* 'the mother tongue.' "[11] Dickinson's poems of captivity, of writing as a burial alive, of identification with a male child, of imagination experienced through the power of a male visitant, and of imagination experienced as torture or as love for a corpse partly rework and revise themes and images out of the prose and poetry of Emily and Charlotte Brontë, along with Elizabeth Barrett Browning. But these poems about the violence of boundaries may also be read for what they suggest about the relationship itself between Dickinson and her literary (m)Others and about the difficulties of conceiving a bounded and unified "women's literary tradition." These poems forge poetic identity out of dangerous relations between self and (m)Other, relations whose difficulties stand at the heart of disputes over the province of psychoanalysis in feminist literary theory.

In Freudian and Lacanian psychoanalytic theory, the psychic locus of violence and boundary tensions between self and other is not so much the id itself but the ego and the superego. The id's desires recognize no boundaries and may not be intrinsically violent (leaving psychoanalytic speculation about the "death drive" aside). It is rather via the ego (the entity Freud described as a perceptual "skin" or boundary between internal and external pressures)[12] and the super-ego (keeper of the ego ideal, through which the child introjects a parental law that is always severely in excess over the "real" parent's authority)[13] that violence and rivalry take on a structuring role in the human subject. In Lacan's account of the instauration of the ego in the mirror phase, aggressivity enters psychic life "by a primary iden-tification that structures the subject as a rival with himself," that is, as someone bound to pursue a bounded, coherent ego-ideal with which his own being does not actually coincide.[14] This primary identification (in Lacan's Imaginary register) starts the subject toward the Oedipal triangle (Lacan's Symbolic register). Identifying himself, under the gaze of the (m)Other, with his ideal image "determines the awaken-ing of his desire for the object of the other's desire . . . from which develops the triad of others, the ego and the object."[15] And along this route, in Lacan's thought, enters the phallus: first as the intuited ob-ject of the (m)Other's desire, with which the child wants to identify himself, then as the paternal signifier laying down the law of sexual difference under the threat of castration, commanding the child to give up his desire for the mother and assume his place with respect to the *non/m du pere.*

My precis of Freudian and Lacanian thought to this point has delib-erately maintained the masculine pronoun for the child. As we saw in the preceding chapter, the girl's story is typically elided in psycho-analytic theory, or presented as a secondary deviation from the story of masculinity. Because castration is beside the point for her—or, in Freud's biologistic literalization of her difference, it has "already hap-pened" to her—she does not react to its threatened violence by aban-doning the mother and reaping a compensatory identification with the father, internalizing his authority as a legalistic superego. What does, then, happen next for her? Freud declared that she turns away from her mother, whom she now indicts for having bequeathed her an inferior lot in life, and moves toward her father, looking for a penis substitute: a baby. Her turn to the father, rather than driving her into channels of identification and aspiration, thus kindles her rivalry with her mother.

Near the end of his life, Freud himself suspected the inadequacy of his own formulations. In clinical experience, he found that the rela-tionship between mother and daughter was scarcely obliterated by the girl's Oedipal turn toward the father: "Almost everything that we find later in her relation to her father was already present in this earlier attachment and has been transferred subsequently on to her father. In short, we get an impression that we cannot understand women unless we appreciate this phase of their pre-Oedipus attachment to their mother."[16] Feminist reinterpretations of psychoanalysis, taking their cue from Freud's own reappraisal of femininity, have relocated sexual difference within girls' and boys' early relations with their mothers. Theorists such as Nancy Chodorow and Carol Gilligan have repossessed Freudian ideas of women's differences in positive terms: women's "lack" of an impersonal superego becomes women's alternative sense of moral relatedness; women's "weak" ego boundaries become women's empathic powers of connectedness.[17]

The problem is that the new feminist reinterpretations of psychoanalysis, reacting against Freud's notions of woman as minus-man, have thus tended to idealize the mother-daughter relationship as a dyadic space of real presence and true mutual recognition. As I argued in chapter 2, this conception of the mother-daughter relationship leaves too much outside it in actual women's writing: the dynamics of Emily Dickinson's rewritings of the Law of the Father, the ambiguities of recognizing the mother in *Aurora Leigh*. Moreover, it can reify binary oppositions between inside/outside, male/female, mother/father, good/bad: violence and oppression can be dismissed as external to the mother-daughter dyad, alien to its space of truth. Freud himself, in coming to an appreciation of the pre-Oedipal mother's overwhelming importance, did not think thereby to exclude rivalry, frustration, and aggression from that relationship. We have seen that Lacan, going further (in reaction against the ego psychology underpinning most feminist revisions of psychoanalysis), has remorselessly made the case for an incipient triangle always already inhabiting the Imaginary would-be dyad of mother and child: the mother's desire inevitably instills a self-dividing desire (to be the object of the mother's desire) in the child. "The Imaginary Father would thus be the mark that the Mother is not All but that she wants . . . who? what? The question is without response other than that which discovers the narcissistic void: 'In any case, not me.' "[18] In this reading, daughters no less than sons—despite the daughter's eventual conscious, sociological identification with the mother's role in the world—unavoidably must ask Freud's notorious question of what Woman wants. Any later rejection of the mother for her failure to provide the daughter with a literal, biological organ is subsequent to this narcissistically wounding initial discovery: I am not that magical thing (that Phallus, eventually) that she desires.

But if the Law of the Father and the Phallus, is, in a certain sense, always already there for Lacan, the mother persists for the daughter, as Freud also came to think, in the Symbolic Order of castration and its prescriptions for women's sexual "maturity." In Lacan's gnomic words, "If there is no virility which castration does not consecrate, then for the woman it is a castrated lover or a dead man (or even both at the same time) who hides behind the veil where he calls on her adoration from that same place beyond the maternal *imago* which sent out the threat of a castration not really concerning her." [19] Lacan's imagery bears taking seriously: both castrating father and son-lover hide, so to speak, behind the mother's skirts. They speak through her veil, her *imago*, through the child's earliest attempts to understand what more—more than the child—the mother wants. No mother-child dyad, for Lacan, Edenically untouched by the division and the Law of the Father; but at the same time, no paternal law or adult sexual relation unmediated by the mother's veiling.

Lacan points toward a way of reconceiving the Oedipal/pre-Oedipal, mother/father dichotomy that vitiates much contemporary feminist psychological theory. Where that theory is applied to ideas of women and literary tradition, Lacan's ideas suggest that we might re-formulate our thinking about women's literary traditions in ways that do not simply reiterate a mother/father, inside/outside dichotomy. For literary daughters, the father is always already there in the mother; the daughter's reading of the mother's desire may lead her to the "Other in the (m)Other." Modeling herself upon the desire of the mother, the daughter internalizes a self-division that is potentially a violence—lit-erally a violence, in much of the poetry we will look at in this chapter. The idea of a women's literary tradition, in this reading, may gain in complexity and power what it loses in reassuring self-identity.

Elizabeth Barrett Browning's *Aurora Leigh* is a case in point. I have already argued that its drama of mother-daughter recognition is equally and fundamentally a drama of misrecognition as well; that the mother-daughter reunion in the poem is not a recovery of full pres-ence, one woman to another; that the "pre-Oedipal" drama of Aurora's relation to the poem's mothers is always already intertwined, for her, with an Oedipal struggle for male recognition. Her dead mother's face is known to Aurora through the mediation of a male gaze, that of the painter who took the mother's portrait after she was dead. Drawn to this picture, Aurora sees in it no reassuring identity but a face that

> was by turns
> Ghost, fiend, and angel, fairy, witch, and sprite,
> A dauntless Muse who eyes a dreadful Fate,

> A loving Psyche who loses sight of Love,
> A still Medusa with mild milky brows
> All curdled and all clothed upon with snakes
> Whose slime falls fast as sweat will; or anon
> Our Lady of the Passion, stabbed with swords
> Where the Babe sucked . . .
>
> (*AL* 1.153–61)

Sexual violation, in these images, seemingly confounds itself with the infant's own feeding. Since it is Aurora herself who "mixe[s] . . . Whatever I last read or heard or dreamed" with her mother's painted face, she participates in the violence of the portrait; it is not in any simple sense a nightmare foisted upon her from outside, from the objectifying and deathly vision of the male painter. Aurora's image of the mother stabilizes somewhat as she gets older, but breasts remain targets of violence, including violence from Aurora's imagination itself. Her most famous image of her poetic project implicitly kills the mother as surely as the male painter's portrait does:

> Never flinch,
> But still, unscrupulously epic, catch
> Upon the burning lava of a song
> The full-veined, heaving, doubled-breasted Age:
> That, when the next shall come, the men of that
> May touch the impress with reverent hand, and say
> "Behold—behold the paps we all have sucked!
> This bosom seems to beat still, or at least
> It sets ours beating . . ."
>
> (*AL* 5. 213–21)

This fiery casting of an image (of absence, not presence—a concave "impress" rather than a rounded projection) sacrifices the maternal flesh to the service of an allegory of the "age," offered up by Aurora to male gazes.

The poem's ambivalent and often violent thematics of Aurora's biographical mother thus play themselves out at another level in *Aurora Leigh*'s relationship to the idea of a women's literary tradition. Helen McNeil notes the paradox of Aurora's image of the age: "The poet is female, her future audience is, interestingly, male. There is still no female tradition"—even though this passage would be "a powerful antecedent" for Emily Dickinson's volcano imagery.[20] Aurora herself participates in the denigration of other women writers as a group, while measuring herself against historical male poets: Keats (explicitly) and Wordsworth and Robert Browning (implicitly). Dorothy Mermin and Cora Kaplan find ample reason to believe that *Aurora Leigh* "must have given Barrett Browning the confidence of writing for the first time in a strong female tradition"; at the same time, however, Barrett Browning "denied what might seem like a specific indebtedness" to Charlotte Brontë's *Jane Eyre* and its final blinding of Rochester.[21] Another woman writer coming to *Aurora Leigh* as a mother text might (consciously or otherwise) have drawn from it the same message young Aurora may have drawn from the silence of her mother's male-drawn portrait: What does she want? Not me.

As an inaugural text of women's literary tradition, then, *Aurora Leigh* is richly, fruitfully contradictory. Is a female-authored text that names male precursors and suppresses literary mothers part of a women's literary tradition? Is a female-authored text that envisions only male readers (whatever the facts of its readership, actual or anticipated) part of a women's literary tradition? Where can the boundaries of that tradition be drawn? *Aurora Leigh* suggests that such boundaries must be seen inside women's texts as well as outside. Like young Aurora's attribution of violence to the portrait of her dead mother, the violent content of what returns from Barrett Browning's repressed mother text—the blinding of the heroine's male lover—further suggests how impossible it would be to segregate violence into the masculine side of literary tradition. Women's relations to literary mothers, like men's to literary fathers, can in their own way be marked by violence and misrecognition, the divided legacy of the Other in the (m)Other.

"A castrated lover, or a dead man": Lacan's reading of the desire that calls to women from "beyond the maternal *imago*" resonates not only with the plot of *Aurora Leigh* itself—the reunion of Aurora and her blinded Romney in Aurora's mother-country—but with the poem's dynamics of influence vis-à-vis the denied mother text, *Jane Eyre*, in which Jane too finds her desire fulfilled, in a blinded, maimed Rochester. Moreover, Lacan cryptically draws a connection between the castrated lover and Christ—"The figure of Christ, which in this light conjures up others more ancient, can be seen here in a more widespread capacity than that which is called for by the religious allegiance of the subject"[22]—a remark that recalls the Christology so prominent not only in *Aurora Leigh* but in Emily Dickinson's poetry, as we have seen. Reading each other's most famous works, nineteenth-century Anglo-American women writers indeed would often seem to have heard a dead or castrated male lover speaking in the accents of their literary sisters and foremothers.

By loving corpses, nineteenth-century women writers were of course following and revising an often male-authored cultural example. As Edgar Allen Poe most notoriously put it, "The death of a beautiful woman is, unquestionably, the most poetical topic in the world."[23] Cynthia Griffin Wolff suggests that Dickinson "performed radical surgery on Poe's pronouncement." One of her strategies for doing so, as we saw in chapter 2, entailed speaking from beyond the grave: in this case, the "death of a woman (though not necessarily a beautiful woman) would be the subject, but the Voice reporting the event would be that of the woman herself."[24] Another strategy, however, reverses the roles, casting the male himself in the role of beloved corpse. I want to look at a group of poems and prose texts by Elizabeth Barrett Browning, Charlotte and Emily Brontë, and Emily Dickinson that revise and reverse the male topos of the beautiful female corpse with reference to a particular father text, Wordsworth's "Lucy" poems. My concern is not only with what each woman writer individually makes of Wordsworth's father text, but with how that father text becomes an alien/familiar Other within the (m)Other, a violence internalized within a women's literary tradition itself.

In the "Lucy" poems, an unknown girl who died young (whether real or no hardly matters) becomes a figure through which the poet himself structures his relation to Mother Nature. Her death makes nature different and other for the male poet. Like the "Tree, of many, one / A single Field which I have looked upon" in the "Intimations" ode, Lucy is retrospectively made singular, not by her own deeds or any naturalistic particularities but by the poet's sense of loss:

> A violet by a mossy stone
> Half hidden from the eye!
> —Fair as a star, when only one
> Is shining in the sky.

> She lived unknown, and few could know
> When Lucy ceased to be;
> But she is in her grave, and, oh,
> The difference to me!
> ("She Dwelt among the Untrodden Ways")

The girl's death (even though her relationship to the poet is mysterious) in these poems localizes what is rendered in "Tintern Abbey" and the "Intimations" ode as a more general loss or difference in the poet's vision of nature. Mother Nature takes Lucy to herself, teaching her (as Wordsworth would be taught in "Tintern Abbey") to "feel an overseeing power" in the outdoors ("Three Years She Grew in Sun and Shower"); but Lucy, unlike the male poet, remains so close to nature that she dies of it, turning into a natural object "Rolled round in earth's diurnal course, / With rocks, and stones, and trees" ("A Slumber Did My Spirit Seal"). Fortunately for him, the poet wakes up—from the stimulus of her loss, as it were. Dreaming along the road in "Strange Fits of Passion Have I Known," he has a "strange and wayward thought"—" 'If Lucy should be dead!' "—which wakes him from his trance. It is as if her life were sacrificed to his, her consciousness to his poetic imagination. Her death leaves him in possession of nature:

> She died, and left to me
> This heath, this calm, and quiet scene;
> The memory of what has been,
> And never more will be.
> ("Three Years She Grew in Sun and Shower")

If irrevocably inflected by Lucy's loss, this scene is at the same time distanced by her difference in a way that saves the poet from Lucy's fate of dying into nature. The loss of boundary that happened between Mother Nature and the girl cannot happen to the poet who is both male and, now, protected by the sacrifice of Lucy's life to nature.[25]

Elizabeth Barrett Browning (then Elizabeth Barrett) took her revenge upon Wordsworth's "Lucy" poems in "The Poet's Vow," a poem published in her volume of 1838, *The Seraphim, and Other Poems*.[26] Full of echoes of Wordsworth's (and, secondarily, Coleridge's) poetry, "The Poet's Vow" tells the story of a Wordsworthian "nature"-poet's rejection of human society and his fitting punishment by the agency of a female corpse, that of Rosalind, his intended bride-to-be.[27] The poet, whose Wordsworthian brow is "Too calm for gentleness," rejects human society, vexed with the blight the human fall has brought upon nature: "O motion wild! O wave defiled! / Our curse has made you so." His withdrawal seems a perverse recoil of the younger Wordsworth's political indignation; rejecting any thought that he too shares the "dessicating sin . . . / The money-lust within," the poet foreswears human society in favor of nature's love, "more deep" (in one of Wordsworth's favorite tropes) than any human tie. Rather than acknowledge that he, too, has bitten of the apple, he will purge himself "to pledge and drink" nature's "wine of wonderment."

Here, however, the woman poet's revenge begins. Elizabeth Barrett identifies this Wordsworthian poet's withdrawal with the fate of Wordsworth's Lucy—a rather threatening development, were the male poet himself conscious of it:

> He dwelt alone, and sun and moon
> Were witness that he made

Rejection of his humanness
Until they seemed to fade:
His face did so, for he did grow
Of his own soul afraid.

Wordsworth's "Maid" who "dwelt among untrodden ways" did not choose that fate; this Poet does, in active rejection of love.

The first person to suffer Lucy's fate in "The Poet's Vow," however, is not the Poet himself but his fiancée, Rosalind. Barrett makes explicit what was implicit in Wordsworth's "Lucy" poems—the causal relation between the Poet's actions and the woman's death. Mother Nature, Barrett would suggest, does not claim Rosalind; the Poet's failure to claim her, to acknowledge human nature, saps her life. Rosalind leaves instructions that her corpse be delivered to the Poet along with an explanatory scroll, "as if she were a suddenly articulate Lady of Shalott,"[28] whose body underwrites the authority of her final speech. Asking her nurse to "heap beneath mine head the flowers / You stoop so low to pull," she intends to remind the Poet of a childhood before language and before any deadly division between human nature and Nature:

The little white flowers from the wood
    Which grow there in the cool,
Which *he* and I, in childhood's games,
Went plucking, knowing not their names,
    And filled thine apron full.

Unlike Wordsworth's "Nutting," in which the boy leaves behind both "Frugal Dame" and his sister to take his solitary exploration into nature, Rosalind remembers to the Poet a childhood expedition that was communal, shared by boy and girl alike, the consequences of which were less destructive than the young Wordsworth's "ravishing" of the bower in "Nutting."

And yet this idyllic childhood moment knew not language, at the time, and was productive of no original language for Rosalind, later; Rosalind does not become a different, alternative kind of nature poet.[29] Flowers remain her mute, literal—and funerary—woman's language. Her written words, carried by the scroll on her breast, bring *Wordsworth's* words back to the Wordsworthian Poet. As Dorothy Mermin notes, "The first stanza of her accusatory scroll in effect gives a voice to Wordsworth's Lucy, speaking from the grave to which Wordsworth's poems consign her"; Wordsworth's "thing that could not feel / The touch of earthly years" becomes Rosalind's "I come to thee, a solemn corpse / Which neither feels nor fears." If Rosalind "cannot avoid

Lucy's fate, silence and death," still "she can make it recoil on the poet."[30] Killed by the repetition of Wordsworth's words, the Poet joins Rosalind in the ground.

On the question of women's access to linguistic authority, the outcome of "The Poet's Vow" is ambiguous. Rosalind's language comes at the price of her death, and her language is not original but the repetion of Wordsworth's. Rosalind appropriates Wordsworth's language of imagination in a literalizing way, literally delivering herself to the Poet as a "thing" and offering him nonlinguistic tokens of nature—her flowers—along with her body. This repetition turns the implicit violence of Wordsworth's poems against themselves and confers destructive power upon the woman. Looking at the the frame of "The Poet's Vow," however, we may question the uses to which Barrett imagines this power being put. An epigraph from Wordsworth himself frames "The Poet's Vow" at the outset:—"Oh, be wiser thou, / Instructed that true knowledge leads to love." The epigraph encapsulates the strategy of the poem, turning Wordsworth's language against him, but it softens its import by suggesting that Wordsworth will survive this act of aggression by turning it into humanizing instruction—indeed, humanizing instruction self-supplied. If Wordsworth can write this, the epigraph implies, he should scarcely need Barrett's instruction. The ending of the poem, the epitaph on Rosalind and the Poet's tomb, is spoken by Rosalind's brother Sir Roland, to his "little son." The boy is tempted to look at nature rather than the funeral heap, but Sir Roland conjures him to look downward,

> "Upon this human dust asleep.
> And hold it in thy constant ken
> That God's own unity compresses
>   (One into one) the human many,
> And that his everlastingness is
>   The bond which is not loosed by any;
> That thou and I this law must keep,
>   If not in love, in sorrow then—
>   Though smiling not like other men,
> Still, like them we must weep."

The instruction purchased at such a price by Rosalind in "The Poet's Vow" passes from men to other men. While Rosalind's and the Poet's corpses are mouldering together in the grave, God's less material "unity" collapses human differences into an ideal one, and that one, clearly, male. Like *Aurora Leigh*, "The Poet's Vow," while searchingly critical of the male romantic tradition, gives rise to no alternative collectivity for women; perhaps it even ends by reinforcing the male tradition's authority to represent all human experience in oneness.

Although "The Poet's Vow," like *Aurora Leigh*, envisions no enabling female literary tradition, its critique of Wordsworth's "Lucy" poems is echoed fifteen years later by Charlotte Brontë in certain extraordinary passages in *Villette*. And unlike Elizabeth Barrett, Charlotte Brontë's critique involves relations between women; a revision of the "Lucy" story becomes part of a story passed from woman to woman, from Miss Marchmont to Lucy Snowe, in an early chapter of *Villette*.

Lucy Snowe arrives at Miss Marchmont's house by a kind of inversion of a bildungsroman quest. Orphaned, she moves not to the city and a wider life, but into an isolated country house to take care of an elderly woman. As Sandra Gilbert and Susan Gubar point out, Lucy Snowe's name recalls Wordsworth's poems, and the story Miss Marchmont tells Lucy of her life inverts one of the "Lucy" poems in particular, "Strange Fits of Passion Have I Known."[31] Wordsworth's poem, too, tells of a strange quest. The speaker recounts riding through moonlight to a cottage, where his lover awaits him. More of his horse's volition than of his own, it seems, the lover nears the cottage. As "the sinking moon" drops nearer and nearer toward Lucy's cottage, the speaker wanders in revery:

> In one of those sweet dreams I slept,
> Kind Nature's gentlest boon!
> And all the while my eyes I kept
> On the descending moon.
>
> My horse moved on; hoof after hoof
> He raised, and never stopped:
> When down behind the cottage roof,
> At once, the bright moon dropped.

And then the unbidden thought interrupts his revery: " 'If Lucy should be dead!' " If she should, who or what would have killed her? The poem does not explicitly say so, but it is Nature's moon that drops upon the cottage; perhaps Nature has taken the girl to herself, as she will in another poem. But the poem also suggests, as we have already noted, that Lucy dies a sacrifice to the male poet's imagination, keeping him conscious, speaking, and apart from nature at the cost of her own existence.

Charlotte Brontë's rereading of the poem in *Villette* draws out and literalizes the implicit action of the male romantic imagination in Wordsworth's poem. Brontë reverses Wordsworth's point of view and "approaches the event from the stationary and enclosed perspective of the waiting woman, whose worst fears are always substantiated."[32] In the story Miss Marchmont finally confides to Lucy Snowe on a stormy Christmas eve (when her own death is imminent), she herself was once the waiting woman. Her lover, Frank (perhaps his name is a male counterpart to "Lucy"—light, lucidity), was killed in an accident while riding to her house on a Christmas eve many years ago. She tells Lucy (as Wordsworth's speaker confides his story to another "Lover") how she sat, with the moon "mounting high," waiting for Frank. But her lover arrives as a body, soon to be a corpse: "a heavy, dragging thing . . . crossing, strangely dark, the lawn," pulled through the moonlight by his horse.[33]

Like Barrett's Rosalind, then, and eventually her Wordsworthian Poet, Frank shares Lucy's fate of becoming a "thing." Does this mean that the waiting woman, Rosalind or Miss Marchmont, has a fearful power of imagination in any way comparable to the power of imagination that Wordsworth's lover seems to fear in himself? She has, perhaps, a derivative power: the power of vengefully literalizing, or substantiating (in Gilbert and Gubar's term), states of mind of the male lover-poet. If Wordsworth's lover seems to have assigned his volition or desire over to his steadily moving horse, he arrives in Charlotte Brontë's text as a literally inanimate object, without volition, pulled by his horse. Wordsworth's lover imagines his beloved dead—a displacement, perhaps, of his own lack of eagerness to arrive at the object of his quest; Miss Marchmont's lover arrives, willy-nilly, on the brink of death himself. The ineffable male romantic subject (envisioned by Brontë's Miss Marchmont as a lover of magical, otherworldly moral and social superiority) arrives at his destination as an unspeakable Gothic horror: " 'How could I name that thing in the moonlight before me?' "

The consequences of this imaginative revenge for Miss Marchmont, however, as for Barrett's Rosalind, are mostly bleak. Like Wordsworth remembering Lucy, she remembers Frank for life. The "difference" of the loss is permanent. But where remembrance of Lucy after she becomes a "thing" merged with Mother Nature confers upon Wordsworth a legacy of power, calm, and freedom in nature ("She died, and left to me / This heath, this calm, and quiet scene"), remembrance of Frank become a "thing" separates Miss Marchmont from nature, as she confines herself to her chamber, increasingly ill and alone. Her fate literalizes another Wordsworthian trope: memory, for her, confines her in "shades of the prison-house," without any compensatory gains in human vision or human fellowship, in bitter parody of the Wordsworthian poetics of memory. And Miss Marchmont passes this story along to Lucy Snowe. The scene of instruction in *Villette* goes from adoptive mother to orphan daughter, rather than from father to son, as in "The Poet's Vow." But memory's legacy for Lucy Snowe, too, is bleakly repetitive, unlike Wordsworth's exalting legacy from Lucy: Lucy Snowe's story, too, will eventually reveal itself as the narrative of a woman pledged to the love of a dead man. If reversing Wordsworth's Lucy story gains a certain imaginative power for both Miss Marchmont and Lucy Snowe, it does so at a terrible price in freedom and fulfillment.

Emily Dickinson certainly knew Charlotte Brontë's *Villette* and Elizabeth Barrett Browning's early poems of *The Seraphim*, as well as their Wordsworthian pre-texts.[34] She must have been alert to the thematics of the castrated or dead male lover that haunted her literary foremothers' pages. Steeped in nineteenth-century popular mourning traditions as well as the poetics of the beautiful dead woman, she too revised, and often reversed, the tradition of the beautiful female corpse.[35] Some of her most famous poems, as Cynthia Griffin Wolff points out, ironically literalize this topos by speaking as the voice of the female corpse—in something of the way that Elizabeth Barrett confers a voice, if a compromised voice, upon the corpse of Rosalind in "The Poet's Vow."[36] As Barrett's poem suggests, however, and psychoanalytic theory stresses, the aggression directed toward the woman poet's own imagined self in such poetic situations can also redound outward, upon the male viewer of the body. Self and other revolve around the disputed axis of the possession of language: is the writing on the scroll Rosalind's, or does it belong to a male other, Wordsworth? Intertextuality in "The Poet's Vow" confounds distinctions between self and other; it is intimately bound up in the poem's covert aggression. So, too, in the Miss Marchmont episode of *Villette*, structured around a more thoroughgoing reversal of Wordsworth's Lucy story: the male lover, rather than the waiting woman, becomes a "thing," and the woman survives to tell the story. Yet the story Miss Marchmont tells could well be read as the scroll on the breast of a corpse, since the violence of her lover's death recoiled upon her in the form of her lifelong imprisonment and invalidism.

Many Dickinson poems draw on a similar reversal of the traditional relationship between living male imagination and female corpse. These are poems about what it is like to love, rather than to be, a corpse. Like *Villette*, however, these poems dramatize the limitations as well as the powers of reversing the masculine tradition's implicit violence. Their passive aggression blurs the boundary between self and other, external and internal violence.

Dickinson's poetic scenarios of surviving the other's death are diverse. In some of them she is denied a final embrace, like Lucy Snowe, who loses her lover Paul in a tempest that she can imaginatively recreate but never actually know. Told of his death by another party, she digs a grave into her own life, which "just holds the trench" (poem 734)—her own identity and writing become the gaping, graven hole of his absence. In other poems she demands Miss Marchmont's privilege of attending to her dying lover. When the lover addressed is still alive, however, her power of envisioning his death at length becomes an implicitly aggressive claim to imaginative power.

> Promise This—When You be Dying—
> Some shall summon Me—
> Mine belong Your latest Sighing—
> Mine—to Belt Your Eye—
>
> Not with Coins—though they be Minted
> From an Emperor's Hand—
> Be my lips—the only Buckle
> Your low Eyes—demand—
>
> Mine to stay—when all have wandered—
> To devise once more
> If the Life be too surrendered—
> Life of Mine—restore—
>
> Poured like this—My Whole Libation—
> Just that You should see
> Bliss of Death—Life's Bliss extol thro'
> Imitating You—
>
> Mine—to guard Your Narrow Precinct—
> To seduce the Sun
> Longest on Your South, to linger,
> Largest Dews of Morn
>
> To demand, in Your low favor
> Lest the Jealous Grass
> Greener lean—Or fonder cluster
> Round some other face—
>
> Mine to supplicate Madonna—
> If Madonna be
> Could behold so far a Creature—
> Christ—omitted—Me—
>
> Just to follow Your dear feature—
> Ne'er so far behind—
> For My Heaven—

> Had I not been
> Most enough—denied?
> (poem 648)

Dickinson's speaker demands full possession of the lover's body, once it becomes a thing that neither feels nor sees. Unlike Charlotte Brontë's Miss Marchmont, she refuses to give her lover up to Paradise. " 'When the dawn of Christmas morning broke, my Frank was with God,' " says Miss Marchmont; appropriately, Christ's sacrifice purchases the lover's redemption in heaven. Not so for Dickinson's speaker; she envisions sacrificing her own body to keep the lover on earth. Suggestions of Victor Frankenstein's overweening ambition (to "renew life where death had apparently devoted the body to corruption") haunt Dickinson's perverse *imitatio Christi*: the speaker proposes to imitate the human corpse, not Christ, pouring out her "Whole Libation" in hopes of restoring the lover again on earth.

The occasion of the poem, however, depends on the lover not rising again, at least not immediately. Although the speaker offers to exchange her life for his, in fact her rhetoric feeds off his corpse. Like Wordsworth in the Lucy poems, Dickinson gains a certain imaginative power over nature through the other's death, as Miss Marchmont does not. Hers is now the power to "seduce the Sun" and command the dews to attend upon the lover's grave; she recenters nature around the lover's corpse. Nature is made different by the loss of the other, as in the Lucy poems, and the poet comes to possess something in it, as Dickinson's insistent reiteration of "Mine" underscores. Where Wordsworth, however, gains possession of a total landscape ("this heath, this calm, and quiet scene"), the landscape of Dickinson's speaker remains dominated by the lover's corpse, pinned to a specific spot. Like the speaker of Emily Brontë's "Remembrance" ("Cold in the earth, and the deep snow piled above thee!"),[37] and like Miss Marchmont, Dickinson's mourner gains voice and power at the expense of a male corpse, in one sense, but in another way remains confined to the grave site in which the lover's corpse sleeps "cold in the earth." If Dickinson, along with the Brontës and Barrett Browning, critiques the male romantic imagination by literalizing and reversing its poetics of the female corpse, she pays a certain penalty for this literalization.[38] Instead of dissolving into the landscape, as Wordsworth's Lucy does, and becoming part of a figurative Mother Nature for the male poet, the male other remains a definite loss, confining the woman writer's voice to a definite grave.[39] As in the after-death poems we looked at in chapter 2, Dickinson over and over insists on the irreducible singularity of the male other. His individual "dear feature" is all she needs of heaven. Importantly, however, the lover's singularity ("Behold the Atom—I preferred—") does not stem from any personal characteristics of his own; it is a sheer putting forth of the woman poet's rhetorical will. But it means that she does not generalize his loss in quite the way Wordsworth can generalize, and so transcend, Lucy's loss.

Wordsworth has the easier task generalizing Lucy's loss, as we have seen, because as a passive "thing" she can be merged into a Nature that Western culture traditionally genders as female. Nature seems female, too, in Dickinson's poem, at least as personified in the "Jealous Grass" whose fondness the speaker solicits for her lover's grave. The relationship between male corpse and nature is a sexualized courting, rather than the merging between Lucy and Mother Nature. Dickinson prays to a "Madonna—/ If Madonna be," as an alternative to the Christ who has "omitted" her (and whose functions the speaker has herself usurped with relation to the male corpse). Perhaps this Madonna stands in for Mother Nature as an alternative to a Christian heaven, but if so, her benevolence toward Dickinson is most uncertain. The most the Madonna can grant is the right of the speaker to follow the male other—whether into an orthodox heaven or into an earthly grave remains ambiguous. Dickinson's power to command, like Orpheus, the natural world with her song seems to abandon her when she, like Orpheus, imagines following the lover into the realm of the dead.

"Promise This—When You be Dying—," if it does tend to fix the poet's imagination to a particular corpse, a particular loss, still does reverse the pattern of waiting woman/questing man that frames the Miss Marchmont episode in *Villette*. It is the woman speaker who will seek out the lover, then reach him only as he becomes a dead thing. This is a standard outcome of many a male quest, of course, and a staple of women's critiques of the genre, like Christina Rossetti's "The Prince's Progress," in which the story alternates between the dallying prince and his woman in waiting: "The bride she sleepeth, waketh, sleepeth, / Waiting for one whose coming is slow:—." So slow, in fact, that the prince arrives to see his bride laid out for burial; the veil becomes a shroud.[40] In the standard quest plot of masculine heterosexual poetic desire, delay gains the male quester space for imagination and adventure. Arriving at the destination too late costs the quester something in fulfillment, of course (adventures must be paid for), but keeps him imaginatively free of the claims of an actual speaking other. The power and action accrue to the male quester along the way, not after the always-deferred arrival at the quest's destination. "Promise This—," by contrast, draws all its power from imagining what happens after arriving at its destination, dwelling on the speaker's services to the beloved's corpse, but it too depends on the silence of the other at the journey's end. An earlier poem plays another variation upon the relationship between the quest and the death of the male other. This time the lover's death inaugurates the speaker's questing rather than ending it. But this poem too, reversing the gender roles of masculine quest romance, draws power at the expense of the other's silence:

> I bring an unaccustomed wine
> To lips long parching
> Next to mine,
> And summon them to drink;
>
> Crackling with fever, they Essay,
> I turn my brimming eyes away,
> And come next hour to look.
>
> The hands still hug the tardy glass—
> The lips I would have cooled, alas—
> Are so superfluous Cold—
>
> I would as soon attempt to warm
> The bosoms where the frost has lain
> Ages beneath the mould—
>
> Some other thirsty there may be
> To whom this would have pointed me
> Had it remained to speak—
>
> And so I always bear the cup
> If, haply, mine may be the drop
> Some pilgrim thirst to slake—
>
> If, haply, any say to me
> "Unto the little, unto me,"
> When I at last awake.
>
> (poem 132)

This poem is often read as a tribute to conventional feminine or religious altruism, but its actual chain of events and its poetic causality are far less reassuring.[41] The speaker's altruism is killing rather than life-giving. Is she responsible for the delay in bringing succor to her neighbor's lips? Like the archetypal male quester, whose delayed arrival symbolically kills the woman waiting for him, the speaker confers love and gratification (her emphasis on lips and "brimming eyes" suggests the erotic, bodily substance of her "unaccustomed wine") when it is too late. Nor does she stay to minister further. The wine works only too well; the corpse (now an "it," its thing-quality underscored) is forever silent. The outcome of her altruism in this case notwithstanding, the speaker offers her cup to other pilgrims and even to Christ himself, should she wake up in heaven to his voice. Would she pit her cup against his?

Dickinson was surely aware of the nineteenth-century American cultural bargain that assigned the virtue of loving altruism, especially maternal altruism, to women while denying them (as Freud later would write) a sense of abstract justice, especially as it exercised itself in public affairs. In this bargain, women became the chief consumers of religion without, for the most part, gaining access to formal religious authority. Dickinson's poem turns this cultural dynamic of consumption around, killing the other with her loving cup, gaining authority of speech for herself at his expense, triumphantly reversing stay-at-home altruism into a sanctified, questing aggression. Contrast her with the muse of many a Romantic and Victorian quest poem (Keats's Moneta in *The Fall of Hyperion,* or the mysterious queen of Elizabeth Barrett Browning's "A Vision of Poets," a companion poem to "The Poet's Vow"), at whose behest a male quester drinks and is initiated into the fraternity of true poets: her male quester is not strong enough to survive his "unaccustomed wine," and the female cupbearer survives to tell the poem.

In these poems and prose passages by Barrett Browning, Charlotte and Emily Brontë, and Emily Dickinson, female self and male other partially or completely change places, reverse roles of activity and passivity, turn aggression directed toward a female object around upon the male other. In these turnings, very often what was latent or figural in a male text (in Wordsworth's "A Slumber Did My Spirit Seal," Lucy's transformation into a "thing" of nature) becomes manifest or literal in an answering text authored by a woman: Rosalind literally carries Wordsworth's words back to the solitary Wordsworthian Poet; Miss Marchmont receives Frank's corpse as a thing; Dickinson's speaker dwells on the male lover's corpse. The rhetorical chiasmus or reversal that structures these texts is not, however, perfectly symmetrical. The female speakers remain themselves to some degree victims of, or imprisoned by, the fates that redound upon the male other. Violence in some way bodily links self to the male other rather than decisively severing their connection. Dickinson figures this connection between self and other, altruism and aggression, in liquid metaphors: while her speaker imagines her life's "Whole Libation" (poem 648) poured out at the other's dead lips, or her eyes brimming over like the cup she carries to the other's parched mouth (poem 132), the transfusion of power in these poems goes at least as much in the opposite direction. Without natural boundaries of their own, these oral, liquid metaphors transgress the bodily boundaries of self and other with covert violence.[42]

As every reader of Dickinson and the Brontës knows, however, the violence of boundaries can also be felt within; conflicts between self and other, woman writer and masculine tradition—partly (but never wholly) externalized in the texts we have looked at to this point—may also be internalized. Here again Charlotte Brontë's *Villette* provides a paradigmatic scene of instruction in self-division, which Emily Dickinson may have mined imagistically. In chapter 12, "The Casket," Lucy Snowe (by now an instructor in Madame Beck's establishment at the Rue Fossette) intercepts a love letter intended for her sometime friend and pupil, Ginevra, while walking in a garden forbidden to Madame Beck's students. Immediately before this prosaic letter from an all-too-human man falls into her hands, however, Lucy's situation and her reveries have, as Sandra Gilbert and Susan Gubar point out, distinctly Wordsworthian overtones: "The English thorn, the experience of interiority in the garden, the ways in which that experience in tranquility recalls an earlier spot in time when Lucy felt the power of infinitude, all are reminiscent of the poetry of Wordsworth."[43] If Lucy intercepts a letter from a romantic lover, her creator intercepts a male Romantic poet, as she had earlier in the Miss Marchmont episode. Anything but tranquility results. In the storm that follows Lucy's discovery of the love letter, she internalizes a natural storm as an interior theater of cruelty:

> One night a thunderstorm broke; a sort of hurricane shook us in our beds: the Catholics rose in panic and prayed to their saints. As for me, the tempest took hold of me with tyranny: I was roughly roused and obliged to live. I got up and dressed myself, and creeping outside the casement close by my bed, sat on its ledge. . . . I could not go in: too resistless was the delight of staying with the wild hour, black and full of thunder, pealing out such an ode as language never delivered to man—too terribly glorious, the spectacle of clouds, split and pierced by white and blinding bolts.
>
> I did long, achingly, then and for four-and-twenty hours afterwards, for something to fetch me out of my present existence, and lead me upwards and onwards. This longing, and all of a similar kind, it was necessary to knock on the head, which I did, figuratively, after the manner of Jael to Sisera, driving a nail through their temples. Unlike Sisera, they did not die: they were but transiently stunned, and at intervals would turn on the nail with a rebellious wrench; then did the temples bleed, and the brain thrill to its core.

The elements of the Miss Marchmont episode are here transformed. There, it was Miss Marchmont who, in the aftermath of a terrible thunderstorm (and unknowingly forecasting her own death), began her Wordsworthian story by saying: " 'I love Memory tonight.' " The instructing relationship between Miss Marchmont and Lucy Snowe, in this chapter, is internalized and made more violent as a split within Lucy herself. Miss Marchmont loses Frank; Lucy's task is to kill her own desires as Jael killed Sisera.[44] The reappearance of Wordsworth in Lucy's story signals that Lucy is doomed to repeat Miss Marchmont's fate. A male "other" intertextually haunting Brontë's own language and imagination, Wordsworth prefigures the intrusion of an "other" desire, figured as male, in Lucy's own head.

The "ode" out of the clouds splits the female subject into two parts, or perhaps more accurately, three: Jael, Sisera, and the narrator, whom we might think of as an ego, observing and assenting to the violence enacted by the superego upon the mental representation of her desire, holding the warring parts into an achieved identity. The ode from the clouds is grander than anything language has ever "delivered to man"—more grandiloquent, certainly, than the nature of Wordsworth's ballads, but also something over which Lucy Snowe claims no mastery. As Patricia Yaeger points out, the mechanisms of projective othering through which male Romantics deliver their own anxieties over to a feminized Nature do not work for Lucy. She "cannot split off these undesirable energies and project them onto some other, since she is already placed in that position of other."[45] Nature for her is not what she half creates, and what perceives; it is all perception for Lucy: its lightnings divide and illuminate; it dominates her own mind, revealing conflict rather than tranquility as her basic condition and the basic correspondence between her mind and nature. She can, however, find figurative language for her internal theater of self-division. What should be the outer boundary of identity—the skull, whole and secure—is, terribly, both internal and violated for Lucy; her inner life turns around the nail in Sisera's temple. Lucy's realistic individual autonomy, her self-determination through paid labor, the privacy of her own thoughts in her own skull (all hallmarks of bourgeois male norms of individualism) cannot defend her from this psychic self-division since she cannot so readily muster figures of projection, the others who assume the anxieties and contradictions of bourgeois (male) identity.[46] Self-division (rather than projection) constitutes her interiority; her sense of boundaries depends on this inward violation.

In fact, self-division is in a very real sense Lucy's internal work and the foundation of her paid, public work. The nail in Sisera's temple terribly parodies women's domestic work—sewing—which is one of the first tasks at which Lucy demonstrates her reliability upon her arrival at Madame Beck's school. The biblical story of Jael and Sisera also makes the metaphoric connection between women's needle and Jael's nail. Wondering aloud why her son is so long returning from battle, Sisera's mother is answered by her "wise ladies" that the men are surely busy dividing the spoils: "to every man a damsel or two; to Sisera a prey of divers colours, a prey of divers colours of needlework on both sides, meet for the necks of them that take the spoil" (Judges 5:30). Jael ironically makes good upon this expectation. No spoil of war herself, her needlework turns Sisera's body into a spoil of war, and the biblical chronicler rejoices in the reversal: "So let all thine enemies perish, O Lord: but let them that love him be as the sun when he goeth forth in his might." For Brontë's Lucy, however, the same metaphor is not a triumphant victory over a people's external enemies but a work of isolated self-execution, and the ending of *Villette* will mock the prayer of the chronicler, as all of Lucy's enemies prosper.

An early poem by Dickinson also ascribes a tormenting self-division, a dreadful forced labor, to the traditional tools of women's work:

> A weight with needles on the pounds
> To push, and pierce, besides—
> That if the Flesh resist the Heft
> The puncture—coolly tries—
>
> That not a pore be overlooked
> Of all this Compound Frame—
> As manifold for Anguish—
> As species—be—for name—
> (poem 264)

Inwardness itself, the experience of subjectivity—what the body's "Compound Frame" presumably contains—is a kind of painful internalization of women's domestic labor. Dickinson's metaphor feminizes one of Wordsworth's favorite (and ambiguous) tropes for experience, the weight of life ("a weight / Heavy as frost, and deep almost as life!" in the "Intimations" ode). The "weight with needles on the pounds," like Lucy Snowe's struggle with Jael and Sisera, adds a dimension of horror to experience and identity beyond the simple deadening freight of custom and habit against which Wordsworth struggles. Uncannily fitted to penetrate every pore, this torture engine, like Lucy's nail in the skull, becomes indistinguishable from the body's own boundaries. The poem turns on the axis of this uncanny boundary. Is the "weight" something inside the speaker, or is it outside? Are "Flesh" and "Compound Frame" metaphors for mind and identity, being attacked from outside through the vehicle of the body, or is the "weight" mind itself attacking its fleshly container? The vehicle and tenor of the metaphor can reverse themselves, but what matters, what constitutes identity in this poem, is the sense of boundary inseparable from its violation.

The privileged figure for this experience of identity in nineteenth-century women writers, as so many feminist critics have pointed out, is the prison. Gilbert and Gubar write that "dramatizations of imprisonment and escape are so all-pervasive in nineteenth-century literature by women that we believe they represent a uniquely female tradition."[47] Other critics, however, point out that imprisonment and escape are to be found in the works of nineteenth-century male writers as well; *Romantic Imprisonment*, to cite Nina Auerbach's title, is a general nineteenth-century motif. Both Emily Dickinson and the Brontë sisters were imaginatively captivated by Byron's "Prisoner of Chillon." (Dickinson cited the poem in several letters, including one of the impassioned "Master" drafts.)[48] This does not so much invalidate Gilbert and Gubar's identification of imprisonment with women's literary tradition, however, as complicate the issues of identity that terms like "unique" and "tradition" assume. If the prison figure, in these texts, represents a self-division within the women writers themselves—if the prison figure is in part an appropriation and internalization of a dominant male Romantic trope, as well as something shared among women writers themselves—then the identity of the "uniquely female tradition" must be self-divided, relational, the product of differences within and between writers (female and male) rather than of simple likeness between women writers. In other words, the prison figure in nineteenth-century women's writing shows that the identity of "tradition" cannot be unique—in the sense of self-sufficient, standing alone. Identity, whether individual or in the sense of a female tradition, never stands alone and is never simply an effect of sameness. If Dickinson shares the prison figure with the Brontë sisters and other women writers, if it is a figure she internalized (among other sources) from her reading of the Brontë sisters, the figure also bears the traces of the female tradition's male "others," and it makes identity an otherness for Dickinson herself.

The Lacanian theory of identity as an Imaginary mirror image is helpful here, I think, because it stresses the alienation involved in projecting any whole, bounded self, whether an individual self or the Imaginary ideal of tradition. In poems like Emily Brontë's poem "The Captive" or Dickinson's prison poems, the prison itself or the voice and gaze of the warden seem virtually to act out the function of the mirror in Lacanian theory. If they imprison the speaking subject, they also mirror back to her a coherent identity:

A Prison gets to be a friend—
Between its Ponderous face
And Ours—a Kinsmanship express—
And in its narrow Eyes—

We come to look with gratitude
For the appointed Beam
It deal us—stated as our food—
And hungered for—the same—

We learn to know the Planks—
That answer to Our feet—
So miserable a sound—at first—
Nor ever now—so sweet—

As plashing in the pools—
When Memory was a Boy—
But a Demurer Circuit—
A Geometric Joy—

The Posture of the Key
That interrupt the Day
To Our Endeavor—Not so real
The Cheek of Liberty—

As this Phantasm Steel—
Whose features—Day and Night—
Are present to us—as Our Own—
And as escapeless—quite—

(poem 652)

A kind of Wordsworthian boy-child and a Wordsworthian poetics of
memory seem to lie imprisoned here; boyhood freedom gives way to
a "Demurer Circuit"—adult female identity, domesticity as a prison.
For this speaker, visionary gleams of a freer past in nature have been
replaced by "the appointed Beam" of the prison's slitted windows, the
"Eyes" of its face. Yet it is important to remember that the prison is not
in any direct way a simply external, masculine force, but an aspect of
the speaker's own identity. Or, to be more accurate, both the speaker's
identity and the prison are effects of the divisions and, at the same
time, repetitions of the poem's language. They are rhetorically dependent upon one another; in the poem's Imaginary metaphor, they echo
each other both visually and aurally. The speaker's coherence and
the prison's "Phantasm Steel" are guaranteed by the internal division
between them.

Dickinson may have found a precursor for this poem's sense of
identity in a long poem by Emily Brontë, edited and published as "The
Prisoner: A Fragment" in 1847.[49] The poem is a dramatic monologue

delivered by a man visiting a woman whom his family has imprisoned; the gaze that Dickinson metaphorically attributes to the prison itself, then, belongs to a dramatic character in Brontë's poem. His visit, his gaze, and his questions prompt the woman prisoner to boast of visionary flight—a visionary flight twice enabled by masculine figures, for he is not her only male visitor:

> "A messenger of Hope comes every night to me,
> And offers, for short life, eternal liberty.
>
> "He comes with western winds, with evening's wandering airs,
> With that clear dusk of heaven that brings the thickest stars;"

The messenger's naturalistic guise, however, gives way to a supernatural " 'mute music . . . —unuttered harmony / That I could never dream till earth was lost to me.' " A better vision, more powerful than nature alone, compensates the speaker for her imprisonment:

> "Then dawns the Invisible, the Unseen its truth reveals;
> My outward sense is gone, my inward essence feels—
> Its wings are almost free, its home, its harbour found;
> Measuring the gulf it stoops and dares the final bound!"

Like the male Romantic poets, Emily Brontë's speaker wants an imaginative vision not confined to naturalistic particulars.[50] The price of that vision for her, however, is not simply growing up and so gaining distance from nature, but this imprisonment caused by men and ameliorated by a masculine "messenger." Brontë's speaker insists that the "Mute music" that "soothes" her imprisonment is superior to the visible and sensory splendor of nature and superior to her own earlier sense of correspondence with nature, before she was imprisoned (" 'When, if my spirit's sky was full of flashes warm, / I knew not whence they came, from sun or thunderstorm' ").

Along with Brontë, Dickinson sees imprisonment in her poem as an alienation from nature, an alienation that nevertheless is the poem's occasion for language and for the speaker's very identity. Nevertheless, Dickinson registers her skepticism at the notion that such alienation makes abundant recompense for the loss of freedom; the music of the prison's planks, echoing herself to herself, are not "so sweet— / As plashing in the pools—." And by personifying the prison as a (presumably masculine) "ponderous face," Dickinson collapses the figures of the dungeon, the male visitor, the Warder, and the masculine "messenger of Hope"—dramatically separated in Brontë's poem—into one identity, which she acknowledges is inseparable from her own.

In its different way, Brontë's poem also implicitly acknowledges that difference and self-division is the foundation of the Prisoner's identity, not only a fate that is imposed upon her from external masculine forces. The Prisoner's coherent rhetorical identity of defiance depends upon and offers itself to the male visitor's mirroring gaze. Her extranatural, visionary flight depends on dividing body from soul, and it is paid for in the same dualistic terms:

> "Oh, dreadful is the check—intense the agony
> When the ear begins to hear and the eye begins to see;
> When the pulse begins to throb, the brain to think again,
> The soul to feel the flesh and the flesh to feel the chain!
>
> "Yet I would lose no sting, would wish no torture less;
> The more that anguish racks the earlier it will bless;"

The metaphoric flight of transcendence that exceeds all boundaries comes back to earth in a series of anguished inside/outside metonymies, one confining boundary leading to the next and the next: soul bound by flesh and flesh by chain. The metonymies expose, however, what the metaphor by itself would deny or efface: the metaphor of flight itself depends on a hierarchical division between body and soul, nature and transcendence.

When Dickinson writes as a poem the kind of speech delivered by Brontë's Prisoner, she overtly makes the same defiant assertion of coherent (because adversarial) identity. But her less conventional, more condensed language holds more surprises about the figurative relationships between body, and soul, prison and freedom:

> No Rack can torture me—
> My Soul—at Liberty—
> Behind this mortal Bone
> There knits a bolder One—
>
> You cannot prick with saw—
> Nor pierce with Scimitar—
> Two Bodies—therefore be—
> Bind One—The Other fly—
>
> The Eagle of his nest
> No easier divest—
> And gain the Sky
> Than mayest Thou—
>
> Except Thyself may be
> Thine Enemy—
> Captivity is Consciousness—
> So's Liberty.
>
> (poem 384)

Dickinson's metaphor for soul, the "bolder" bone behind the "mortal Bone," frankly admits that metaphors for soul and transcendence may really be metonymies; soul and body are contiguous, not different essences but the effect of a mysterious inward and linguistic boundary between bone and its "bolder One—." Her very wordplay suggests that soul is an inward division in the *word*, bone. The convoluted syntax of the second and third stanzas, untangled, seems to say that the soul can transcend as easily as the eagle can fly out of its nest, but the language of the poem calls into question this easy metaphorical belief in transcendence. It is hard to abstract this paraphrasable "meaning" from these lines, as hard as it would be to detach "mortal Bone" from the "bolder One" knit up behind it and, linguistically, *with* it. The final stanza's alliteration and reflexive syntax explicitly assert that there is no easy way to transcend this situation, no easy separation of body and soul; identity is this inward division. The reflexive, mirroring, Imaginary wholeness of the speaker's identity is the effect of that elusive division. If Gilbert and Gubar are right in suggesting that a poem like this participates in a distinctive nineteenth-century women's literary tradition, we must acknowledge the poem's difficult implications for the identity of that tradition.

Surveying the field of feminist literary criticism in 1981, Myra Jehlen proposed the topographical notion of the border as governing metaphor for a "radically comparativist" feminist criticism. Revising Elaine Showalter's map (in *A Literature of Their Own*) of an exclusively female literary topography, Jehlen argued, "Comparison reverses the territorial image along with its contained methodology and projects instead, as the world of women, something like a long border." The border itself, not the supposed integral essence of the territory contained, is the place of definition.[51] Jehlen's metaphor is a suggestive alternative not only to Showalter's female topography but to Sandra Gilbert and Susan Gubar's eschatological metaphor of the "single woman artist, a 'mother of us all,' "—the unified, Imaginary individual woman behind the textual "fragments" assembled by feminist criticism.[52] As Jehlen pointed out, the actual matter of what Showalter, along with Gilbert and Gubar, found in the female territory undermined such eschatological visions of a promised land or a giant mother of capable imagination. If the "women's tradition" means anything, it means a common set of problems—of definition and ambivalence. It is a relational, not an absolute, identity.

And, as Jehlen implies, that border is within, as well as without, women writers. The border, the difference within, makes its insistence felt in the kinds of figures I have examined in this chapter: figures of internalized self-division; chiastic reversals of subject and object, of violence and cause and effect; the metaphor of identity as a prison. To push the deconstructive point of Jehlen's argument a little further: the kind of split internalized as a prison in these texts is not, in my view, an unhappy accident that befalls a preexisting, once-unified female identity, an identity that can somehow be recovered later by assembling the divided fragments. Rather, for the purposes of these texts and their historical frame, this split *is* female identity. In Lacanian terms, the subject exists in the very split that opens between its disorganized reality and the would-be totality of its mirror-stage image, its Imaginary *moi*. The border—whether internal or external—defines identity, which is irremediably relational. But this general (perhaps) problematic of human identity afflicts the women writers under study here in historically specific, particular ways, at least some of which can be considered under the rubrics of literary tradition, literary influence, and literary internalizations.

These texts prompt, however, one more deconstructive turn around the metaphor of the border. If the border defines entities—female/ male, self/other—that only exist relationally and in relation to the border, what about the border itself? Over and over in these poems and prose passages, borders and boundaries exist to be breached, or they make their existence (often painfully) felt through a breaching or violence. The soul's inviolable borders are not thinkable, for Dickinson, without "saw" or piercing "Scimitar." The border might be seen deconstructively, not as irreducibly "primary," but as the effect of its own undoing. If women's literary tradition constitutes itself, in Jehlen's metaphor, as a long borderline, or if women writers of the nineteenth century repeatedly constitute their own identities along the inner boundary of a prison, those are, as these texts often suggest, not stable constructions, even if the violence associated with these borders has an uncanny way of repeating itself. If the borderline is a painful place, then, it is also—as Adrienne Rich's "From an Old House in America" insists—the possible place of change.

NOTES

1. Rich's "From an Old House in America" and "Face to Face" (below) are cited from the *Poems: Selected and New, 1950–1974* (New York: W. W. Norton, 1975).

2. "Each time the psychoanalytic description of internal conflict and psychic division is referred to its social conditions, the latter absorb the former, and the unconscious shifts—in that same moment—from the site of a division

into the vision of an ideal unity to come." Jacqueline Rose, *Sexuality and the Field of Vision*, 9.

3. Rose, *Sexuality and the Field of Vision*, 15.

4. Ibid., 16.

5. Adrienne Rich, "Vesuvius at Home: The Power of Emily Dickinson" (1975), repr. in *On Lies, Secrets, and Silence: Selected Prose 1966–1978* (New York: W. W. Norton, 1979), 172. Albert J. Gelpi's essay "Emily Dickinson and the Deerslayer," in Sandra Gilbert and Susan Gubar, eds., *Shakespeare's Sisters* (Bloomington: Indiana University Press, 1979), 122–34, drew on Rich's insights. Joanne Feit Diehl notes some of the more recent feminist interpretations in "Murderous Poetics: Dickinson, the Father, and the Text," in Boose and Flowers, eds., *Daughters and Fathers*, 326–43. Important, although not explicitly feminist, readings have been advanced by Robert Weisbuch, in *Emily Dickinson's Poetry*, 27–35, and Sharon Cameron, in *Lyric Time: Dickinson and the Limits of Genre*, 65–74.

6. Feit Diehl, "Murderous Poetics," 329.

7. Ibid., 326.

8. See Rich's brief remarks in "Vesuvius at Home," 161, 174–75, which, along with Ellen Moers's *Literary Women*, helped inaugurate serious consideration of Dickinson's relations to the Brontës as well as Barrett Browning and George Eliot.

9. Sandra M. Gilbert, "Notes toward a Literary Daughteronomy," in Boose and Flowers, *Daughters and Fathers*, 256–77.

10. To take perhaps the most influential example, Elaine Showalter's "Feminist Criticism in the Wilderness" called in 1981 for the displacement of "feminist critique," based upon "the feminist as *reader*," with a new "gynocritics," based on "the study of women *as writers*"; gynocritics would yield a description of "the evolution and laws of a female literary tradition." "Feminist Criticism in the Wilderness," repr. in Elizabeth Abel, ed., *Writing and Sexual Difference* (Chicago: University of Chicago Press, 1982), 12, 14–15, emphasis in the original. Showalter's separation of women as readers from women as writers seems to me wholly untenable, and, indeed, it does not survive the conclusion of her own essay, in which women's cultural productions are seen (in the context of women's situation as a "muted" group) "as a double-voiced discourse," inevitably bearing the traces of women's reading of the dominant culture. There have since been too many reexaminations of the ideal of "women's literary tradition" from too many critical angles to survey here. Nina Auerbach, writing on the Brontë sisters in the context of Romanticism, registers her own difficulties with "the female tradition" in thematic and psychological terms very close to my concerns in this chapter: "Female traditions are often celebrated as a nurturing, even a swaddling, ambience for a woman writer supposedly unheard in patriarchy. I want to free these traditions from their potential for constricting cant and self-flattery, their hypocritical protestations of womanly feeling. Like violence, self-deception is a human, not a male, instinct." *Romantic Imprisonment: Women and Other Glorified Outcasts* (New York: Columbia University Press, 1986), xxi.

11. Jane Gallop, "Reading the Mother Tongue: Psychoanalytic Feminist Criticism," 130.

12. For an interpretive survey of Freud's thought on the ego, see Jean Laplanche, *Life and Death in Psychoanalysis*, trans. Jeffrey Mehlman (Baltimore: Johns Hopkins University Press, 1976), chapter 3, "The Ego and the Vital Other."

13. See Freud, *New Introductory Lectures on Psychoanalysis*, trans. James Strachey (New York: W. W. Norton, 1965), 55–56.

14. Lacan, "Aggressivity in Psychoanalysis," in *Ecrits*, 22.

15. Ibid., 19.

16. Freud, "Femininity," in *New Introductory Lectures*, 105.

17. Carol Gilligan, *In a Different Voice*; Nancy Chodorow, *The Reproduction of Mothering*. See chapter 2 above.

18. Julia Kristeva, "L'abject d'amour," trans. and cited by Cynthia Chase in "Desire and Identification in Lacan and Kristeva," in Richard Feldstein and Judith Roof, eds., *Feminism and Psychoanalysis* (Ithaca, N.Y.: Cornell University Press, 1989), 79.

19. Lacan, "Guiding Remarks for a Congress on Feminine Sexuality," in Mitchell and Rose, eds. *Feminine Sexuality*, 95.

20. Helen McNeil, *Emily Dickinson*, 154.

21. Dorothy Mermin, *Elizabeth Barrett Browning*, 185; see also Cora Kaplan's introduction to the Women's Press edition of *Aurora Leigh and Other Poems*, 20–26.

22. Lacan, "Guiding Remarks for a Congress on Feminine Sexuality," 65.

23. Poe, "The Philosophy of Composition," in *The Complete Works of Edgar Allan Poe*, ed. James A. Harrison (New York: Thomas Y. Crowell & Co., 1902), 14:201. Poe's relationship to this nineteenth-century cliché was, however, complex indeed; see Joan Dayan, *Fables of Mind: An Inquiry into Poe's Fiction* (New York: Oxford University Press, 1987), chapter 3, "Convertibility and the Woman as Medium."

24. Cynthia Griffin Wolff, *Emily Dickinson*, 222.

25. For more on the "Lucy" poems in the context of male romanticism, see Margaret Homans's discussion in *Women Writers and Poetic Identity*, 20–29.

26. All citations of "The Poet's Vow" in this chapter are taken from *The Complete Works of Elizabeth Barrett Browning*, ed. Charlotte Porter and Helen A. Clarke, vol. 1 (New York: Thomas Y. Crowell & Co., 1900).

27. For a full and excellent discussion of the poem's revisions of Wordsworth's "Lucy" poems and Coleridge's *Ancient Mariner*, see Dorothy Mermin, *Elizabeth Barrett Browning*, 63–67.

28. Mermin, *Elizabeth Barrett Browning*, 65.

29. According to Mermin, Elizabeth Barrett confronted "her exclusion from the Romantic tradition" in *The Seraphim, and Other Poems*, realizing that "she could see no way for a woman to establish an appropriate poetic relationship with nature." *Elizabeth Barrett Browning*, 63.

30. Mermin, *Elizabeth Barrett Browning*, 65, 66.

31. Gilbert and Gubar, *The Madwoman in the Attic*, 405.

32. Ibid., 405–6.

33. All *Villette* citations are taken from the Penguin edition, ed. Mark Lilly (Harmondsworth: Penguin, 1979).

34. Jack L. Capps remarks on the similarities between Dickinson's "I Died for Beauty" (poem 449) and Barrett Browning's "A Vision of Poets" in *Emily Dickinson's Reading: 1836–1886* (Cambridge, Mass.: Harvard University Press, 1966), 83–84.

35. Barton Levi St. Armand discusses Dickinson's negotiations with "the Victorian way of death" in *Emily Dickinson and Her Culture*, 39–77.

36. Wolff, *Emily Dickinson*, 221–22.

37. "Remembrance" is the title given the poem in the 1846 edition of *Poems by Currer, Ellis, and Acton Bell* (London: Aylott and Jones).

38. Margaret Homans finds such literalizations a consistent strategy in nineteenth-century women writers' negotiations with masculine myths of linguistic authority; see *Bearing the Word*, chapter 1, "Representation, Reproduction, and Women's Place in Language."

39. The outcome of Emily Brontë's "Remembrance" is more perhaps more ambivalent about the woman's fixation on the dead male lover than either Dickinson's or Barrett Browning's poems. See chapter 5, note 13, below, for contrasting feminist readings of "Remembrance" and other heroic mourning poems by Emily Brontë.

40. Christina Rossetti, "The Prince's Progress," in *The Prince's Progress and Other Poems* (1866), repr. in *The Complete Poems of Christina Rossetti: A Variorum Edition*, ed. R. W. Crupp (Baton Rouge: Louisiana State University Press, 1979).

41. Jack L. Capps sees the poem as piously Christian, noting its quotation of Matthew 25:40. *Emily Dickinson's Reading*, 48–49. For Cynthia Griffin Wolff, the poem competes with orthodox Christianty, offering instead a humanized "simple charity" and "shared hope"; yet this reading too seems to miss something crucial in the poem's expressive causality. *Emily Dickinson*, 213–14.

42. For a reading of women's orality as an emancipatory boundary-breaking figure in women's writing, see Patricia Yaeger's *Honey-Mad Women: Emancipatory Strategies in Women's Writing* (New York: Columbia University Press, 1988), 1–34.

43. Gilbert and Gubar, *The Madwoman in the Attic*, 411. For a brilliant and detailed interpretation of Brontë's revisions of male Romanticism in *Villette*, see Yaeger's *Honey-Mad Women*, chapter 2, "The Bilingual Heroine," 35–76. Yaeger's reading of *Villette* in this respect is more positive than Gilbert and Gubar's or mine.

44. In the biblical story, Jael invites Sisera to turn in to her tent and offers him a bottle of milk to drink, above and beyond the requirements of hospitality: "He asked water, and she gave him milk; she brought forth butter in a lordly dish" (Judges 5:25). Like Dickinson's "unaccustomed wine," Jael's hospitality is death-dealing.

45. Patricia Yaeger, *Honey-Mad Women*, 65. Yaeger also points to Coleridge's presence in this passage, in the form of allusions to "Dejection: An Ode."

46. This status of self-division and romantic desire in this episode and

others like it are at the heart of an extremely important feminist debate about *Villette*. For Judith Lowder Newton's marxist-feminist perspective, such episodes are something of an embarrassment. They draw attention away from the autonomy Lucy achieves through work and self-discipline, locating her subjectivity instead in romantic longings. *"Villette,"* in *Women, Power, and Subversion: Social Strategies in British Fiction 1778–1860* (Athens: University of Georgia Press, 1981). By contrast, Mary Jacobus, writing from a psychoanalytic and perhaps romantic perspective, locates the book's most important subversive energies in just such moments. "The Buried Letter: *Villette,"* in *Reading Woman: Essays in Feminist Criticism* (New York: Columbia University Press, 1986). Cora Kaplan has cogently argued that these opposed readings are historically symptomatic of feminism's historical roots and its present difficulties mediating between social and psychic realms. She notes however that "for both critics, female sujectivity is the site where the opposing forces of femininity and feminism clash by night, but they locate these elements in different parts of the text's divided selves." "Pandora's Box: Subjectivity, Class and Sexuality in Socialist Feminist Criticism" in *Sea Changes: Culture and Feminism* (London: Verso, 1986), 154. Locating division and violence is exactly the issue of my concern with "women's literary tradition" and its internal/external boundaries. It is important to observe, in this context, that even if Lucy Snowe does not project her self-division onto others in this particular passage, elsewhere in *Villette* and in Charlotte Brontë's other novels the heroine does find projective Others—most infamously in *Jane Eyre's* Bertha Rochester. As Kaplan puts it, "Imperiled bourgeois femininity takes meaning in relation to other female identities" ("Pandora's Box," 168).

47. Gilbert and Gubar, *The Madwoman in the Attic*, 85.

48. See *The Letters of Emily Dickinson*, ed. Thomas H. Johnson (Cambridge, Mass: Harvard University Press, 1958), 2:374, 393, 433 (hereafter cited as *Letters*), and Auerbach, " 'This Changeful Life': Emily Brontë's Anti-romance," chapter 13 in *Romantic Imprisonment*, 212–29.

49. The poem, originally part of a longer dramatic work, was published as "The Prisoner" in *Poems by Currer, Ellis, and Acton Bell*. For more on the complex textual history of the poem, see chapter 4 below.

50. For a discussion of Wordsworthian echoes and presences in this poem, see Margaret Homans, *Women Writers and Poetic Identity*, 118–21.

51. Myra Jehlen, "Archimedes and the Paradox of Feminist Criticism," *Signs* 6, no. 4 (Summer 1981): 585.

52. Gilbert and Gubar, *The Madwoman in the Attic*, 101.

4

An Ear outside the Castle

Then there's a noiseless noise in the Orchard—
that I let persons hear—
—Dickinson to Thomas W. Higginson,
August 1862

Though your ear be next-door to your brain, it is forever removed
from your sight. It is because we ourselves are in ourselves, that
we know ourselves not.
—Melville, *Mardi*

Reading the poetics of Emily Dickinson's home space is an enterprise complicated by the biographical fact of her withdrawal into her father's house and grounds, and by the nearly inevitable formal analogies drawn between that withdrawal and the condensed difficulty of her poetry. Fact and analogies alike make it difficult to think about what Dickinson's work really neighbors, to what traditions she may be related.[1] I read Dickinson's poetics of home as the outgrowth of her engagement with Romanticisms American and English, with male-authored texts and women's revisionary efforts. In so doing, I am perhaps temporarily shifting the focus of many recent feminist analyses of Dickinson's withdrawal away from biographical and generally social/historical determinations and onto more narrowly literary/textual grounds. This is in no way to deny the importance of such determinations; rather, it is to insist that literary texts and relations among literary texts express social relations, albeit (to borrow Althusser's formulation) with relative autonomy. Nor is it to draw a fixed line of demarcation between historical facts and literary texts; the new historicism reminds us that there is no way of reading texts directly out of "facts" without the interposition of texts. Rather, what I propose is a heuristic move, intended to revise the debate over Dickinson's withdrawal as it is now typically framed in feminist literary criticism.

The parties to the feminist debate over Dickinson's withdrawal to her father's estate, the Homestead, argue, on the one hand, that this withdrawal imaginatively liberated Dickinson to work or, on the other, that it was a costly assumption of literary "madwomanhood" that finally rendered her "helpless agoraphobic"; these positions can, of course, be dialectically combined with finesse and sensitivity. Wendy Martin argues the most optimistic side of the feminist debate: "By remaining single and living in her father's house for her entire life, Dickinson created a haven in which she wrote nearly two thousand poems. . . . In a historical period that required women, even women writers, to conform to standards of piety and purity that were inimical to the creation of enduring poetry, she created the conditions necessary for her art."[2] Her reading explicitly counters Sandra Gilbert and Susan Gubar's characterization of Dickinson as a "helpless agoraphobic," trapped in her father's house and in a fictive identity, acting out the madwoman fictionalized by other nineteenth-century women writers. They see Dickinson as the culmination of a nineteenth-century women's tradition of identifying the house with the female body, the tomb, and the prison; women's nineteenth-century "confinements"—to the house and the functions of maternity—turned the house into a "negative space" in women's Imaginary.[3] Following the connection written into patriarchal culture between home and female biology, Gilbert and Gubar find that "in the fiction of her life, a wound has become Dickinson's ontological home" and her poetry, a self-haunting house.[4]

For a recent philosophical critic of American literature, by contrast, the space of the house is neutral or neuter. Drawing on Kant as a philosopher of Romanticism, Evan Carton's study of American romance[5] persuasively links Dickinson's pervasive trope of the house-as-boundary with the epistemological quests of writers like Poe and Hawthorne:

> The issues of transgression (moral, conceptual, and linguistic) and the definition or construction of a home . . . are crucial and connected in American romance. . . . They will persist in this study, as they do for Kant, who later acknowledges that "the understanding is forced out of its sphere" by reason's need to complete its own, that the mind *commits itself* to an "unavoidable illusion." Against this bleak necessity, however, Kant once again pits the notion of the "boundary," skillfully and suggestively representing it not as a line of defense but as "a narrow belt" of mediation. . . . A boundary, Kant insists, "is something positive which belongs as well to that which lies within, as to the space that lies without the given complex." It is at once a division and a connection, the locus of relation.

In Carton's analysis, Dickinson's poetic project "defines this boundary in poem after poem." This epistemological home has nothing explicitly to do with a gendered social reality in which men and women are assigned different relations to the image that defines for Kant and Carton "the locus of relation." Unsexed and bodiless, the subject of the generically "American" romantic quest is in a position to idealize its material home as "a 'narrow belt' of mediation" rather than a site of labor or confinement or irreducible opposition.

These two strong readings by Gilbert and Gubar and Carton (whose work appeared after *The Madwoman in the Attic*) are each to each a sealed church, not yet communing. The criticisms to which each approach is most clearly liable become evident in their juxtaposition. Gilbert and Gubar can be faulted for amalgamating under the metaphor of a universalized female body (the symbolic "mother of us all") the specific frustrations of women whose situations, with respect to their writing *and* their bodies, were more particular and varied than Gilbert and Gubar's exclusive gender dimorphism can admit. The Imaginary (in a Lacanian sense) house of women's literary tradition represses difference within its own space, projecting it outward as an all-encompassing difference with a monolithic male-authored tradition. Carton's philosophical study, on the other hand, locates Dickinson within the house of American romance, bypassing issues of the social construction of gendered body, house, and boundaries.[6] His paradigm of home space as a mediating boundary is at once more nuanced and more abstract than Gilbert and Gubar's phenomenologically "negative space" of the imprisoning body-home, and, as we shall see, it does respond (as does Gilbert and Gubar's) to important currents in Dickinson's language of home.

The distance between Gilbert and Gubar's and Carton's ways of reading Dickinson's home space has been eloquently mediated by Helen McNeil. McNeil emphasizes that the function of the house changes from poem to poem in Dickinson's canon; while some of Dickinson's houses indisputably embody Gilbert and Gubar's gothic, feminized "negative space," others do not. Biographically and culturally, the house is heavily "overdetermined," a patriarchal space as well as the locus of women's labor. It is not neuter, but has masculine and feminine "facets," differently investigated in different poems. The architecture of the house signifies culturally as both a locus of masculine transcendental philosophical subjectivity (as Carton sees it) and of women's historically particular confinement to immanence (as Gilbert and Gubar see it). In McNeil's reading, Dickinson's choice of the house as a paradigm for boundaries reflects the way Dickinson experienced patriarchy in her family: "Since being in her father's house was a circumstance Dickinson considered beyond her control, the house is the most apt image possible (except perhaps the body) for writing about the borderline between inner and outer, between what one has generated and what is given, between present and past."[7] More so than the body, McNeil argues, which often "encourages an easy dualism" of inside and out (the kind of Imaginary dualism—more violent than easy—explored in chapter 3, above), the house allows Dickinson to devise "a highly innovative poetics of container and contained." Dickinson often strives to figure a house that is not Imaginary in the Lacanian sense, not "a house which is always resembling something in a mentality in which all ideas of resemblance originate in the mirror image of oneself."[8] The house can indeed (as we have seen) be an embodied prison, a tensely fraught either-or boundary of conflict with the others of identity. It can also be something else.

The something else—a different relationship to what is other, a different configuration of the relationship between the internal and the external—is the topic of the poems I will discuss in this chapter. In these poems Dickinson undertakes what might be called a cure of the house and its allied metaphysics of female identity. She reforms that specular and violent body-centered imaginary of women writers' identity without abandoning her critique of male-authored tradition. As McNeil's argument suggests, one of the things the house as a "borderline . . . between what one has generated and what is given" can figure is intertextuality, the relationship between the present writing and past writings. Both the outer world mediated by the house-boundary and the boundary itself are inscriptions made by prior texts, rather than ahistorical ontological givens of the human mind. Dickinson's poetics of the house revise, among other things, the way one woman's poetic identity intersects with the projects of male romantic poets, especially (as Carton's study suggests) their questing into nature. Her poetics of the house presents one alternative to the literalizing reversal of the quest, the kind of violent revenge, at times practiced by Dickinson and other nineteenth-century women writers she read.

The central trope of the poems I will discuss in this chapter is the organizing idea of a sound, usually melodic, overheard from within a human shelter that draws a fluid boundary for consciousness. Often these boundaries are silently understood to be enabling conditions of perception, rather than painfully present barriers. The house implicitly frames Dickinson's perception, and we are allowed to infer the degree of her separation from events she describes as taking place "abroad" (poem 321). The location of the author herself and the character of whatever construction shelters her are not always determinable, and this indeterminacy is fundamental to the shelter's power as a mediating boundary. Dickinson's sense of boundary in these poems may be historically analogous to, yet different from, that of canonical male writers of the American Renaissance. Sharon Cameron also finds that "the phenomenon of voice—that which exists but is not visible—offers an exemplification of why the self has trouble knowing the boundaries between itself and the world."[9] On the basis of her reading of male writers, Cameron suggests that this confusion is psychologically regressive and connected to a distinctively American poetics of violence and dismemberment, with British analogues confined chiefly to the Gothic tradition. Dickinson's sometimes violent representation of bodily boundaries, as Gilbert and Gubar have argued, is indeed related to a Gothic tradition that is perhaps central, not marginal, from the standpoint of many women writers. The strategies of voice and boundary discussed here, however, seem less violent; Dickinson more often connects violence to a specular confrontation than to encounters in which voice, however embodied or disembodied, enjoys primacy. Cameron's reading of male writers presumes a standard of individualism: the adult (male) self is firmly certain of boundaries between self and world, and anything less than this certainty counts as unhealthy regression. Dickinson's voices challenge this standard of identity and raise the question of how including Dickinson might complicate questions of what makes a distinctively "American" poetics.

In her strategy of overhearing sounds from within shelter, Dickinson draws on, while distancing herself from, a central issue of the male Romantic tradition. As John Hollander points out, "For the English Romantics, although steeped in a poetic tradition which acclaimed the significance and power of music, it is by and large sounds heard out of doors which are worthy of imaginative concern."[10] Natural sounds, unlike those of made music, fictively promised the imagination an original and unmediated encounter with the world. Sensual barriers constructed by habitual and conventional perception would break down from the outside and the inside in this encounter. As Harold Bloom has shown, one of the central Romantic hopes for this outdoor music was that it fulfill a longing "for a composite, originary sense that combined rather than opposed seeing and hearing. . . . The joy of what they [Wordsworth and Coleridge] considered to be a fully active imagination expressed itself for both poets in a combined or synaesthetic sense of seeing-hearing."[11] Poetic imagination for them, however, on further exploration, turned out to be the decay of this hope, a product of the struggle between hearing and sight rather than their wished-for synthesis.[12]

In contrast to the male Romantic investment in sounds of outdoor nature, Dickinson consistently hears outdoor sounds from indoors, within an explicit or implicit framing dwelling. And this is both more than the simple reflection of Dickinson's biographical withdrawal, significant as that was, and different from imprisonment within a gothically confined, nightmarish, self-haunted female space. Dickinson's posture of hearing, in these poems, revises the male Romantic plot of the errand into nature. To put it as baldly as possible, she goes nowhere, and yet nature is still there to be experienced in some way. It is there to be heard and overheard. Domesticating male Romanticism's outdoor music, Dickinson de-specularizes the structure of its quest romance. In Dickinson's indoor Romantic music, the characteristic Wordsworthian struggle between hearing and sight is often transposed either into the single register of sound (looking is not so privileged for her indoors), or into a synaesthesia of sound and touch, rather than sound and sight. In this latter synaesthesia Dickinson seems to retain (despite her renunciation of the male Romantic originary dream of a supersensual seeing-hearing) some claims for the independent transforming power of imagination as against simple, passive perception. Yet she does not wholly internalize the outside other (the natural phenomenon), any more than she is wholly estranged from the natural world by her withdrawal to the house—internalization and estrangement, Harold Bloom insists, being "humanly one and the same process."[13] Neither an object of nor an accessory to specular quests, in these poems Dickinson at home (home that becomes an organ of reception, an ear) selectively hears in Romantic nature what she can use, what she can lure into propinquity.[14]

The house in these poems also revises the dungeon of female Romantic imagination as delineated by Emily and Charlotte Brontë, who, like Dickinson, are uneasy readers of male Romantic poetry. Figuring the house as a shelter for the ear rather than as a dungeon in which one consciousness struggles for visionary authority against another, who is always already defined as the master, Dickinson moves away from the always-given binary terms of Emily Brontë's dramatic lyrics. Her shelter enables her, for intervals at least, to question, pluralize, and humanize the claims of the originary Master voice. She shifts attention away from the dualistic metaphysics of poètic identity (the aggressive Imaginary struggles of a fictive central consciousness against an other) to the rhetoric of poetic agency, discovering the figurative defenses that allow a poem to be written despite prior inscriptions.

An early strategy in this shift is parody. Dickinson plays with the situation of the central consciousness, bound to defend its inside against its outside, in a short poem spoken from the castle of consciousness with the voice of the royal "we":

> The Spirit is the Conscious Ear.
> We actually Hear
> When We inspect—that's audible—
> That is admitted—Here—
>
> For other Services—as Sound—
> There hangs a smaller Ear
> Outside the Castle—that Contain—
> The other—only—Hear—
>   (poem 733)

In a resourceful reading that takes the poem as nonironic, Albert J. Gelpi aptly connects Dickinson's "Conscious Ear" with Keats's melodies that play "Not to the sensual ear, but, more endeared, / Pipe to the spirit ditties of no tone" ("Ode on a Grecian Urn"). According to Gelpi, Dickinson in this poem transcends the mechanistic delineations of faculty psychology, dissolving them in an Emersonian " 'background of . . . being' ": "Emily Dickinson's conception of the soul went beyond the old categorical definitions of intellect and will, memory and imagination; to her the importance of these faculties was their function in the activity through which the sensibility penetrated and absorbed and reacted to the impressions that impinged without interruption upon the individual." The poem, in Gelpi's reading, exhibits a Dickinson "heartily" in agreement with Emerson's idealism of consciousness, his enthroning of the soul as "master" of its body and senses.[15]

Attention to the poem's language, however, suggests that Dickinson may be repeating Emerson and male Romanticism with a parodic, deconstructive difference. Simply reading the poem aloud sets the difference vibrating; the reader will struggle to assimilate Dickinson's puns, to assess aurally as well as visually the difference between "here" and "hear." The two great Romantic idealist metaphors for the poet's authority—the mastering, creative eye and the certainty of bardic voice—come quietly to loggerheads in this small poem. "Hear" and "here" are both alike and different; alike in voice, different to the eye. These homophones recall the "eye"/"I" pair in Emerson's famous "transparent eyeball" passage in *Nature*. In the course of Dickinson's poem, however, the difference within the pair widens to a critique of the ideology of the encastled, mastering, self-present consciousness. (The manuscript variant for "Contain," line 7, is "present.") Rather than dissolving consciousness as "mechanism," she accentuates it. This alienated soul virtually treats its senses as servants who do the soul's living for it. It reduces its body to a mere doorknob—the hanging ear—for consciousness. The encastled consciousness needs constant and slightly anxious in(tro)spection in order to know that it is alive. It privileges sight as the medium of its own self-reflections and holds such mere "Services—as Sound—" in contempt.

Yet the poem inevitably approaches readers through the despised medium of sound, as well as through the eye, and its language, as over and against its manifest content, subverts the hierarchies that rank consciousness over the senses, soul over body, mind over matter. The poem's conspicuous alliteration insists on the importance of sound. It first supplements, then subverts the hierachies of consciousness. Consciousness—the castle that contains—segregates below it the smaller service of sound and sense. Yet the subject of the verb "Contain" is not so clear as it might be. Is the soul unambiguously the "container" of presence, when it stoops to language—when, after all, it takes its metaphorical form, the "Conscious Ear," from the despised body? The "smaller Ear" hovers closer to the verb; consciousness only exerts its claim to be the subject of "Contain" through the despised medium of sound, alliteration. Finally, the two stanzas' play on hear/here/ear closes with "Hear," giving sensory process the last word over the protestations of consciousness as self-presence or self-sufficient "here"-ness.

Dickinson's poem takes the powerful Romantic ideology of solipsistic self-consciousness—which Dickinson's own withdrawal, of course, acted out in some degree—and linguistically undercuts it.[16] The body —for Emerson part of Nature's "NOT ME," against which consciousness defined itself—inevitably insinuates itself into the deliberations of the would-be separate consciousness. Romantic transcendentalist internalizations of the world, in this poem, entangle themselves in a language that refuses to sort itself out into signifier/"natural fact" versus signified/"spiritual fact," the hierarchy Emerson worked out in the "Language" chapter of *Nature*. Dickinson's punning, alliterative parody of Romantic encastled consciousness in this poem recalls the way she mimes (to borrow a much-debated concept of Luce Irigaray's) God the Father's "Verily" vicarious statements, and the point is similiar: the mediating incarnation of language deconstructs the authority of a self-present but humanly absent, disembodied voice—be it the voice of God the Father or the ideal Transcendentalist consciousness, "I" as "transparent eyeball." "To play with mimesis is thus, for a woman, to try to recover the place of her exploitation by discourse, without allowing herself to be simply reduced to it. It means to resubmit herself—inasmuch as she is on the side of the 'perceptible,' of 'matter'— to 'ideas,' in particular to ideas about herself, that are elaborated in/

by a masculine logic, but so as to make 'visible,' by an effect of playful repetition, what was supposed to remain invisible: the cover-up of a possible operation of the feminine in language." [17] Irigaray shares with Dickinson's poem the putting into quotation marks of the "visible" through repetition.

Dickinson's occupation of the castle ("the place of her exploitation by discourse"?) thus subverts its transcendentalist ideology of the relationship between the "perceptible" and "ideas," ideas and the body. (Dickinson's phraseology reminds us as well that the social analogue of consciousness as king of the body may be the happy cliché of nineteenth-century gender roles: "A man's home is his castle.") As Christopher Benfey remarks, "A major strain in Dickinson's poetry seeks an affirmation of the body," even if, as here, that affirmation takes the form of a double negative, linguistically subverting the body's negation. [18] Benfey admits that this argument is bound to strike readers "perversely," given the prevailing conception that Dickinson is a characteristically disembodied poet. [19] This conception may stem partly from reluctance to acknowledge the unconventional, startling, sometimes violent ways that Dickinson deploys conventions of the body. As Luce Irigaray and other French feminists would be the first to argue, it may also stem from the poverty of Western thought in envisioning women's bodies except as "the blind spot of an old dream of symmetry." In connection with Dickinson's ear-as-doorknob or doorbell, it is tempting to recall a twentieth-century controversy about a brass knob in another context: the infamous "little brass knob just beneath the middle of the mantlepiece" in Poe's "The Purloined Letter"—and remember, too, the connection Freud draws between a remembered "noise" and a woman's clitoris—her inner ear, as it were. [20]

Is there a Romantic alternative to alienating the body and nature in the interests of consciousness? Speaking in a more definitely feminine persona in a slightly earlier poem, Dickinson envisions a house and occupant that are more hospitable to sensual guests:

> The Wind—tapped like a tired Man—
> And like a Host—"Come in"
> I boldy answered—entered then
> My Residence within
>
> A Rapid—footless Guest—
> To offer whom a Chair
> Were as impossible as hand
> A Sofa to the Air—
>
> No Bone had He to bind Him—
> His Speech was like the Push

Of numerous Humming Birds at once
From a superior Bush—

His countenance—a Billow—
His Fingers, as He passed
Let go a music—as of tunes
Blown tremulous in Glass—

He visited—still flitting—
Then like a timid Man
Again, He tapped—'twas flurriedly—
And I became alone—

(poem 436)

Like the much more famous "Because I could not stop for Death—"
(poem 712), this poem is organized around a male visitor, but in
this case the visitor's power does not carry off the female speaker.
In Evan Carton's beautiful oxymoron, this is the romance of the "receptive quester,"[21] going nowhere and possessing nothing. Far from
disdaining the ministration of external sounds, the speaker courts
and hosts them. Her visitor's only being is in sound, the sound the
speaker reproduces in the assonance of her similes: "Like the Push /
Of numerous Humming Birds." For this speaker, the consonance between "Here" and "Hear" is as welcome as it was undermining to "the
Conscious Ear" and its hierachies in poem 733. Unlike the alienated
consciousness that confirms auditory sense impressions by subjecting
them to in-spection, the confirmation of inward sight (a kind of me-
chanical version of Keatsian synaesthesia), the "Host" of this poem
onomatopoetically recreates the original auditory sense impression
in her poetic refiguration of the event. Her similes (not the original
wind's presence, but a sensual re-presentation) do elaborate a form of
synaesthesia, but one that makes sound and touch, rather than sound
and sight, convertible: speech is a "Push," tactile; the visitor makes
music as one makes a delicate glass "sing" by brushing it with a wet
fingertip. Lower by convention in the imaginative hierarchy of the
sense than sight (the long-distance, comprehensive, mastering sense,
for Wordsworth as for Emerson), touch requires proximity, an ac-
knowledgment of (and contact with) materiality, consequently of vul-
nerability. Reason enough, perhaps, for the male visitor's timidity and
the speaker's complementary requirement of boldness. Touch denies
"the Conscious Ear" the privilege of regarding the body as a "smaller"
ear. The reward for renouncing this privilege, however, is pleasure, is
romance (in every sense of the word), as the tonal contrast between
the two poems can hardly fail to suggest.

In this poem, unlike those we looked at in chapter one, there is no

"Shylock," no father figure to whom Dickinson's language of nature must appeal for authority or currency. Indeed, the language of nature in this poem is not a hard currency at all, unlike the rubies and gold of other poems. In economic terms, it is a language of use-value rather than exchange-value: a language, as Helen McNeil puts it, "not subject to any contract, outside of the economy of 'gain.' "[22] Nor does Dickinson's wind as male vistor, the poem's muse, possess the distinct—if perfectly abstract and willed—individuality that she claimed for her "Atom"-muse in the poems we discussed in chapter 2. The "Atom's" identity was all boundary, in effect: that of a point with no concrete extent, knowable only in terms of its difference from all other points. A billowing cloud with no bone "to bind Him—," Dickinson's guest in this poem has no fixed boundary of identity. (Recall how Dickinson figured identity as prison with a metaphor of bone within bone in poem 384.) In a sense, then, putting this encounter with nature inside the imagined frame of a house allows Dickinson to revise the terms on which she represented Nature, the authority of a "Shylock," and her own poetic romance of a masculine muse in other poems. The poem illustrates what Helen Michie has defined as a persistent dream of (twentieth-century) feminist discourse: a language in which "the production of metaphor can take place without the phallus"; Dickinson's caller is masculine but notably not phallic.[23]

"The Wind—tapped" also rings changes on prior Romantic texts. Richard Chase suggestively compares Dickinson's "tired musician" to "the neo-Platonic or pantheistic spirit which the romantic poets heard strumming delicately upon the Aeolian harp."[24] And indeed Coleridge's famous poem on the Aeolian harp is structured, like Dickinson's, around a courtship scenario for the operations of nature upon consciousness:

> And that simplest Lute,
> Placed length-ways in the clasping casement, hark!
> How by the desultory breeze caressed,
> Like some coy maid half yielding to her lover,
> It pours such sweet upbraiding, as must needs
> Tempt to repeat the wrong! And now, its string
> Boldlier swept, the long sequacious notes
> Over delicious surges sink and rise,
> Such a soft floating witchery of sound
> As twilight Elfins make, when they at eve
> Voyage on gentle gales from Fairy-Land,
> Where Melodies round honey-dripping flowers,
> Footless and wild, like birds of Paradise,
> Nor pause, nor perch, hovering on untamed wing!
> ("The Eolian Harp," ll. 13–25)

Dickinson's poem condenses the courtship scenario of Coleridge's poem. Where "The Eolian Harp" features not one but two heterosexual couples (the pairing of caressing breeze with yielding harp doubles the human pairing of Coleridge and Sara), Dickinson leaves only the female speaker and the masculine wind. This leaves the speaker without an audience in Dickinson's poem: a typical situation for Dickinson, as we saw in chapter 1, since the sexual poetics of audiences in male-authored Romantic poems (Dorothy as William Wordsworth's listener, Sara as Coleridge's in "The Eolian Harp") apparently did not seem imaginatively accessible to Dickinson. Without an audience built into the poem itself, Dickinson narrates the wind's visitation in the past tense, rather than in the immediacy of the typically Romantic present tense. No other consciousness was there to corroborate or be receptive to her experience.

The contraction of Coleridge's courtship scenario in Dickinson's poem has other effects, however. Coleridge imagines the wind half seducing—that is, half raping—the harp. Nature herself is female, recumbent, violable; the active wind figures the Platonic "intellectual breeze, / At once the Soul of each, and God of all" that animates all nature. If the human couple in Coleridge's poem does not by any means act out this imagery without contradiction (Coleridge lies "indolent and passive," l. 41), still this gendered account of poetic imagination may have troubled Dickinson. In her poem, wind and speaker do not divide up along the lines of a passive/active, male/female, soul/body, supernatural/natural Platonic opposition. The wind passing through the casements in Dickinson's poem is his own harp, without need of a coyly passive female body to make his ministrations heard. And the female speaker does not merely vibrate in immediate response. It is she who acts "boldly," the quality Coleridge's poem attributes to the breeze acting on the harp. Likewise, the very pastness of the event in Dickinson's narration—the absence of another consciousness on the scene—helps underscore the female speaker's activity in the present. Her language reproduces the wind's humming assonance, and so recreates the pleasure of the encounter actively, for herself and her audience. Part of the poem's pleasure, for Dickinson and for a contemporary feminist audience, may lie in the way it preserves the Romantic pleasures of Coleridge's Aeolian harp while tactfully extricating those Romantic pleasures from the implicitly violent gender dualism in which Coleridge's poem embeds them. Tact is the leitmotiv of the entire encounter in Dickinson's poem: both in the sense of a politeness that does not clutch and in the word's original etymological relation to touch.

The departure of the visionary experience—a difficult moment, in

Romantic poems generally—comes more gently in Dickinson's poem
than in Coleridge's. Less happy in his poetic audience than William
Wordsworth was with Dorothy, Coleridge links his sexualized Romantic Platonism with guilt; Sara's punitive eye rebukes his ravished ear
and pantheistic speculations:

> But thy more serious eye a mild reproof
> Darts, O beloved Woman! nor such thoughts
> Dim and unhallowed dost thou not reject,
> And bidst me walk humbly with my God.
> Meek Daughter in the family of Christ!
> Well hast thou said and holily dispraised
> These shapings of the unregenerate mind;
> Bubbles that glitter as they rise and break
> On vain Philosophy's aye-babbling spring.
>
> (ll. 49–57)

Coleridge's docile female auditor turns on him, not to protest the
sexual politics of his myth of poetic imagination, but to reenlist him
into religious orthodoxy. Whatever pleasure the poet took in imagining the "coy maid half yielding to her lover" gives way before the
reconstitution of the family of the church, in which the lovers are
to walk as brother and sister in Christ. The noise of waters—one of
Wordsworth's and Coleridge's favorite auditory tropes for the combined voices of nature and imagination—diminishes to the "babbling"
of a mindless repetition.

   Whatever her distance from and disagreements with male Romanticism (distance and disagreements that varied from poem to poem),
Emily Dickinson would hardly have identified with Sara's punitive
role of chastising Romantic imagination with religious orthodoxy. If
no conventional sexual relationship is consummated in the wind's
visit with her, perhaps by the same token (unlike other poems in
which Dickinson pits human love against divine) there is no punish-
ing father in view, no guilt and no reparation made for the experience
of pleasure. (The poem virtually anticipates Higginson's account of
his 1870 visit to Dickinson at the Homestead: ". . . a house where each
member runs his or her own selves. Yet I only saw her.")[25] Dickinson
does not fall out of a realm of imagination with Keats's sense, in the
"Ode to a Nightingale," of being left "forlorn," collapsed back into his
sole self. The wind's departure leaves her, indeed, "alone," but not
forlorn. Dickinson's choice of verb—"And I became alone—," softly
emphasizes imagination's lingering aftertones; presence is not a gift
that the sensual visitor can immediately retract with him. Imagination
(Dickinson almost agrees with Hobbes) is departing sense.

Dickinson's way of listening to the wind within a homely "frame" recalls not only Coleridge's Aeolian harp, but the many poems Emily Brontë wrote on similar themes, several of which were published in Dickinson's lifetime.[26] As we saw in the previous chapter, however, Brontë's most ambitious poems often remain within the metaphorical or Imaginary "dungeon" of poetic identity conceived over and against (and therefore dependent upon) a spectral other. And, relatedly, Brontë's poems in this vein mirror "The Eolian Harp" in being shadowed by threats of punishment: poetic imagination in this framework seems inextricable from punishment. In many poems, Dickinson repeats Brontë in this oppositional figuration of poetic identity. Yet some of her poems framed within the house, like "The Wind—tapped," reach toward less violent and less dualistic alternatives.

The lines that Charlotte Brontë edited and published after Emily Brontë's death as "The Visionary" seem remarkably close in inspiration to Dickinson's poem. Like Dickinson's poem, Brontë's "The Visionary" tells the story of a woman waiting in a house for a lover-like visitation; eventually the male other arrives in the form of a wind. Originally an introduction to the longer dramatic poem, "The Prisoner," discussed in chapter 3, "The Visionary" appeared separately in 1850 in the edition of *Wuthering Heights* edited by Charlotte Brontë, with two final stanzas silently added by Charlotte herself. In its original form, then, "The Prisoner" / "The Visionary" made the association between the woman waiting in a house for inspiration and the woman imprisoned, the undoing of which I am attempting to trace out in Dickinson's work. In Emily Brontë's original version of the poem(s), the house narrative frames the prison dramatic narrative—but only on one side, giving the last word to the prison dialogue and suggesting the inadequacy of the house to conceal or contain the "dungeon crypts" over which it stands. The prison, for Emily Brontë, seems to be the repressed truth of the dynastic house. "The Visionary,"[27] which frames the world of the prison with the world of the house, is itself unexpectedly invaded, in the third stanza, by the dramatic rhetoric of defensiveness and defiance that rules in "The Prisoner" 's world of the dungeon:

> Frown, my haughty sire! chide, my angry dame!
> Set your slaves to spy; threaten me with shame:
> But neither sire nor dame, nor prying serf shall know
> What angel nightly tracks that waste of frozen snow.

For the woman speaker to dream and desire is automatically to call up the threat of punishment, in the house of the father. The concluding stanzas Charlotte Brontë supplied for the poem turn the "angel" more explicitly into a figure for imaginative power itself but continue Emily's association of imagination with defiance and punishment:

> What I love shall come like visitant of air,
> Safe in secret power from lurking human snare;
> Who loves me, no word of mind shall e'er betray,
> Though for faith unstained my life must forfeit pay.

> Burn then, little lamp; glimmer straight and clear—
> Hush! a rustling wing stir, methinks, the air:
> He for whom I wait, thus ever comes to me;
> Strange Power! I trust thy might; trust thou my constancy.

Brontë's stanzas throw the accent upon the power of the stranger and the speaker's rigid fidelity to his inspiring might; both fidelity and power are to be measured by the human snares opposed to them. While Dickinson's poem recalls a good deal in the situation of "The Visionary," she emphasizes her own role as "host" and makes no promise of fidelity. His identity does not, in the end, overshadow hers ("And I became alone—") as the "Strange Power" overbalances the Visionary's. Moreover, Dickinson's poem materializes the visiting male other, in auditory and tactile form, as a humming "Push" of air. Dickinson's muse comes to her embodied but not bounded, erotic but not phallicized; unlike Brontë's, he is not an identity upon which hers depends, not an identity that confines her to sole fidelity to him. Like the poems we looked at in the previous chapter, Charlotte Brontë's concluding stanza invokes the rhetorical figure of the chiasmus for explaining the relationship between the female speaker and her male "visitant" ("I trust thy might; trust thou my constancy"), and that rhetorical figure sketches the specular interdependence of the two identities mirrored in its structure. The figure of chiasmus suggests inescapable closure, imprisonment. So, too, the combination of "The Visionary" with "The Prisoner" suggests that Brontë's "Strange Power" is complicit with the powers of imprisonment. Not so Dickinson's "visitant of air."

Coleridge's, the Brontës', and Dickinson's poems about the visitants of air all turn on different Romantic ways of engendering the relationship between consciousness and its inspirations. That the Brontë sisters and Emily Dickinson, unlike Coleridge, engender this relationship within the imaginative confines of house or dungeon says much, as Gilbert and Gubar (along with others) have argued, about women writers' felt barriers to inspiration. For both the Brontës and Dickinson, the receptive consciousness is gendered as a woman waiting for a male muse, a "visitant" from nature. For the woman to be waiting within the house is to acknowledge a mediated, to some extent disempowered, relationship to nature. Yet there is room for difference and change within this paradigm; Dickinson's reception of her "timid" visitor is not the same, imagistically or rhetorically, as the Visionary's reception of her visitant in the Brontës' poem. Unlike some women writers of their times, neither Dickinson nor the Brontës, in these poems at any rate, want uncritically to celebrate the ideology that confined middle-class women to the home, nor even the familial relationships fostered there. While the gendered social division of nineteenth-century labor surely made its force felt in Dickinson's decision to keep to the house, Dickinson turns housekeeping into a poetic model of perception and reception: the house as ear, as permeable but protective boundary-organ.

What does Dickinson gain from this model of home space? Unlike the eye laid upon the windowpane and in pain (poem 327: the eye "put out"), Dickinson's ear seems metaphorically and painlessly enlarged by its situation within the sheltering house.[28] And despite her literal withdrawal from contact with the social and natural worlds beyond the confines of her father's property, the poems record a lingering engagement with the materiality of that world and of other people. Unlike sight, the distancing and mastering sense, which tends to register presence or absence absolutely (if sometimes erroneously), hearing seems to leave a certain residue behind it in Dickinson's imagination, like the elusive withdrawal of the wind in poem 436. The privileged Imaginary sense, sight, traces abstract boundaries of identity, whereas hearing embodies identity in less constricting ways. One of Dickinson's favorite tropes for the residual embodiment of presence in sound is "accent," the material quality voice or sound has above and beyond its lexical signifying function. This aspect of sound is to be desired, for Dickinson, but also to be feared, as a late quatrain suggests:

> The Treason of an accent
> Might Ecstasy transfer—
> Of her effacing Fathom
> Is no Recoverer—
> (poem 1358, version I)

Dickinson incorporated this quatrain into a letter of February 1876 to Higginson. In context, the lines may comment on Dickinson's gift of a book, probably George Eliot's *The Legend of Jubal and Other Poems,* or on the sympathy Higginson had extended to Dickinson in the loss of her father—or both.[29] Cryptic in either case, the quatrain links "accent," a quality of voice, to one of Dickinson's ruling erotic tropes, the sea. While accent is a mark of difference and individuality, too much of it is "treason" to identity; the ocean transfers, levels, flows, erases differences. Looking at the lines in context, perhaps they suggest that to hear the "accent" of the dead father's voice, or George Eliot's voice in her poetry, would level distinctions between self and other, reader and text, heaven and earth.[30] As a property of language, "accent" has much in common with figuration itself. Like metaphor, accent draws attention to the workings of language itself, foregrounding its own texture rather than its referential functions. It exceeds lexical identities of definition; it transfers meaning, ecstatically multiplying it, but to the point, perhaps, of losing it in a sea of blissful likeness. For voice to be flooded with too much "accent" would be the end of language.

Many of Emily Brontë's poems end in just that way. Overwhelmed by the "Strange Power" she has summoned, the speaker loses her own speech; as Margaret Homans writes, "Ecstatic mergence with spirit or wind takes place at the price of language and perhaps of life."[31] Dickinson defends herself against this possibility, however, by choosing to *over*hear accents—and I mean the prefix to suggest both her hyperbolic overvaluation of things heard and her refusal to come directly into their presence. Mabel Loomis Todd's anecdote about visiting the Homestead to sing for Dickinson illustrates this strategy as Dickinson lived it out in the last years of her life: "I used to sing to Emily frequently, in the long, lonely drawing-room. But she never came in to listen—only sat outside in the darksome hall, on the stairs. But she heard every note. When I had finished she always sent me in a glass of wine on a silver salver, and with it either a piece of cake or a rose—and a poem, the latter usually impromptu, evidently written on the spot."[32]

The poem Dickinson sent her, on the first occasion of these repeated performances, once again connects "accent" to paradise postponed, "Elysium" just across a threshold:

> Elysium is as far as to
> The very nearest Room
> If in that Room a Friend await
> Felicity or Doom—
>
> What fortitude the Soul contains,
> That it can so endure
> The accent of a coming Foot—
> The opening of a Door—
>
> (poem 1760)

"Accent" almost, but never quite, breaches the boundary between presence and absence, the here-and-now and Elysium. In Dickinson's later years, the quality of accent in voices almost replaces her earlier favored eschatological drama of the face-to-face confrontation. A prose fragment written in the last decade of her life and perhaps intended for Judge Otis Lord defines Dickinson's late erotics of the accent overheard: "[A group of students passed the House—one of them said Oh no, like you—the same vagabond Sweetness. I followed the voice—] You know I have a vice for voices—That way lies—(pleading lies) yearning—pathos—." [33] Embodying desire itself in the overheard "no" of a seemingly familiar voice, staying inside the House to follow the voice only in imagination, Dickinson ensures that she will never merge with the other's voice at the price of her own. As she wrote to Thomas Higginson in 1874, after his last visit to Dickinson's house, "The Ear is the last Face. We hear after we see." [34]

These are not only biographical choices, however; as I have suggested, Dickinson's strategies of the ear join her, perhaps consciously, to a body of Romantic and post-Romantic concerns about the relationship between perception and imagination. If many of the most famous conversation poems and odes of the male Romantic tradition, as Bloom notes, are structured around a complicated dialogue of sight and sound, through which the poet struggles to establish the authority of his own human imagination (greater than any single sense, or the sum of the senses), many of Dickinson's finest poems of nature limit themselves to nature overheard. The sound of waters typifies nature in many of these poems, in a way that recalls the "soft inland murmur" of the waters Wordsworth heard revisiting Tintern Abbey, or the "rapid river" that carries "sounds of inland life and glee" to the ocean in Elizabeth Barrett Browning's "Sounds." But Dickinson's waters are more inland still than Wordsworth's or even Barrett Browning's, and they often come from scenes that she cannot or will not recover to sight. As so often in Dickinson's work, these poems define themselves against precursor texts in part by what they leave out. [35] In "Tintern Abbey," the temporal distance between the remembered expedition of five years earlier and the present visit to Tintern Abbey, as well as the spatial and sensory distance between the landscape seen and the sea heard from a distance, provide Wordsworth's questing imagination with space in which to work. Imagination can invest now one, now another sense with power, or it can give the inward senses of memory priority over present sensory data. Dickinson typically gives her imagination far less space in which to work. Not only does she write shorter, less expansively meditative poems, but these poems usually represent her vantage point as fixed in time and space. She is not a quester or a "vagabond" herself, in these poems; the powerful male I/eye moving in nature, as we saw earlier, was not an assimilable role for her. Without Wordsworthian recourse to movement, distance, and the contest of faculties, Dickinson has a much smaller range of dislocations in which to invest imagination with power over nature—and nature, it will be clear by now, inevitably means the "nature" given to her through prior texts as well as the nature literally outside the windows of her father's Homestead.

What she has to work with is, first of all, the fiction of the house: an initial dislocation from nature that defends her imagination against absorption and allows her desire, at least, to be vicariously "vagabond." And the house allows her imaginative space to figure and refigure the sounds heard (and the texts read) from within its shelter, the way she turns the wind into a timid caller and his sounds into her similes in "The Wind—tapped" (poem 436). More elaborately figured, less "naturalistic" than Wordsworthian nature writing, Dickinson's language thus asserts its own human space of power against nature and against other writings.

The process can be seen operating, assimilating the pressure of an actual human male visitor and his writing into her own poetics, in the 1874 letter to Higginson that I have already cited, in which she tells her visitor that "the Ear is the last Face." Dickinson pays her visitor a compliment: "I was re-reading 'Oldport' "—Higginson's volume of sketches, *Oldport Days*—"Largest last, like Nature." Her comment is cryptic; perhaps she means that she was saving the longest of the essays for last, or that among the books she was reading at the time, Higginson's volume was the most important. Unmistakably, however, she praises Higginson's book for its likeness to nature itself. This praise leads Dickinson to a question: "Was it you that came?" Her answer to her own question takes the form of a poem (she sent Higginson only the final quatrain, perhaps deliberately withholding the poem's most forbidding lines):

> A wind that rose
> Though not a leaf
> In any Forest stirred
> But with itself did cold engage
> Beyond the Realm of Bird—
> A Wind that woke a lone Delight
> Like Separation's Swell—
> Restored in Arctic confidence
> To the Invisible.
>
> (poem 1259)

The answer is, implicitly, no: not Higginson but an impersonal, quasi-natural muse had visited her. Like a sleeper awakened by a wind rising outdoors, she feels "Delight" and "confidence" from the experience: delight with the sense of the wind's power, confidence in that power but also in the shelter that keeps nature separate and invisible. Earlier in the letter her description of Higginson's arrival and departure recalls the language she used about her visitor in "The Wind—tapped." "Of your flitting Coming it is fair to think. Like the Bee's Coupe—vanishing in Music." The point is clear: no matter what the value Dickinson placed on Higginson's personal visit, its meaning has been anticipated by, and will be subsumed into, her own system of meanings. Higginson and his text first become part of nature, but a nature from which Dickinson herself is adequately separated. Given that initial separation, nature can then be refigured in the mind's own terms: her "Arctic confidence."

The strategies of this letter and of Dickinson's poems of nature overheard, as we shall see, bring with them their own questions. Is there any check to refigurations of nature in these poems? Are these refigurations, like Emerson's idea of language in *Nature*, in some sense authorized by, and ultimately returned to, a spirit or idea behind the natural world—an "Arctic confidence" in "the Invisible"— or must they be guaranteed only by Dickinson herself? The distance these strategies set between nature and nature's listener forestalls the archetypal Romantic trap of merging woman into nature (as the letter suggests, in which Higginson, not Dickinson, is assimilated into nature). Dickinson would have known this trap not only through male-authored Romantic texts, but in poems authored by women whose work she read and admired. Emily Brontë's poem "The Night Wind" (so titled by Charlotte Brontë), for instance, dramatizes this fate. Here too we have a speaker awakened to a "lone Delight": the night wind at her window urges the speaker to leave her shelter for nature. She resists, telling the seductive masculine wind to

> "Play with the scented flower,
> The young tree's supple bough,
> And leave my human feelings
> In their own course to flow."

It is, however, too late for that. She is already a lover of nature, and for her, as for Wordsworth, human feelings cannot at will be disentangled from natural stimuli and natural metaphors (are feelings rivers, that they flow in their own course?). The wind answers the speaker's plea, and ends the poem, with a vision of the woman's death and burial. In a sense, this answers both their desires: the buried natural metaphor of human feelings "flowing" will end with the speaker literally incorporated into nature.[36]

Dickinson's often awkward mannerism, her distinctive "accent," defends her against the seductive, naturalizing language of Brontë's nightwind. Unlike Brontë's speaker, she does not ask the wind to go his own way and let her go hers, a hierarchical and dualistic strategy (as Margaret Homans notes) that inevitably exists to be undermined— her speaker's refusal only allows the wind more thoroughly to colonize her language. Nor does she abandon herself to a literal nature. Dickinson's poems let the wind in, not to resist its sounds but to refigure and refigure them. These conspicuous refigurations maintain Dickinson's powers of independent language and resist any literalizing merger with nature. If "accent"—figuration, overhearing, a voice without a face—represents paradise deferred, it may also represent the grave deferred.

The distance sounds can travel between their natural or human sources and their representation in Dickinson's poetry is the point of a poem written down around 1862. This distance—the speaker's inability literally to repeat something she heard—is a kind of fortunate fall for the poet:

> Better—than Music! For I—who heard it—
> I was used—to the Birds—before—
> This—was different—'Twas Translation—
> Of all tunes I knew—and more—
>
> 'Twasn't contained—like other stanza—
> No one could play it—the second time—
> But the Composer—perfect Mozart—
> Perish with him—that Keyless Rhyme!
>
> So—Children—told how Brooks in Eden—
> Bubbled a better—Melody—
> Quaintly infer—Eve's great surrender—
> Urging the feet—that would—not—fly
>
> Children—matured—are wiser—mostly—
> Eden—a legend—dimly told—
> Eve—and the Anguish—Grandame's story—
> But—I was telling a tune—I heard—
>
> Not such a strain—the Church—baptizes—
> When the last Saint—goes up the Aisles—
> Not such a stanza splits the silence—
> When the Redemption strikes her Bells—
>
> Let me not spill—it's smallest cadence—
> Humming—for promise—when alone—

> Humming—until my faint Rehearsal—
> Drop into tune—around the Throne—
> (poem 503)

The sound that initiates the poem cannot be categorized as natural or as human; the poem does not start with that opposition, unlike Brontë's "The Night Wind." "It" is other, but its otherness cannot be defined by relation to a source, only by difference (it is a "Translation" of other tunes—"and more—") and by unrepeatability ("No one could play it—the second time—").[37] If its "Composer" were to repeat it, he would be consumed with the melody, like "perfect Mozart" (Mozart was famous for being able to reproduce any melody on one hearing). The pronoun "him" (line 8), which logically refers to the melody, implies that the composer who could repeat this melody would disappear into it, even grammatically. This poem glosses another that Dickinson wrote around the same time, "I would not paint—a picture—" (poem 505), in which the speaker wonders about the consequences: "Had I the Art to stun myself / With Bolts of Melody!" The perfect coincidence of creation and perception, the Composer's ability perfectly to repeat his "Keyless Rhyme," might be death.

To go on living in relation to this "Keyless Rhyme"—since Emily Brontë's speakers all too often do not go on living in relation to their powerful inspiring sounds heard from abroad—is to abandon ideas of coinciding with its source, to abandon originary claims on it and go on telling one's difference from it. The speaker's inability to repeat the melody exactly is exactly what allows her to go on. If a male Romantic poet typically would prefer to originate sound, even at the cost of violating some natural order (compare Wordsworth's story of the Boy of Winander's calls, *Prelude* V, or the violent "crash / And merciless ravage" with which the boy in "Nutting" shatters the "quiet being" of his bower), Dickinson's language in this poem makes claims to strength out of the very secondariness of hearing. The idea of a "perfect Mozart," a godlike male creator, source and proper name for the unknown melody, is suggested only to be discredited. The dichotomy of absolute male creator/passive female perceiver does not hold in a world where, as Derrida puts it, "what is called perception is not primordial, . . . somehow everything 'begins' by re-presentation."[38]

Instead of reproducing the melody—by definition an impossible task—Dickinson elaborates its significance by analogy, signaled in the third stanza's "So—," which confesses its own distance from literal repetition. The next two stanzas of the poem temporalize the difference between ordinary "Music" and the unrepeatable better sound by projecting the difference onto the Christian story of the Fall. Once upon a time, children learn at their female caretakers' knees, nature was unfallen and its melodies more gorgeous. What we hear now in nature is a faint echo of that better music. The cause of all this, the children "Quaintly infer," is Eve's disobedience. Interestingly, what the children imagine—given the female environment in which, according to this poem, they are raised—is an Eden (a childhood) without a masculine father-god. Where "Mozart" stood in the first two stanzas, insert God: the perfect but absent, impossible male creator. For these children his place is, in a sense, taken by Eve, the "Grandame," and Dickinson herself. Eve, the Grandame, and Dickinson are each of them fallen in the sense that they inadequately repeat melodies or stories they have heard elsewhere. "Eve's great surrender" was just such a repetition: she imitated Satan's desire to be as God. The poem subversively insinuates, however, that such female repetitions, the stuff of our childhood, are all there is to know of Eden. Wiser and sadder children may forget them or take their "Anguish" to the church for consolation—not Dickinson. The "tune" she repeats is not sanctified by sacrament or redemption, she insists in the fifth stanza.

The poem's conclusion does not sustain this subversion. Instead, the final stanza relegates Dickinson's tune to a part in a greater, perfect music, presumably authored by the invisible God who sits on the throne. If she contains her tune faithfully enough, bearing it into heaven without "spill[ing]—its smallest cadence" (if there are no more falls), she will join the heavenly choir of perfect repetition. Dickinson's smaller music will then be perfectly contained in the greater. Like so many of Emily Brontë's poems, this ends with the female speaker's subsumption into a larger, culturally masculine power. If, to recall Helen McNeil's argument, Dickinson's poetics of the house are related to "an innovative poetics of container and contained,"[39] the ending of this poem retreats from the most innovative aspects of her poetics. A poem like "The Spirit is the Conscious Ear" questions the notion of an all-containing consciousness; the contained self-presence of consciousness is undermined by the differences in language (like the difference between "here" and "hear," a repetition that does not coincide with itself) through which consciousness asserts its own sameness. The ending of this poem, however, merges female repetitions—the fallen language of a possible earthly paradise—into a heaven of perfect sameness, collapsing the differences that made the poem possible in the first place.

Other poems on the music heard abroad, however, do not submit the speaker's voice to containment in a greater power, whether of nature or of a heavenly music:

Of all the Sounds despatched abroad,
There's not a Charge to me
Like that old measure in the Boughs—
That phraseless Melody—
The Wind does—working like a Hand,
Whose fingers Comb the Sky—
Then quiver down—with tufts of Tune—
Permitted Gods, and me—

Inheritance, it is, to us—
Beyond the Art to Earn—
Beyond the trait to take away
By Robber, since the Gain
Is gotten not of fingers—
And inner than the Bone—
Hid golden, for the whole of Days,
And even in the Urn,
I cannot vouch the merry Dust
Do not arise and play
In some odd fashion of it's own,
Some quainter Holiday,
When Winds go round and round in Bands—
And thrum upon the door,
And Birds take places, overhead,
To bear them Orchestra.

I grave Him grace of Summer Boughs,
If such an Outcast be—
Who never heard that fleshless Chant—
Rise—solemn—on the Tree,
As if some Caravan of Sound
Off Deserts, in the Sky,
Had parted Rank,
Then knit, and swept—
In Seamless Company—

(poem 321)

While this poem pays homage to natural forces, there is no question of the speaker's merging with them. She is doubly sheltered, first by the house from the confines of which she perceives the wind, and then by the language with which she represents it and humanizes it. In the first section of the poem, her simile for the wind's action is vividly tactile, like Dickinson's language for the wind in "The Wind—tapped" (poem 436). Like Shelley's "Ode to the West Wind," the poem seems to imagine the cloud-scudding sky as streaming hair, but for Dickinson the wind combs the sky, letting down not only clouds but "tufts of Tune—." Sound is a godlike touch. Yet the audacity of Dickinson's simile calls attention to the poem's language itself, ensuring that the luxurious seductions of touch do not collapse into merging or indifferentiation between natural realm and human speaker.

In similar situations, Emily Brontë's poems would often allow the wind to speak for himself, overwhelming and containing the voice of the female speaker; "The Night Wind," as we have seen, follows just such a plot. Dickinson's poetics of the container and the contained, in this poem, take a different course. She does not allow the wind to speak for her. Nor does she trace the wind back to a supernatural source, as "Better—than Music" eventually brings its "tune" back to celestial music. The focus here remains on the human use of the wind's "Inheritance." Again, as usual in Dickinson's poems of nature as music, this "Inheritance" cannot be reified, alienated, or turned into an object of exchange for "Robber" or Shylock. It is contained in a way too "inner" for that, "inner than the Bone—," and yet it is external and other at the same time. The wind's "Inheritance" amounts to a kind of permanent sympathy between what is contained inside and what is outside. In a kind of materialist version of an afterlife, very different from the resurrection she finally imagines in "Better—than Music," Dickinson imagines the dust inside a funerary urn vibrating responsively when the winds "thrum upon the door." The container or boundary, door or enclosing urn, that separates the human realm from the realm of nature, is precisely what registers the vibrations of contact and sympathy. The bounding, containing house is the poet's thrumming ear.

The final section of the poem pronounces a benediction in the tradition of Wordsworth's and Coleridge's conversation poems. Dickinson turns to another imagined auditor of the wind and begs grace for him, recalling Wordsworth's turn to Dorothy in "Tintern Abbey" ("Therefore let the moon / Shine on thee in thy solitary walk") and Coleridge's prayer for his son at the end of "Frost at Midnight" ("Therefore all seasons shall be sweet to thee"). As we have seen, the power of so mediating an imaginative experience for someone who has not directly experienced it is difficult for post-Romantic women poets to assume, for in male-authored Romantic poems it is typically women or children who are the beneficiaries of the male poet's experienced (in every sense of the word) grace. When Dickinson imagines telling the "Buried Gold" to someone else in her early poem 11, it is guilt rather than a blessing that comes with her language of nature. Insofar as Emily Brontë's poems invoking the wind typically end with the speaker's absorption into earth and sky (as in "Ay—There It Is!"), or in a dramatic dialogue in which the wind has the last word on the speaker's death ("The Night Wind"), the woman heeding the wind loses the human power of mediating her experience to others, in language. In "Shall Earth No More Inspire Thee," it is the voice of nature itself, "Genius of a solitary region" (as Charlotte Brontë's note put it), that offers a seductive benediction:

> Then let my winds caress thee;
> Thy comrade let me be:
> Since nought beside can bless thee,
> Return—and dwell with me.

Dickinson's contrasting emphasis in the second stanza of this poem on an active but bounded correspondence between consciousness (even after death) and wind, rather than a mutual absorption, seems to ground her power of Romantic benediction.

Unlike Wordsworth and Coleridge, however, Dickinson asserts no familial or particular relation to her imagined auditor in her benediction. Her wish for "Him" does not carry that "natural" authority of brother over sister, or father over son, that lends weight to the wishes of Wordsworth and Coleridge in their benedictions. Her poetic authority, like her imagined audience, therefore remains more abstract than theirs. Unlike the male poets, she does not insert her own imaginative autobiography of experience into her benediction, as Wordsworth tells Dorothy to "remember me, / And these my exhortations!" or as Coleridge rather differently laments the imaginative poverty of his own rearing "'mid cloisters dim."[40] Instead, her benediction describes the wind itself in terms of a remotely anthropomorphized "Caravan of Sound"—a collective personification, closer to the procession on Keats's Attic urn and the "multitudes" driven before Shelley's West Wind.[41] Less static and silent than Keats's urn and its verities of sameness, more recuperative and playful than Shelley's revolutionary spirit, Dickinson's "Caravan" is, like them, of this earth, rather than being contained by a larger heavenly music.

The sky is rarely a desert in Dickinson's poems about the sounds abroad. More often, as we noted earlier, it is a vehicle for the sound of inland waters—waters that "transfer" ecstasy (as in poem 1358, version I) or bear "Mediterranean intonations" to a landlocked listener:

> I think that the Root of the Wind is Water—
> It would not sound so deep
> Were it a Firmamental Product—
> Airs no Oceans keep—
> Mediterranean intonations—

> To a Current's Ear—
> There is a maritime conviction
> In the Atmosphere—
>
> (poem 1302)

Merely to be listening to the wind in Amherst, then, is potentially to be "Rowing in Eden." Like Shelley's West Wind, Dickinson's wind bears Mediterranean accents, but where his wind shatters and uproots, hers gives security of a world larger than Amherst: the Mediterranean, for Dickinson, was the place of hope's "blue Peninsula," Elizabeth Barrett Browning's romantic Italy, a warmer south. If not revolutionary, Dickinson's wind nevertheless challenges certain local pieties, at least. The poem's language alludes to the account of creation in Genesis 1:6–7: "And God made the firmament, and divided the waters which were under the firmament from the waters which were above the firmament." Why, Dickinson might have asked, did the Father leave the winds—active, desiring, sweeping—out of the story of creation? Verse 2 of the creation story suggests that God himself is wind, breath, or spirit, brooding over the face of the deep. This is a heavenly usurpation, however, that Dickinson implicitly corrects in her poem. The wind is her spirit, and she ascribes a watery rather than a heavenly origin to it; oceans, not the firmanent, promise the combination of fluidity and reliability that characterizes boundaries and identity in these poems written to "a Current's Ear—."

Another storm poem written about the same time also rewrites the Old Testament in naturalistic terms:

> Like Rain it sounded till it curved
> And then I knew 'twas Wind—
> It walked as wet as any Wave
> But swept as dry as sand—
> When it had pushed itself away
> To some remotest Plain
> A coming as of Hosts was heard
> That was indeed the Rain—
> It filled the Wells, it pleased the Pools
> It warbled in the Road—
> It pulled the spigot from the Hills
> And let the Floods abroad—
> It loosened acres, lifted seas
> The sites of Centres stirred
> Then like Elijah rode away
> Upon a Wheel of Cloud.
>
> (poem 1235)

The onset of the storm is signaled to the senses of hearing and touch (the wind sounds wet, but its onset sweeps dry), the senses Dickinson often presents as particularly attuned to the wind. Only as the storm retreats into the distance does it assume the retrospective outlines of a prophetic vision. On its way to becoming a vision, the storm allusive touches on Old Testament history from the creation of dry land and the gathering of the seas, to the flood, to the age of kings and prophets. A decreation as much as a creation, however ("It loosened acres, lifted seas"), the storm happily disturbs local "Centres" on its general way to renewing the world.

But who is the speaker of this poem, and what is her relation to the power she describes? After "I knew" in the poem's second line, she disappears: rhetorically, the storm becomes the object of a personification; grammatically, the storm becomes the subject of constructions (it "was heard") in which the speaker's agency is displaced from awareness. Looking to the biblical story of Elijah, however, a reader might indentify Dickinson with Elisha, who waited on the ground to assume the mantle dropped when Elijah "went up by a whirlwind into heaven" (2 Kings 2:11). With the mantle came "the spirit of Elijah," the power of his word, including the power to part waters and walk on dry land, and the power to cleanse the waters of barren Jericho: "So the waters were healed unto this day, according to the saying of Elisha which he spake" (2:22).

For readers alert to her allusive claims, then, Dickinson may have written a poem of naturalistic election, in which her own language inherits something of the wind's power to divide and heal nature's waters. While this poem thus displaces the question of Dickinson's own poetic identity and power, that displacement itself may be its strongest move, for it radically distinguishes Dickinson's text once again from Emily Brontë's characteristic invocations of the wind as power. In those invocations, all too often, the wind threatens to obviate the conscious perception of the female auditor who heeds him all too well. In "Ay—There It Is!" a third observer intuits the effects of the wind upon the woman who listens:

> "Yes—I could swear that glorious wind
> Has swept the world aside,
> Has dashed its memory from thy mind
> Like foam-bells from the tide"

Without embracing a full-fledged "poetics of renunciation," Dickinson's poem and others like it in her oeuvre eschew this total submission to overwhelming, otherly natural force. There is a house between

her and the storm—a house of rhetorical strategy, intertextual awareness, and allusion—through which she figures the wind's approach,
preserves consciousness, and is able to report the experience herself,
rather than leaving it for a third party to infer from her rapt silence.
Brontë's listener speaks only in a nonverbal bodily language of her
immersion in nature; her "altered cheek" and "eyes' full gaze" (recalling "the shooting lights" of Dorothy Wordsworth's "wild eyes" in
"Tintern Abbey") stand in for words. Dickinson, by contrast, removes
herself as an object to be looked at from this poem (as she often did in
social encounters during her life) and de-centers sight, leaving us to
appreciate the shaping, figurative powers of her word over nature.

Poem 1235 implies that the storm Dickinson witnessed elected her
to an untrumpeted but nevertheless prophetic identity. A very late
poem, probably written within a year of her death, swells this implication into a retrospective allegory of her poetic career. This very
considerable poem combines her typically visual metaphors of election, poetic and erotic—lightnings and noons—with her other mode
of overhearing sounds abroad from within a sheltered place:

> The farthest Thunder that I heard
> Was nearer than the Sky
> And rumbles still, though torrid Noons
> Have lain their missles by—
> The Lightning that preceded it
> Struck no one but myself—
> But I would not exchange the Bolt
> For all the rest of Life—
> Indebtedness to Oxygen
> The Happy may repay,
> But not the obligation
> To Electricity—
> It founds the Homes and decks the Days
> And every clamor bright
> Is but the gleam concomitant
> Of that waylaying Light—
> The Thought is quiet as a Flake—
> A Crash without a Sound,
> How Life's reverberation
> Its Explanation found—
>
> (poem 1581)

Struck by lightning, Dickinson is forever different from those whose
life is only owed to the dailiness of breathing. Yet her election does not
shun domesticity altogether; this very lightning bolt is what "founds

the Homes and decks the Days." Dickinson's wit concedes that internalizing one's original lightning inspiration can be a form of domestication, like the exchange of lightning for light bulbs, but it is a power that goes on living. Shelter is not to be despised. In this self-consciously belated state of life, sound—as much as (or more than) vision—testifies to the ongoing vitality of the original experience. Visionary gleams, scattered from that first bolt, continue to manifest themselves in synaesthetic "clamor bright." If, for Hobbes, all imagination was decaying sense, Dickinson suggests that an original sense-impression of lightning is changed, but hardly decaying, in her still-bright synaesthetic imagination. The thunder overheard rumbling still is what remains of "torrid Noons." Memory and imagination still connect Dickinson to an earlier self's desires; "Life's reverberation" confirms their persistent power. Desire and memory, "Crash" and "reverberation," found poetic "Homes."

Home, defined in so many ways by Dickinson, may best be characterized in this poem (and in the part of her career that this poem sums up) as a mediating boundary that, over and over again, returns sound to the speaker. Home returns to and revises the specular agonies of female poetic identity conceived of as a prison; election's bolt does not split the speaker into warring, self-punishing parts, as it does Lucy Snowe in *Villette*. This return, this repetition with a difference (the lightning is never repeated in the same way), creates the space in which meaning can be made of "Life's reverberation." Again and again, as the etymology of "reverberation" suggests, words can be found.

"The poetry of earth is never dead," Keats's famous sonnet proclaims. Joanne Feit Diehl suggests that Dickinson may have challenged these lines in a relatively late poem, "Further in Summer than the Birds" (poem 1068), that takes issue with "the benignity at the heart of [Keats's] poetic vision."[42] If so, at some time she returned to Keats's sonnet on the grasshopper and the cricket and to the "Ode on a Grecian Urn" to write her own elegy for the poetry of earth:

> The earth has many keys.
> Where melody is not
> Is the unknown peninsula.
> Beauty is nature's fact.
>
> But witness for her land,
> And witness for her sea,
> The cricket is her utmost
> Of elegy to me.
> (poem 1775)

Contemplating her own death and looking (as elegists will) for the appropriate mourners, Dickinson settles on the cricket who, in Keats's poems, sustains the sounds of summer even when winter has driven life indoors. In her own indoor life, "melody" became her most consoling trope for nature, Emerson's "NOT ME." If nature was melody, then the possible afterlife is not the rigid, spectral, eschatological confrontation between the Father's and a human face, but a more inscrutable absence—a place not of melody, without "keys." Unlike Keats regarding the urn, Dickinson seems unwilling to assert that the "unknown peninsula"'s unheard melodies are "sweeter" than those of the world she knows. If the earth's melodies are not absolute but plural, if they do not tell her that Beauty is Truth, still they allow her to say that "Beauty is nature's fact."

In Dickinson's poetics, however, "nature's fact" does not paralyze imagination before the givens of the sensory world. Perception is always already imagination, figuration, "reverberation." Another way to say this is that perception is always already intertextual (or historical). In this elegiac poem, as also in a note addressed to Susan Gilbert Dickinson, Dickinson seems to ring changes on Keats's letter to Benjamin Bailey: "What the imagination seizes as Beauty must be truth—whether it existed before or not—. . . . The Imagination may be compared to Adam's dream—he awoke and found it truth." [43] Joanne Feit Diehl points out that "what Adam found when he awoke was woman. . . . The Imagination engenders a distinct, antithetical reality: the creation of the feminine form out of the marrow of the masculine self." [44] Dickinson's version of this process does not employ the figures of sexual difference that gender and ground (if temporarily and ambiguously) Keats's fable of the imagination. She writes, "No dreaming can compare with reality, for Reality itself is a dream from which but a portion of Mankind have yet waked and part of us is a not familiar Peninsula—." [45]

Imagination's other place, afterlife or Italy, the "blue peninsula," is inside one's identity and outside it at the same time. Rather than rendering imagination as a retelling of the familiar and hierarchical relationship between Adam and Eve, Dickinson plays out her complex poetics of the container and the contained. Dreaming and reality exchange places as container and the contained. Rhetorically, the problem of containment is allied to the figure of synecdoche, the relation of part to whole. In Dickinson's fable of imagination, a chain of synecdoches—a portion of mankind, a part of us, a peninsula as part of a presumed mainland—keeps deferring the whole, of which the individual links are presumably a part. Keats's couple is, in ideological or

Imaginary terms, complete, as Dickinson's peninsula by definition is not. The internal-external difference the "unknown peninsula" represents (like the difference between the sea and her "unsown Peninsula" in poem 474) cannot be contained by projection onto binary sexual difference.[46] Like Dickinson's figure of home, the peninsula is a figure of connection as well as isolation, indeed a figure that deconstructs that binary opposition—a metafigure of synecdoche itself, undoing its hierarchical opposition between part and whole, container and contained. She could hardly have chosen a more apt elegiac emblem for her own uncanny poetry of earth and home.

NOTES

1. Barton Levi St. Armand's comprehensive study of Dickinson's cultural context, for instance, is organized around the premise that England and English literature was distant, and Amherst near, in terms of Dickinson's assimilation of cultural materials. See, for instance, his comparison of Oliver Wendall Holmes's "The Professor at the Breakfast-Table" against Charlotte Brontë's *Jane Eyre* as a model for Dickinson's "portfolio" verse; Holmes is "the closer analogue" because "fully American." *Emily Dickinson and Her Culture*, 5. Feminist literary criticism, on the other hand, has often been interested in identifying a women's literary tradition across national and period boundaries. St. Armand's method is, so to speak, metonymic (contiguity rules); the idea of a women's literary tradition is, often, metaphoric (likeness imported across distances of time and space). The idea of a women's literary tradition has its problems of likeness (see chapter 3, above), but Virginia Woolf reminds us that nationalism, even literary nationalism, may not explain women's situations. The daughters of the professional classes (which certainly would include Dickinson) are stateless in ways that their fathers might be hard-pressed to imagine. *Three Guineas* (1938; repr., New York: Harcourt Brace Jovanovich, 1966).

2. Wendy Martin, *An American Triptych: Anne Bradstreet, Emily Dickinson, Adrienne Rich* (Chapel Hill: University of North Carolina Press, 1984), 80.

3. Gilbert and Gubar, *The Madwoman in the Attic*, 87–88.

4. Ibid., 604, 624.

5. Evan Carton, *The Rhetoric of American Romance: Dialectic and Identity in Dickinson, Poe, and Hawthorne* (Baltimore: Johns Hopkins University Press, 1985), 8–9. Carton is citing Kant's *Prolegomena*.

6. Stanley Cavell, the best philosphical critic now writing on American literature, has recently come to wonder about the implicit gendering of philosophical issues hitherto regarded as universal, or at least universal, for "Modern Man." Skepticism in particular, or the problem of knowing—to which Kant addresses himself in the passages from which Carton derives the terms of his study—seems "a male business." Women may "get into the way of skepticism" but not in the same way. See "Psychoanalysis and Cinema: The

Melodrama of the Unknown Woman," in Françoise Meltzer, ed., *The Trial(s) of Psychoanalysis*, 248. Christopher Benfey's excellent study of Dickinson's relation to skepticism, *Emily Dickinson and the Problem of Others*, indebted to Cavell, does not directly address issues of skepticism and gender, although many of his insights are resonant in feminist contexts.

7. Helen McNeil, *Emily Dickinson*, 114. McNeil does not cite Carton or list him in her bibliography; her book followed very closely upon his. It is the more fortuitous, then, that McNeil's argument both parallels Carton's and makes effective rejoinder to his omissions.

8. McNeil, *Emily Dickinson*, 114, 115, 113. I would take issue, however, with McNeil's claim that the body, unlike the house, is not cultural and does not bear the inscriptions of the past (114). Chapter 3 above made a case for the inscriptions of other women's literature in Dickinson's textual "body."

9. Sharon Cameron, *The Corporeal Self: Allegories of the Body in Melville and Hawthorne* (Baltimore: Johns Hopkins University Press, 1981), 8.

10. John Hollander, *Images of Sound: Music and Sound in Romantic Poetry* (Cambridge: W. Heffer and Sons, 1970), 7.

11. Harold Bloom, *Poetry and Repression* (New Haven, Conn.: Yale University Press, 1976), 57.

12. Bloom's illustrative text is Wordsworth's *Tintern Abbey*. *Poetry and Repression*, 76–77.

13. Bloom, *Poetry and Repression*, 65.

14. See Christopher Benfey's chapter on "Nearness and Neighbors" in *Emily Dickinson and the Problem of Others*, 63–79. For Benfey, many of Dickinson's poems on natural subjects are "about a willingness to forgo certainty and knowledge, and accept intimacy and 'nearness' " (78).

15. Albert J. Gelpi, *Emily Dickinson: The Mind of the Poet*, 98–99.

16. Here my reading diverges from Joanne Feit Diehl's, for whom this poem represents an unquestioning intensification of Romanticism's "solipsistic inclinations." *Dickinson and the Romantic Imagination*, 43.

17. Luce Irigaray, *This Sex Which Is Not One*, 76.

18. Benfey, *Emily Dickinson and the Problem of Others*, 7.

19. Voiced most recently in Jerome Loving's *Emily Dickinson: The Poet on the Second Story* (Cambridge: Cambridge University Press, 1986).

20. Sigmund Freud, "A Case of Paranoia Running Counter to the Psychoanalytic Theory of the Disease" (1915), trans. Edward Glover; repr. in *Sexuality and the Psychology of Love*, ed. Philip Rieff (New York: Collier, 1963). For a feminist rereading of the "Purloined Letter" controversy and Freud's essay, see Naomi Schor, "Female Paranoia: The Case for Psychoanalytic Feminist Criticism," *Yale French Studies* 62 (1981): 204–19.

21. Carton, *The Rhetoric of American Romance*, 55.

22. McNeil, *Emily Dickinson*, 121.

23. Helen Michie, *The Flesh Made Word: Female Figures and Women's Bodies* (New York: Oxford University Press, 1987), 148. While this poem draws on a masculine, if nonphallic, figure in generating its language, another poem

in Dickinson's canon shows a similar metaphor emerging, in Michie's words, "parthenogenically from the bodies and texts of women":

> I saw the wind within her
> I knew it blew for me—
> But she must buy my shelter
> I asked Humility
> (poem 1502)

In a sense, however, even Dickinson's more phallically masculine figures of inspiration may be seen "parthenogenically," if part of their impetus comes from Dickinson's inspiration by the tradition of women's poetry represented in this study by the Brontës and Elizabeth Barrett Browning.

24. Richard Chase, *Emily Dickinson* (Westport, Conn.: Greenwood Press, 1951), 162.

25. *Letters*, 2:342a.

26. Margaret Homans brings these poems together and discusses both their published and their manuscript versions in *Women Writers and Poetic Identity*, 116–29.

27. Again, I am citing the 1850 text as edited by Charlotte Brontë because this is the version of the poem to which Dickinson would have had access. She certainly knew Charlotte's "Biographical Notice" to this edition; see Jack L. Capps, *Emily Dickinson's Reading*, 167.

28. Dickinson's eye ailments are, of course, an important part of the biographical record, if still somewhat mysterious medically (see Richard Sewell, *The Life of Emily Dickinson*, esp. 606–7n). But it would be pointlessly reductive to try to peg all of the texts under discussion here to particular biographical episodes of illness. Elizabeth Phillips surveys the poetic "personae" of Dickinson's eye troubles in *Emily Dickinson: Personae and Performance* (University Park: Pennsylvania State University Press, 1988), 60–75.

29. *Letters*, 2:450.

30. The quatrain exists in another version that may have been sent over the fence to Susan Gilbert Dickinson. According to this version, "the Treason of an Accent" might "corrode the rapture / Of Sanctity to be—": that is, anticipate (and so corrupt) heaven on earth. More pessimistic about the consequences of accent's leveling powers than the other version, perhaps this quatrain needs to hold its recipient more rigidly at a distance than does version I.

31. Homans, *Women Writers and Poetic Identity*, 124.

32. Cited in Sewall, *The Life of Emily Dickinson*, 218.

33. *Letters*, prose fragment 19, 3:914.

34. *Letters*, 2:405. Perhaps Dickinson's comment glosses the poem she enclosed with this letter, "Because that you are going" (poem 1260), which is a fine late example of her eschatological love story centered upon the vision of the beloved's face. As always, heaven for Dickinson lacks meaning "Unless in my Redeemer's Face / I recognize your own—."

35. For a stylistic discussion of Dickinson's modes of compression, with

illuminating comparison to her contemporaries, see Christanne Miller, *Emily Dickinson: A Poet's Grammar*, 24–44.

36. See Margaret Homans's reading of this poem in *Women Writers and Poetic Identity*, 124–29.

37. Christanne Miller notes that Dickinson often begins her definition poems with an "it" that defies straightforward definition. Often "it" is defined through negation. "*No* opens the doors that normal definitions close. Negation keeps the poet honest to her own sense of a changing world and experience, and it allows her to create her own boundaries of definition and meaning." *Emily Dickinson: A Poet's Grammar*, 99–101.

38. Jacques Derrida, *Speech and Phenomena*, trans. David B. Allison (Evanston: Northwestern University Press, 1973), 45.

39. McNeil, *Emily Dickinson*, 115.

40. Noting that Dickinson sent copies of the poem to both Susan Gilbert and Higginson, Ruth Miller persuasively argues that the poem responds to (though it may or may not have been composed in reply to) Higginson's queries about her reading and his suggestions for revision. "Let *him* seek instruction, *he* is the Outcast who has never heard such new song as her fleshless chant." *The Poetry of Emily Dickinson*, 74. Neither in life nor in her own imagination did Dickinson enjoy interlocutors quite like Dorothy Wordsworth or Sara Coleridge.

41. Joanne Feit Diehl notes that the Dickinson family copy of Shelley's poems bears marks that may be Dickinson's, including the page turned down at "Ode to the West Wind." *Dickinson and the Romantic Imagination*, 138. According to Feit Diehl: "If Shelley's world mirrors to serve his apocalyptic vision, Dickinson internalizes the forces that surround her, assuming their cosmic rage and power. Isolating images from their intended poetic structure, she places them within her own context, identifying the self as an antetype, the origin for all naturalistic metaphors" (158). While this accurately characterizes many of Dickinson's strategies, I think it is too absolute to do justice to the poems discussed in this chapter, which explore the (perhaps oxymoronic) possibility of a more fluid but sustainable boundary between self and other. Again, Christopher Benfey makes a similar point in his response to Feit Diehl in *Emily Dickinson and the Problem of Others*, 109–14.

42. Feit Diehl, *Dickinson and the Romantic Imagination*, 96.

43. Keats to Benjamin Bailey, November 22, 1817, cited in *John Keats: Selected Poems and Letters*, ed. Douglas Bush (Boston: Houghton Mifflin, 1959), 257–58.

44. Feit Diehl, *Dickinson and the Romantic Imagination*, 75.

45. *Letters*, 3:911. Prose fragment 2 is part of a group transcribed by Susan Gilbert Dickinson, and therefore it cannot be dated on the basis of Emily Dickinson's handwriting.

46. Helen Michie points out that synecdoche is the favored trope in Victorian literature for the woman's body. "Victorian novels are frequently about women's hands: hands that stand for hearts, and hands that are won and offered by themselves. . . . The synecdochal chain shifts the burden of female

sexuality away from the body as a whole." *The Flesh Made Word*, 98. Dickinson herself often deployed such synecdoches in anatomizing other women or even herself, sometimes to grotesque effect, as in "Rearrange a 'Wife's' Affection!" (poem 1737). In this prose fragment, however, Dickinson finds another way of using the figure of synecdoche.

5

"All we are strangers—dear—"
Elegy and (Un)knowning

"All *we* are *strangers*—dear—," Emily Dickinson wrote in the spring
of 1859 to Catherine Scott Turner, a woman she may have loved.
She imagines them simultaneously isolated from the world ("not acquainted with us, because we are not acquainted with her") and from
each other, "owing to the smoke" of a battle in which enemies and
friends alike are obscured. From behind this imagined veil, Dickinson
asks for intimacy and distance at the same time: an intimacy not necessarily contingent upon presence or vision, a distance not reducible
to physical separation. A century and a quarter later, Adrienne Rich
would cite this letter in her poem, "Spirit of Place," trying to say her
own *ave atque vale* to Dickinson's spirit. To do this, Rich recognized,
she needed "a place large enough for both of us" and, like Dickinson,
a veil—"the river-fog will do for privacy"—to achieve intimacy and
distance at the same time.[1]

The elegy is an essential testing ground for any idea of literary
tradition and women's particularity of tradition, as Celeste Schenck
has argued. For male poets, the tradition of pastoral elegy has stood
as gatekeeper to the poetic canon. The pastoral elegy is traditionally
"modelled on archaic initiation rituals of younger man by an elder"; it
"marks a rite of separation that culminates in ascension to stature; it
rehearses an act of identity that depends upon rupture." By contrast,
"the female elegy is a poem of connectedness; women inheritors seem
to achieve poetic identity in relation to ancestresses, in connection to
the dead."[2]

As my initial citations of Dickinson and Rich will suggest, in keeping with my readings of Dickinson's poetry and feminist psychoanalytic theory, I think it necessary to introduce a measure of distance
and difference into Schenck's eloquently proposed countertradition
of connectedness in women's elegies. I am not sure that the "female
funeral aesthetic" enjoys an "unsettling coherence," as Schenck suggests, "across centuries";[3] or at least it seems no more startlingly

coherent than do male-authored elegies through the centuries, especially as Peter Sacks's recent study describes the male tradition.[4] I see
more ambiguity in women's elegiac gestures of connectedness than
does Schenck, and less than an absolute distinction (although this
is not my main concern here) between women's connectedness and
men's rituals of separation. If identities are constructed asymmetri-
cally for women and men in patriarchal culture, as the new feminist
psychologies suggest, and if women's identities depend more on connectedness than do men's, still certain psychic processes inherent to
identification surely overlap between the genders, and not all women
accede to their gender identification in exactly the same degree of connectedness. (To think otherwise would be to subscribe to a thoroughgoing functionalism in the psychic realm, in which identity always
reproduces itself identically.)[5]

Women's resolutions of identity, broadly speaking, do differ from
men's, but also from each other's. So too may women's elegiac representations of identity differ in their degree of connectedness. Moreover, psychoanalysis and deconstruction, as we have already seen,
point to how difference and otherness inhabit connectedness. As
Dickinson's figuration of home as a receptive boundary suggests, what
divides may also connect; one may forge connections to otherness
through the bonds of difference and deferral rather than through an
Imaginary dream of sameness and simultaneity. Language as such,
language as it structures psychic possibility, may consign us to a different "dream of a common language," in Adrienne Rich's phrase.

The texts I want to explore are not all, strictly speaking, elegies
nor lyric poems, but they are all concerned with issues of memory
and psychic continuity. All contribute to an intertextual network, encompassing works by Emily and Charlotte Brontë, Adrienne Rich,
and Emily Dickinson, that does include formal elegies. They differ
from the traditional masculine "initiatory" models in that they fall
toward the middle or end of their authors' writing careers. And they
differ from most of the women's elegies cited by Schenck insofar as
they address other women as precursors. Schenck finds that "women
writers, lacking mentors, tend to mourn their personal dead rather
than predecessor poets."[6] These elegiac texts, in their varying ways,
constitute exceptions. In these works women writers elegiacally reread and re-present their own writing as well as other women's. Perhaps for this reason, questions of difference and power for these texts
are more acute than when women poets mourn their more strictly
"personal dead."

Is poetic space then at a premium—as Rich's language of "privacy" might suggest—even in a women's countertradition? Not in any simple way, in these texts; yet poetic power and its possession are still to some degree contested. The issues for these elegies seem to be: How "other" is my female precursor's power? How "other" was her power to her? If I connect myself with her, do I also connect myself to her possibly alienated or oppressed sense of the sources of her own power, and its relation to male precursors? In these elegies, connections can be dangerous, and separation is sometimes sought after, for a variety of reasons. Identifications are double-edged. These elegies, in my reading, radically qualify—without abandoning—what Schenck identifies as the female elegist's drive to connect. They relate the poet ambivalently to "the piece of us that lies out there" (Rich, "The Spirit of Place") or in the other, dead or alive.

Finally, these elegiac texts revise our understanding of the elegy's traditional relationship with sexuality. According to Sacks, the elegist's figurations of "loss and gain" must "work toward a trope for sexual power."[7] Sacks's paradigm for this work is, not surprisingly, the male castration complex and its resolution. If, as feminist revisionary psychoanalysis insists, women's psychosexual development is different (and all too poorly understood), do women elegists also work for tropes of sexual power, and, if so, how? Schenck approaches this question in her reading of Anne Sexton's elegy for John Holmes, "Somewhere in Africa," the only truly "vocational" woman's elegy in her essay. Sexton there indeed powerfully images her sexuality; the "God who is a woman" bears Holmes away in her hold. Maternity and female sexuality, in this troped consolation and consolidation of power, merge. But are there alternatives to the merging of maternity and female sexuality, which is after all the patriarchally prescribed resolution of women's psychosexual development? The elegiac texts I discuss here, by contrast, profoundly distrust heterosexual resolutions. And Rich explicitly undertakes to find other tropes of female sexuality, other resolutions.

Editing a selection of her sister Emily's poems for the posthumous 1850 edition of *Wuthering Heights* and *Agnes Gray*, Charlotte Brontë gave the final place to the poem now often known (through her title) as "No Coward Soul Is Mine."[8] She prefaced it with a note saying simply, "The following are the last lines my sister Emily ever wrote." In this poem Emily addresses the "God within my breast," exulting (in the final two stanzas) that

> Though earth and moon were gone,
> And suns and universes ceased to be,

And Thou wert left alone,
Every existence would exist in Thee.

There is not room for Death,
Nor atom that his might could render void:
Thou—THOU art Being and Breath,
And what THOU art may never be destroyed.

Charlotte's note and her editorial placement of the poem have probably done much to make "No Coward Soul Is Mine" the best known of Emily Brontë's poems (and one that was important to Dickinson; Higgins read this poem at her funeral), but Charlotte's strategies are a little deceptive. The last poem of which Emily made a fair copy may indeed—for all we know—have been "No Coward Soul Is Mine," but she *composed* the poem nearly three years before her death.[9] Charlotte Brontë apparently wanted "No Coward Soul Is Mine" to have the last word on her sister's heroism in the face of death—to be, in effect, Emily's self-authored elegy—and Emily seems in fact to have died in that poem's spirit, refusing consolation and medical aid until her last hour.[10] "There is not room for Death," the poem says, and Emily gave it none.

I would like to propose as a counter-elegy, however, the penultimate poem in Charlotte's 1850 arrangement, "Stanzas." More directly concerned with the traditional elegiac matter of memory and pastoral nature, these second-to-last words (as Charlotte, in her editorial role, cast them) movingly revise the account of female heroism that Emily and Charlotte collaborated upon in their writing and reading of "No Coward Soul is Mine."[11]

Often rebuked, yet always back returning
    To those first feelings that were born with me,
And leaving busy chase of wealth and learning
    For idle dreams of things which cannot be:

Today, I will seek not the shadowy region:
    Its unsustaining vastness waxes drear;
And visions rising, legion after legion,
    Bring the unreal world too strangely near.

I'll walk, but not in old heroic traces,
    And not in paths of high morality,
And not among the half-distinguished faces,
    The clouded forms of long-past history.

I'll walk where my own nature would be leading:
    It vexes me to choose another guide:

Where the grey flocks in ferny glens are feeding;
Where the wild wind blows on the mountain-side.

What have these lonely mountains worth revealing?
More glory and more grief than I can tell:
The earth that wakes *one* human heart to feeling
Can centre both the worlds of Heaven and Hell.
                                                  ("Stanzas")

The poet in "Stanzas" is rereading her own life and, implicitly, her own poetic production, with acknowledged difficulty. She feels "rebuked" for doing so since she herself is not sure that her own "first feelings" ("the fountain light of all our day," Wordsworth said, and "master light of all our seeing") do not amount to "idle dreams of things which cannot be."

Can her own life sustain a Wordsworthian retrospective? Unlike the speaker of "No Coward Soul Is Mine," who addresses a unified immortal power that leaves no room for death, doubt, or other existences, the speaker of "Stanzas" looks into a visionary realm without initial certainties. In "No Coward Soul Is Mine," Brontë protests too much that the immortal power really does reside within the poet's own breast: in fact, as Margaret Homans has put it, that "the spirit rests in her and she draws power from it is not an equal relation but a hierarchical devotion that operates only in one direction."[12] In "Stanzas," by contrast, Brontë admits to the uncanniness of the quasi-external visionary realm that comes "too strangely near," and her admission of the vision's elusive otherness-in-nearness renders her relationship to the visionary realm more equal. The speaker is powerful enough, by the third stanza, to get by the "shadowy region" with its "legion after legion" of visions (almost a poetic underworld); now she becomes a powerful Romantic figure, the poet walking, or rather wandering, since at this point in the poem she still must decide where she is going by where she is not. The "shadowy region" of the second stanza gives way here to slightly more determinate forms. The "old heroic traces" and "paths of high morality" refer Brontë back to her own youthful heroic poetry—perhaps even to "No Coward Soul Is Mine"—but these memories are still for her uncanny, like the "half-distinguished faces" of history, in part because they are implicated in the male literary-historical tradition of Byronic heroism. Brontë cannot, over the course of this poem, repossess these heroic traces wholly for herself, but it is a gain to know and image in this poem, as she does not in "No Coward Soul Is Mine," their cloudy, half-determinate, divided allegiance—to know, and keep journeying.

In the final two stanzas Brontë at last finds, so to speak, a place to walk: in nature, or in the nature of William Wordsworth's poetry of the "first affections." Marked by Wordsworthian ideas and his diction of "glory" (and vexation), this nature is not unambiguously Brontë's own in an originary, Edenic sense; someone has walked here before. Like Byronic heroism, nature after Wordsworth is intertextually marked with the "trace" of another, but the question of poetic power's connection to otherness in this Wordsworthian nature is at least posed differently. The wind of inspiration blows wild here without Brontë's defensive claim that she includes it, or that it includes her and all the universe besides. This poem does not rely upon invoking the (always dualistic, and potentially violent) boundaries between self and other. The Wordsworthian earth that wakes us to feeling "centre[s] both the worlds of Heaven and Hell" but leaves the poet free still to wander, rather than nailing her to the spot to await a visionary lover or mourn a dead one (as in the plot of so many of Emily Brontë's poems).[13]

The romantic figure of the poet walking works for Emily Brontë's freedom in "Stanzas" and leads her to a less alienating courage than that she proclaims in "No Coward Soul Is Mine" or other of her poems of "romantic imprisonment." And unlike Cathy at the ending of *Wuthering Heights*, the speaker here is still alive to know this glory. But the Wordsworthian romantic poet walking in nature is still traditionally alienated from both the nature he sees (using the pronoun "he" advisedly) and the society he leaves behind to go walking, as Brontë's defensive emphasis on *one* in the last stanza suggests. To what degree does visionary imagination transgress both upon nature and upon human or women's community? Over the course of Emily Brontë's career, Nina Auerbach finds, imagination transgresses indeed.[14] Brontë's elegiac rereading of her own poetic career, its dangers and attractions, is only in part an adventure in connectedness. Reconnected to her own "first feelings," she still insists on separateness in her reimagined freedom. But if connectedness is complicated in this poem, so is separateness. Separateness does not mean the isolation of a unified, self-present single self, the "*one*." The self walking here is in some ways divided from itself, other to itself, walking among the half-discerned shadows of its own younger dreams. The subject is, in a certain, difficult sense, a community even when it walks alone.

Emily Brontë died while Charlotte Brontë was writing her third novel, *Shirley*. As many readers have recognized, Shirley Keeldar, one of the novel's two heroines, is Charlotte's portrait of her sister. Among many remarkable visionary prose passages in the novel is a long prose-poem elegy for Emily that, among other things, seems to reread Emily's poem "Stanzas" while trying to come to terms with the alienation of Emily's self-figurations in this poem and in her other works. Although not the most celebrated of the visionary prose passages in *Shirley*,[15] this is perhaps one of Charlotte's best moments as a reader of her sister's poetry.[16] The passage is conspicuously lyrical not only in its elevation of style and use of the continuous narrative present, but in its underdetermination by its narrative context. At this point in the novel's plot, Shirley has nothing much to do but wander her house in distraction, reading and waiting for a man with whom she is secretly in love to turn up. Charlotte Brontë strews plenty of hints about the sources of Shirley's distraction and, later in the novel, produces the man by a stratagem that hardly pretends to credibility. What matters for this passage, however, is that the narrator here explicitly denies that her romantic plot in any way explains Shirley's visionary mood, marking this lyric revery as an unassimilable other in the narrative:

> At last, however, a pale light falls on the page from the window: she looks, the moon is up; she closes the volume, rises, and walks through the room. Her book has perhaps been a good one; it has refreshed, refilled, rewarmed her heart; it has set her brain astir, furnished her mind with pictures. The still parlour, the clean hearth, the window opening on the twilight sky, and showing its "sweet regent," new throned and glorious, suffice to make earth an Eden, life a poem, for Shirley. A still, deep, inborn delight glows in her young veins; unmingled—untroubled; not to be reached or ravished by human agency, because by no human agency bestowed: the pure gift of God to His creature, the free dower of Nature to her child. Buoyant, by green steps, by glad hills, all verdure and light, she reaches a station scarcely lower than that whence angels look down on the dreamer of Beth-el, and her eye seeks, and her soul possesses, the vision of life as she wishes it. No—not as she wishes it; she has not time to wish: the swift glory spreads out, sweeping and kindling, and multiplies its splendours faster than Thought can effect his combinations, faster than Aspiration utter her longings. Shirley says nothing while the trance is upon her—she is quite mute; but if Mrs Pryor speaks to her now, she goes out quietly, and continues her walk upstairs in the dim gallery.

The narrator claims that Shirley's vision owes nothing to any particular human connectedness. Even the book Shirley has been reading, whatever it may be, does not explain this elevation—or if it does, it does so only insofar as the book's authorship is attributable to something exceeding human agency. Charlotte bows to the uncanny otherness of Shirley/Emily's visionary experience, as Emily Brontë herself does in "Stanzas," but in a way that tries to cure this uncanniness, retrospectively, of its anxiety. Shirley reads and moves on, again like the poet of "Stanzas," without being wholly *authored* either by the book she sets down or by Charlotte Brontë's narrator, whose plot (by the narrator's own admission and desire) does not quite enclose her.[17]

Yet there is something to be gained from connectedness in this passage, for Charlotte Brontë as elegist has something to give to Emily's memory through the novelistic character by whom she remembers her. As we saw in chapter 3, Emily's poetry, along with *Wuthering Heights*, again and again imagines the world claustrophobically or agoraphobically or both: those on the inside wanting to escape, those on the outside wanting to get in (think of her mourners longing to enter the beloved's grave, or Cathy's ghost at Lockwood's window), each place defined as being not the other, the boundary of an impossible and violent desire. What Charlotte imagines for Emily instead is a less absolute architecture of remembrance, one that is inside and outside at once; an architecture reminiscent of Emily Dickinson's figurations of home. The "green steps" and "glad hills" by which Shirley's vision mounts are the same steps that lead her to her home's dim upstairs gallery. She can wander freely in an internalized nature and at the same time enjoy the protection of a human shelter.

Charlotte's reading of Emily in this passage is both generous and delicately poised. She softens the violence of Emily's struggles with the male romantic visionary tradition, while preserving an allusion to struggle in the narrator's reference to "the dreamer of Beth-el"— Jacob, who, on another memorable night, wrestled with God himself (in the biblical episode Emily Dickinson so often recalled). She provides Shirley/Emily with cosmic parents familiarly gendered as male and female, God and Nature. These parents have dowered Shirley, but no fixed marriage has yet taken place—no cosmic "crowning epithalamium" through which male romantic poets often figured the relationship between nature and the human mind.[18] Shirley is still free, although not without loss. The narrator glides over the pain of Mrs. Pryor and Shirley's mutual incomprehension; apparently there are no visionary human foremothers for Shirley. Still, Charlotte's elegiac passage makes a shelter for Emily Brontë while striving to honor her otherness, and it seriously represents at least one half of Emily Brontë's working poetic life, her *reading*, as an experience of power and self-possession serenely mingled with self-forgetfulness.

If the scene omits or arrests the other half of poetic vocation—composition, utterance—it still renders a woman in the full power of a vision out of the romantic sublime. And if we recall the romantic figure of the poet walking from Emily Brontë's own "Stanzas," we may think of composition as intertextually encoded in the scene's ending, which juxtaposes Shirley's muteness with her pacing. As Charlotte Brontë's narrator goes on pointedly to say, "If Shirley were not an indolent, a reckless, an ignorant being, she would take a pen in such moments"; as Emily Brontë, reckless being that she was, in fact often did. As Gaskell recalls the Brontës' work patterns: "The sisters retained the old habit, which was begun in their aunt's life-time, of putting away their work at nine o'clock, and beginning their study, pacing up and down the sitting room. At this time, they talked over the stories they were engaged upon, and described their plots. Once or twice a week, each read to the others what she had written, and heard what they had to say about it. . . . the readings were of great and stirring interest to all, taking them out of the gnawing pressure of daily-recurring cares, and setting them in a free place."[19] Charlotte's elegiac interlude recreates this free place. And silent as she is, Mrs. Pryor's presence may be indirectly helpful. Shirley replies to Mrs. Pryor not directly in speech but through the active imagination of her pacing. Relationships between women, the scene suggests, can encompass difference and still be enabling. The architecture of this elegiac passage respects distance as a form of connection.[20]

This communion of Shirley, Mrs. Pryor, and the narrator, elegiac and tenuous as it is, is better than Shirley's eventual fate in the novel. Charlotte's plot ushers Shirley into marriage through pedagogical scenes of reading as dominance and submission that alienate Shirley's own visionary powers from her more completely than the elegiac passage even begins to hint is possible. By the end of the novel, Shirley's visions are no longer hers to command; instead, she recalls her early dreams (in the shape of her ancient devoirs, her French homework) at the behest of a male master (the former tutor whom she will eventually marry). It is as if Charlotte Brontë's inevitably social narrative of the vicissitudes of female desire had to pay for the freedom of the elegiac lyric vision, including its implied freedom from heterosexual desire (Shirley there "has not time to wish"—for the absent lover, among other things). In the lyric passage, Shirley enjoys a mental and bodily "delight . . . not to be reached or ravished by human agency," a kind of pre-Oedipal, nearly prehuman, sexual plenitude overseen by the distantly benevolent parents, God and Nature. But what this prose-poem elegy proposes in the way of presocial female sexual delight, the narrative punitively disposes.[21] It remains for Adrienne Rich, invoking Emily Brontë and other female precursors more than a century later, to break up this unwillingly Oedipal narrative's resolution.

In the poem that closes Adrienne Rich's collection *Poems: Selected and New, 1950–1974,* "From an Old House in America,"[22] Rich takes farewell of her poetic career up to *The Dream of a Common Language* (1978), which openly announced her lesbian-feminism. This poem also marked an important step in Rich's (still ongoing) elegiac representations of her former husband, Alfred Conrad. Rich begins the poem's fourth section with an italicized and scrupulously annotated borrowing from Emily Brontë's "Stanzas":

> *Often rebuked, yet always back returning*
> I place my hand on the hand
>
> Of the dead, invisible palm-print
> on the doorframe
>
> spiked with daylilies, green leaves
> catching in the screen door
>
> or I read the backs of old postcards
> curling from thumbtacks, winter and summer
>
> fading through cobweb—tinted panes—
> white church in Norway
>
> Dutch hyacinths bleeding azure
> red beach on Corsica
>
> set-pieces of the world
> stuck to this house of plank

Why, then, this scrupulous appropriation of Emily Brontë's words? Like the poet in "Stanzas," Rich in this poem is acknowledging the difficulty of undertaking an elegiac rereading of her own life, a difficulty compounded both by the suicide of Conrad in 1970 and by the pressures that Rich's emerging lesbian identity exerts in mid-life upon her organization and understanding of her own memories. This elegy is thus clearly posed upon the threshold of defining new sexual powers, to recall once again Sacks's description of the male elegy— but sexual powers not encompassed by a heterosexual prescription from women's maturation. Borrowing the opening of Brontë's "Stanzas" in this section of "From an Old House in America," Rich at once admits to and displaces her own defensiveness toward the dead, her own guilt and need to return to the scene of loss. Lead by her female precursor, Rich ventures into a realm of half-effaced traces, elegiac inscriptions, the faded writing exchanged on old postcards that is Rich's counterpart to Brontë's "half-distinguished faces" and "clouded forms of long-past history." This trace or writing symbolically half-externalizes memory, suggesting that its power comes both from within and without the self. As Rich describes it, the impulse to the work of memory is material yet invisible, a palimpsest, rewriting over writing that is already there:

> I place my hand on the hand
>
> of the dead, invisible palm-print
> on the doorframe

On the doorframe, the liminal place, neither inside nor outside the house of self or history, this uncannily doubled handprint anticipates the involuntary return of memories through writing. But these memories, like the "old heroic traces" of Brontë's poem, are not wholly to be (re)possessed by Rich, because they are implicated with the power of a masculine other—once, for Rich, a living man, now a signature: the handprint, the postcards. Unlike Brontë in "No Coward Soul Is Mine," however, Rich refuses to take consolation or draw vicarious power from locating her being "inside" the masculine other, the other who, in Rich's case, has been subsumed himself into the powers of "Non-being." Rich's involuntary memories may be implicated with the life they shared, but not to the point of confusing life with death. On the threshold between being and nonbeing, she will look and listen, but not merge with the dead:

> The other side of a translucent
> curtain, a sheet of water
>
> a dusty window, Non-being
> utters its flat tones
>
> The speech of an actor learning his lines
> phonetically
>
> The final autistic statement
> of the self-destroyer
>
> All my energy reaches out tonight
> to comprehend a miracle beyond
>
> raising the dead: the undead to watch
> back on the road of birth

If this poem eventually becomes a ritual of connectedness, it depends also upon an imperative separation, dividing Rich from this ultimately alienated voice. Bearing Brontë's words with her into the world of the dead—a feminist version of Aeneas's golden bough—she returns from the underworld more knowing, and alive, seeking connections in other directions. Where elegies in the masculine tradition look forward to raising the dead ("So *Lycidas,* sunk low, but mounted high / Through the dear might of him that walk'd the waves," ll. 172–73), Rich prefers a feminist trope of birth. Yet she revises not only male-authored literary tradition, but that of many nineteenth-century women poets as well (including the Emily Dickinson of Rich's essay "Vesuvius at Home" and the Dickinson fascinated with the idea of resurrection), by turning away from tropes of power as a transcendent, otherworldly, overmastering masculine otherness. Behind the veil, that ancient metaphor of hope and disillusion, is not God or truth or power but nonbeing. Look elsewhere.

What happens, then, to the elegiac mode later in Rich's career, when issues of memory and community, power and sexuality, are addressed from a woman-centered (if not necessarily separatist) literary perspective? Several poems in *A Wild Patience Has Taken Me This Far* address the challenges of the work of elegiac remembering and re-reading within the bounds of an interpretive community of women.[23] I would like to conclude by looking at two poems from *A Wild Patience,* "For Memory" and "The Spirit of Place," which bear directly on the questions already addressed to elegy and memory within the context of Rich's earlier poetry. "The Spirit of Place," moreover, takes a long last farewell of Rich's haunting sister-other, Emily Dickinson.

Rich knows in "For Memory" that "there are gashes in our understandings / of this world"; she addresses another with whom she at one time "came together in a common / fury of direction / barely mentioning difference." To understand differences, there must be memory, and it must somehow be shareable. But where there is memory, can there be freedom to change? The poem concludes with an attempt to work out the difficult association between freedom and memory, difficult because (as in "From an Old House in America") the power of memory comes in part from its involuntariness, its estranging community of unconscious implication with things both past and other, hence not fully open to repossession. On the other hand, what else but memory holds a life together and makes retrospective conscious sense of even its most radical changes of direction—"that common life we each and all bent out of orbit from"? (This is also the problematic of memory for Rich's coming-out poems in *The Dream of a Common Language.*) Rich weighs memory's powers of estrangement and powers of connection in the poem's end, and at last she coerces an ideologically freighted choice between them.

> Freedom. It isn't once, to walk out
> under the Milky Way, feeling the rivers
> of light, the fields of dark—
> freedom is daily, prose-bound, routine

remembering. Putting together, inch by inch
the starry worlds. From all the lost collections.

To borrow Freud's and, more recently, Derrida's distinction between different representations of memory,[24] Rich here decides for memory as recollection (self-continuous, self-possessed, self-present, voluntary, laborious, communal, and prosy) over memory as trace, that is, as a writing not altogether continuous or self-present or voluntary, and communal only in the difficult sense of bearing witness to the voice(s) of the other(s) underlying individual identity.

Rich's decision has clear political pertinence and a kind of ethical insistence in scholarly terms as well. Feminist scholars, whatever the contradictions of that identity, all know that we should be working in the library all the time, scavenging in the lost collections and producing well-wrought prose, inch by painful inch. We all believe that the history so produced will re-member something important for women, will foster community by making difference historically intelligible; and we tremble at the self-aggrandizement besetting other, more romantically "poetic" ideas of freedom. Poetry's aggrandizing tropes of power bear a guilt toward history (certainly in the academy today, and perhaps elsewhere) that seemingly might be exorcised by a life spent reading in the American suffrage archives (as is part of Rich's project in other poems of this volume), by a voluntary ascesis disciplined through prose and history.

But it is also worth reflecting on what this poem says freedom is not. Why is it only "once" that one could walk out under the Milky Way, as Emily Brontë too walks into nature, but "always back returning"? What power or what tradition denies this experience repeatability? Part of the answer, as so often in Rich's poetry, seems to lie in this poem's revisionary stance toward her own earlier poetry. The ending of "For Memory" alludes to Rich's earlier poems about male figures of power and identification up in the sky, the most conspicuous example of which is "Orion" (written in 1965), in which she says to that alien being of whose nature she ambivalently wishes to partake:

> You take it all for granted
> and when I look you back
>
> It's with a starlike eye
> shooting its cold and egotistical spear
> where it can do least damage.
> Breathe deep! No hurt, no pardon
> out here in the cold with you
> you with your back to the wall.

In back of "Orion" and its evocation in "For Memory" is the male romantic tradition of the egotistical sublime, identified in literary history with William Wordsworth and characterized by a poetics of memory as trace rather than recollection, memory as involuntary, intermittent, and bound up with powers of repression. The Wordsworthian "spots of time" do ground a lifetime's worth of feeling but they indeed happen only "once," as Rich says by way of rejecting this poetics in "For Memory." [25] Already a tradition of alienated subjectivity even for men, the egotistical sublime is twice so for women, who traditionally do not have direct access to its involuntary, eruptive powers, but who, like Dorothy Wordsworth in her brother's poem "Tintern Abbey," have memory only in order to be a storehouse of male gleanings of power. "Remember me," Wordsworth says to Dorothy, "And these my exhortations." [26] The egotistical sublime for women, Rich suggests, is not freedom, not outdoors, not a place in which to walk out under the Milky Way, but just another confining patriarchal architecture. She indirectly repudiates what Emily Brontë does in "Stanzas," walking out in the company of Wordsworth, and chooses not to identify herself with the cold male hunter (a situation that again invokes Dickinson's poem "My Life had stood—a Loaded Gun"). Her work of memory chooses instead the libraries of prosy recollection, where prose encloses and confines poetry, binding its energies to the reconstruction of women's collective presence to one another.

We may or may not regret what "For Memory" does to the male tradition of the egotistical sublime, and we may not regret Rich's rereading of her own earlier "Orion" and its brother poems. But at last, I think, the attempt to separate memory as recollection from memory as trace, to deny an unconscious or repressive poetics of memory in order to reconstitute a fully present women's tradition (in literature or history) does not work, intellectually or practically. The always-othered nature of language, let alone human beings, may not allow it to work. It does not work that way, I will argue, in Rich's "The Spirit of Place," concerned with remembering the words of Emily Dickinson. And something important in Rich's own career falls between the cracks of the distinction "For Memory" draws—between what memory and freedom are not, "once," and what they are, daily and routinely. Between "Orion" in 1965 and its revision in "For Memory," came "Planetarium" (1968), another poem in which Rich symbolically reengages "Orion"'s problem of the starry male egotistical sublime. The quarrel (at least one of the quarrels) Rich has with the romantic sublime—its failure to relate visionary moments to the work of dailiness—was always a quarrel within Romanticism itself as well.

For Percy Bysshe Shelley or the young Wordsworth, not less than for Rich, the political question was and is how "Apocalypse becomes immanent; the sublime, a daily habit."[27] And Rich's visionary answer, in "Planetarium":

> I am bombarded yet   I stand
> I have been standing all my life in the
> direct path of a battery of signals
> the most accurately transmitted most
> untranslatable language in the universe
> I am a galactic cloud so deep   so invo-
> luted that a light wave could take 15
> years to travel through me   And has
> taken   I am an instrument in the shape
> of a woman trying to translate pulsations
> into images   for the relief of the body
> and the reconstruction of the mind.

If the speed of light itself is finite (fifteen years in the journey) when it travels through the instrument of the woman poet's body, then there is no imaginable revelation in the universe that is not continuous rather than ("once") instantaneous and unrepeatable; no power so alien and other that it cannot be translated into the immanent "relief of the body"; and, in political terms, no revolution that is not continuous. Rich uses scientific knowledge brilliantly to transform the romantic trope of light as instantaneous revelation into sustained political recollection. Of all Rich's many and searching representations of the mind of the poet at work, "Planetarium" perhaps rejects the least and transforms the most in the "battery of signals" whence its language comes.

Writing her elegiac "The Spirit of Place," by contrast, Rich discovers, or chooses, the limits of her assimilative and transforming powers with respect to Emily Dickinson. Like Charlotte Brontë in the elegiac passage from *Shirley*, Rich here remembers and rereads a powerful and difficult woman poet who resembles the earlier Emily (and the younger Rich) in her tendency to figure her own poetic power in the alienated form of a masculine other. Like Charlotte Brontë, Rich belatedly tries to give comfort to a woman who would not be helped to die. Dickinson's ghost, to use the (historically feminized) language of nineteenth-century spiritualism, needs help "crossing over" and until she does, she is dangerous: in Dickinson's own words, "I have but the power to kill / Without the power to die" (poem 754). Like Charlotte Brontë, Rich nevertheless tries to protect and honor Dickinson's strangeness. As traditional elegies often do, "The Spirit of Place" castigates the dead one's venal or inadequate mourners, in clearing its own space.[28] They are ready to hand:

> In Emily Dickinson's house in Amherst
> cocktails are served   the scholars
> gather in celebration
> their pious or clinical legends
> festoon the walls like imitations
> of period patterns

Rich wants to protect Dickinson from the academic industry of which Dickinson is herself the capital, the worldly literary critics who consume her words to foster their own legends and drink over her corpse in crass parody of Dickinson's observation that "A Word made Flesh is seldom / And tremblingly partook" (poem 1651).

But what, then, can distinguish the poet's own mourning from that of the bad mourners? Their oral greed is related, at bottom, to Rich's confession that she had "taken in" and brooded over Dickinson's "My Life had Stood—" (poem 754) for many years.[29] The gesture left to her is to stop taking. No more transformations of Dickinson's words, no more passing her signals through the poet's invo / luted body for revision and reconstruction. As antidote to the scholar's mixed drinks, Rich faithfully offers up Dickinson's own words, from a letter to her beloved friend Catherine Turner, italicizing them with respect for their otherness:

> and you   whose teeth were set on edge by churches
> resist your shrine
>   escape
>   are found
> nowhere
>   unless in words   (your own)
> *All we are strangers—dear—the world is not*
> *acquainted with us, because we are not acquainted*
> *with her. And Pilgrims!—Do you hesitate? and*
> *Soldiers oft—some of us victors, but those I do*
> *not see tonight owing to the smoke.—We are hungry,*
> *and thirsty, sometimes—We are barefoot—and cold—*

The scholars batten greedily on her words; Dickinson herself hungered; turning away from the temptation to consume further, Rich puts Dickinson to rest in privacy, like a daughter, a sister, a mother. The setting for this consciously revisionary ritual of mourning and of feminist intertextuality is a naturalistic underworld:

> This place is large enough for both of us
> the river-fog will do for privacy
> this is my third and last address to you
>
> with the hands of a daughter I would cover you
> from all intrusion   even my own
> saying   rest to your ghost
>
> with the hands of a sister I would leave your hands
> open or closed as they prefer to lie
> and ask no more of who or why or wherefore
>
> with the hands of a mother I would close the door
> on the rooms you've left behind
> and silently pick up my fallen work.

Freighted with dignity, self-denying, scrupulously faithful to Dickinson's own words, this elegy is nevertheless for me haunted by a Dickinson poem that it half-remembers, half-represses. Rich's choice of Dickinson's prose for citation, rather than her poetry, and the gesture of closing the door upon the older poet, uncannily recall Dickinson's protest:

> They shut me up in Prose—
> As when a little Girl
> They put me in the Closet—
> Because they liked me "still"—
>   (poem 613)

It is eerily as if Dickinson had anticipated Rich's motherly compassion and rejected it in advance. Dickinson's poem brings into sharp relief the double edge of the protection Rich offers her memory. Rejecting a sublime poetics (Orion, later in the poem, "plunges like a drunken hunter,"—a figure of this rejection) in favor of the prose of dailiness, Rich's architecture of remembrance is spatially more restrictive than the elegy Charlotte Brontë offers to Emily in *Shirley*, more housebound. Seductive as Rich's compassionate dignity is, something about words (Dickinson's own) escapes it. That room with the door shut, I would prefer to think, is empty.

"The Spirit of Place" is a ritual of separation as much as connectedness. Rich separates Dickinson's voice from her own both typographically and stylistically. As in "From an Old House in America," she insists on the necessary separation between the living and the dead, although in this case the dead is a woman and a precursor. Although she names herself Dickinson's mother, she does so in the context of a separation, untying the identification between herself and

Dickinson through the rite of mourning. In some ways, "The Spirit of Place" answers closely to Schenck's characterization of the male, rather than the female, elegy: it "marks a rite of separation that culminates in ascension to stature," although the stature here envisioned is, importantly, maternal rather than paternal. Moreover, Rich's elegiac separation uncannily recalls aspects of Harold Bloom's schema of male poetic careers, the kind of Oedipal schema Rich's poem and Schenck's essay seem to want to hold at a distance from women's writing. In Bloom's schema, the final revisionary ratio in the career of a strong (male) poet is labeled "apophrades," "the Return of the Dead," in which the dead precursor returns but in the voice of the living poet, who thus celebrates a triumph over time and "the return of the early self-exaltation that made poetry possible," inverting the subjection of his initiatory identification with his precursor.[30]

Rich diverges from Bloom's paradigm in crucial respects: she allows Dickinson to retain her own voice rather than subsuming it; she sternly disciplines any attendant narcissistic exaltation; and, to the extent possible, she wants to work within, rather than against, time. Yet there are points of similarity. Rich and Dickinson change places, as do Bloom's ephebe and precursor, in a chiasmus of poetic identity. And Rich could indeed be said to invert her "initiatory identification" with Dickinson, as she herself traced it in her essay "Vesuvius at Home." How far, then, does the poem at last partake of what Bloom describes as the central irony of the "great pastoral elegies" of the male tradition? "The later poets, confronting the imminence of death, work to subvert the immortality of their precursors, as though any one poet's afterlife could be metaphorically prolonged at the expense of another's."[31]

Rich's challenge to the conventions of male elegy is eminently serious and not in any simple sense self-defeating. Her differences are real. I would only want to suggest that there is difference within, as well as difference without—difference within the poems of individual authors and within any idea of a women's literary tradition.[32] For instance, Charlotte Brontë's prose remembrance of Emily in *Shirley* resembles Rich's elegy for Dickinson in its commitment to respecting the other woman's silence. Yet the Brontës (and Dickinson as well) remain committed (not uncritically) to a poetics of the romantic sublime that Rich deliberately, and for many reasons, rejects. If historically male-identified, this poetics nevertheless works in some positive ways for Charlotte Brontë's remembrance of Emily. Charlotte Brontë's elegiac passage offers a sympathetic rereading of Emily's romantic desire, as well as a hospitable place for it. *Shirley*'s imaginative flight and the mysteriously expansive character of the house itself[33] speak to

Emily Brontë's restlessness within the categories of inside and outside, nature and the house. Charlotte's lyricism, for a moment, figuratively disarms these categories of their cultural power over women in general. By contrast, Rich's very effort to revalue the historically female sphere of the house against the sphere of the romantic natural sublime in a certain way preserves these ideological categories and immures Dickinson's desire inside them.

Yet part of Rich's problematic distance from Dickinson in this poem comes from her need to see what has changed, and not changed, since Dickinson's time. The poem's mourning of Dickinson is enmeshed in a difficult context of mourning for history, for things done and not done. Rich puts history into this elegy—exactly what is missing from the female elegy in Schenck's reading of its changelessness over centuries. She connects her own public lesbian identity with Dickinson's passionate but still private and sexually undecodable letter, while respecting the historical distance between them. Rich also mourns, without resignation, the insufficiency of her own freedom in the Berkshire hills, and the existing liability of living things to violence.

> as it is   not as we wish it
> as it is   not as we work for it
> to be

What is at stake in these readings is the possibility of a nonidealizing "countertradition" of women's writing. The texts I have discussed here seem to me a fascinating concatenation of relationships; they make a powerful case for a "tradition," but not a tradition possessed of a mirror-like smoothness and coherence, the idealizing mother in which to discern the perfectly connected mother. This tradition encompasses differences among and within women, different readings of separateness and connection, different attitudes to and figurations of power. One of feminist criticism's anxieties today is whether this tradition can survive readings impelled by one version or another of the "hermeneutics of suspicion"—whether deconstructive, psychoanalytical, or marxist. What theoretical challenges to the metaphysics of self-presence, what forms of psychic ambivalence, what gaps between revisionary intentions in language and actual linguistic performances, what absences, what distances, what differences (apart from those with the male-authored tradition) can feminist critics entertain with respect to women writers? As Laurie Finke has argued, we need such theoretical challenges in order to understand the actual complexity of the "interrelationships" constituting women's texts and women as subjects.[34] Interrelationship, connection, is not the same as full presence or the absence of difference. Rich puts it best: we need some form of the "hermeneutics of suspicion" in order to think process and pain in identity:

> Ourselves as we are   in these painful motions
> of staying cognizant: some part of us always
> out beyond ourselves
> knowing   knowing   knowing
> ("The Spirit of Place," 1980)

NOTES

1. *The Letters of Emily Dickinson,* 2:349. Rich's "Spirit of Place" is in *A Wild Patience Has Taken Me This Far: Poems 1978–81* (New York: W. W. Norton, 1981).

2. Celeste Schenck, "Feminism and Deconstruction: Re-Constructing the Elegy," *Tulsa Studies in Women's Literature,* 5, no. 1 (Spring 1986): 13–15.

3. Schenck, "Re-Constructing the Elegy," 23.

4. Peter M. Sacks, *The English Elegy: Studies in the Genre from Spenser to Yeats* (Baltimore: Johns Hopkins University Press, 1985). Sacks's book—and particularly his provocative contention that the elegiac work of mourning-by-separateness applies "with similar force to both genders" (12)—helps impel Schenck's argument. Sacks's anatomy of the elegy is more richly suggestive for feminist criticism than either Schenck's essay or this chapter can show.

5. Jacqueline Rose argues this point in her critique of Chodorow's and others' "sociological accounts of gender," in "Femininity and its Discontents," *Sexuality in the Field of Vision,* 90–91.

6. Schenck, "Re-Constructing the Elegy," 15.

7. Sacks, *The English Elegy,* 32.

8. C. W. Hatfield, ed., *The Complete Poems of Emily Jane Brontë* (New York: Columbia Univ. Press, 1941), 243–44. I quote the poem in the version Charlotte edited and published in 1850, because one of the issues at stake in this argument is how Charlotte re-presents Emily.

9. Ibid., 243. The manuscript is dated January 2, 1846.

10. As Elizabeth Gaskell's *Life of Charlotte Brontë* (1857; repr. Harmondsworth: Penguin, 1975) narrates Emily Brontë's illness: "She made no complaint; she would not endure questioning; she rejected sympathy and help" (354).

11. The collaboration between Emily and Charlotte Brontë on "Stanzas" may have been more one-sided than Charlotte's attribution of Emily's authorship suggests. Hatfield notes that no manuscript of "Stanzas" survives and gives his opinion that the poem "savors more strongly of Charlotte than Emily, seeming to express Charlotte's thoughts about her sister, rather than Emily's own thoughts" (255). Sandra Gilbert and Susan Gubar, however, in *The Norton Anthology of Literature by Women* (New York: W. W. Norton, 1985), acknowledge "speculation" about the poem's authorship but declare that "the poem

seems to express much of Emily's characteristic vision," and print it as hers (751). I will treat the author, provisionally, as Emily Brontë; but the possibility of Charlotte's forgery (to put it strongly) underlines the problem of how literal faithfulness and connectedness to the dead (typical of women in Schenck's reading of women's elegies) perhaps crosses over, here, into literally claiming the signature of the dead—a powerful usurpation of the dead woman poet's identity and autonomous voice.

12. Margaret Homans, *Women Writers and Poetic Identity*, 132.

13. Brontë's more typically heroic mourning poems can be seen as the ultimate instance of women's insistence on connectedness. As Schenck comments: "In #182 [Cold in the earth, and the deep snow piled above thee!], Rosina even asks to die when Julius does, knowing that in time she will forget to mourn him: as that 'divinest anguish' of grief now defines her relation to him, it is as if she fears that ceasing to mourn would most threaten her sense of self" (24), whereas continuing to mourn (contrary to Freud's thesis) emphatically exalts her sense of self (as superior to "the empty world"). But the poems are more complicated than this would suggest. In fact the speaker of #182 says she has "Sternly denied [her young soul] its burning wish to hasten / Down to that tomb already more than mine!" And she speaks fifteen years after Julius's death. In the context of the Gondal saga, Rosina/A. G. A. is outstandingly successful in what Schenck and Sacks suggest is the *male* elegist's activity—figuratively and literally substituting new gratifications for old. She has it both ways: getting through (while gorgeously, orgulously mourning) lots of men. See, for instance, #110 (To A. G. A.), where A. G. A. figures a change in love objects as the substitution of sun for moon (eerily recalling Shelley's figurative love astronomy in the "Epipsychidion"). See Nina Auerbach for a more extended reading of what Auerbach eloquently calls "A.G.A.'s sin against relationship, and her gift to it as well." *Romantic Imprisonment*, 218. The character in the Gondal saga who best lives out what Schenck sees as a female will to stay connected, the inability to sublimate or refigure desire, is actually Lord Alfred of Aspin Castle, who kills himself for love of A. G. A.

14. Auerbach, "Emily Brontë's Anti-Romance," esp. 218–19.

15. Sandra Gilbert and Susan Gubar discuss the famous Eve passage of chapter 18 in *The Madwoman in the Attic*, 193–96.

16. Legions of critics have complained of Charlotte's treatment of *Wuthering Heights* in the preface she wrote for the posthumous edition of 1850. "An interpreter ought always to have stood between [Emily] and the world," Charlotte wrote in the 1850 edition's "Biographical Notice." Repr. in Mark Schorer, ed., *Wuthering Heights* (New York: Holt, Rinehart, 1966), xxix. Charlotte, to the extent that she could, assumed that role of interpreter.

17. Charlotte Brontë, *Shirley*, ed. Andrew and Judith Hook (1849; repr. Harmondsworth: Penguin, 1974), chapter 22, 373–74.

18. Emily Brontë's own poems often turn back the expected romantic epithalamium in one way or another; see Auerbach, "Emily Brontë's Anti-Romance," 220.

19. Gaskell, *The Life of Charlotte Brontë*, 307–8.

20. Mrs. Pryor's difference from Shirley is literalized inasmuch as she is not Shirley's own biological mother but rather Caroline's (the novel's other heroine). Psychologically, Mrs. Pryor's participation in the scene recalls the good-enough mother described by object-relations psychologist D. W. Winnicott, who can stand by—even be temporarily forgotten—while the child explores her separate autonomy. See D. W. Winnicott, "The Capacity to be Alone," in *The Maturational Processes and the Facilitating Environment* (London: Hogarth Press and the Institute of Psychoanalysis, 1965); and *Playing and Reality* (London: Tavistock Publications, 1971), 47–48.

21. Helen Michie also notes of this passage that "Shirley's visionary re-writings cannot sustain themselves; by the end of the novel her authorial voice speaks out only in schoolgirl compositions corrected and interpreted by her teacher/lover Louis Moore, to whom, like so many Brontë heroines, she defers as "master." *The Flesh Made Word*, 116. Within the novel's own narrative frame, this is true enough; but in the larger context of the Brontë sisters' achievement, something in this passage *is* sustained in my reading.

22. Rich has since reissued her collected poems in volumes incorporating later work, so that the special concluding force of "From an Old House in America" is no longer felt in the same way; even in 1975, however, one would have read "From an Old House" both as conclusion and as initiation.

23. I regret that I am not able to include a discussion of Rich's next volume, *Your Native Land, Your Life*, which begins with the sustained elegiac sequence, "Sources."

24. Sigmund Freud, "A Note upon the 'Mystic Writing Pad' " (1923); trans. James Strachey, repr. in *General Psychological Theory*, ed. Philip Rieff (New York: Collier Books, 1963), reinterpreted by Jacques Derrida in "Freud and the Scene of Writing," *Writing and Difference*, trans. Alan Bass (Chicago: Univeristy of Chicago Press, 1978).

25. Wendy Martin has also remarked that in these lines Rich is "rejecting the romantic exaltation in freedom from everyday concerns." *An American Triptych*, 220. Neither Wordsworth nor Romanticism, of course, so simply rejected the everyday. Neither Martin's discussion nor mine can do justice to Rich's complicated relationship with the ideological underpinnings of that particularly Wordsworthian Romanticism which sought exaltation as "A simple produce of the common day" ("Prospectus" to *The Excursion*)—one of the ancestors of Rich's own "dream of a common language."

26. See Margaret Homans's discussion of Dorothy and William Wordsworth, *Women Writers and Poetic Identity*, 41–103.

27. Thomas Weiskel, *The Romantic Sublime*, 50.

28. Sacks discusses this move in Milton's "Lycidas" and Shelley's "Adonais." *The English Elegy*, 90–117, 138–65.

29. Rich, "Vesuvius at Home." See chapter 3 above.

30. Harold Bloom, *The Anxiety of Influence* (New York: Oxford University Press, 1973), 147.

31. Ibid., 151.

32. On the political importance of thinking difference in deconstructive

terms, see Barbara Johnson, *A World of Difference* (Baltimore: Johns Hopkins University Press, 1987), 1–11.

33. Compare Lucy Snowe's apostrophe to imagination in *Villette:* "A dwelling thou hast, too wide for walls, too high for dome—a temple whose floors are space—" (chapter 21). Her vaunting lament for her love of Graham Bretton is cast in similar terms: "Graham's thoughts of me were not entirely those of a frozen indifference, after all. I believe in that goodly mansion, his heart, he kept one little place under the skylights where Lucy might have entertainment, if she chose to call. . . . I kept a place for him, too—a place of which I never took the measure, either by rule or compass: I think it was like the tent of Peri-Banou. All my life long I carried it folded in the hollow of my hand—yet, released from that hold and constriction, I know not but its innate capacity for expanse might have magnified it into a tabernacle for a host" (chapter 38). As Mary Jacobus points out, however, this dwelling may also contract into a prison in which Reason and Imagination alternately keep guard. "The Buried Letter: *Villette*," 59–60; see chapter 3 above.

34. Laurie Finke, "The Rhetoric of Marginality: Why I Do Feminist Theory," *Tulsa Studies in Women's Literature*, 5, no. 2 (Fall 1986): 252–72.

Index

Anderson, Charles, 61
Arac, Jonathan, 2–3
Armand, Barton Levi St., 1–2, 3, 40n.13, 76n.9, 114n.35, 147n.1
Auerbach, Nina, 106, 112n.10, 157, 172n.13

Benfey, Christopher, 45n.54, 124, 147n.6, 150n.41
Bible: Genesis, 64, 65, 142; 2 Kings, 143; Revelations, 62, 64. *See also* Eschatology; Higher Criticism; Jesus
Blake, William, 67; *The Book of Urizen*, 65, 66, 78n.24
Bloom, Harold, 1, 30, 120, 121, 169
Bowles, Samuel, 43n.33
Brontë, Charlotte, 84–85, 91, 102, 106, 121, 129–30, 135, 149n.27, 153, 154–55, 172n.17; works: *Jane Eyre*, 69, 75–76, 78n.28, 79n.41, 90, 114n.46, 147n.1; *Shirley*, 157–60, 166, 169, 173n.20; *Villette*, 95–97, 100, 103–5, 114n.46, 145, 174n.33
Brontë, Emily, 84–85, 91, 102, 106, 121, 132, 138, 153; works: "Ay—There It Is!," 140, 143–44; "The Night Wind," 135–36, 137, 140, 141; "No Coward Soul is Mine," 154–55, 156, 162; "The Prisoner: A Fragment" ("In the dungeon crypts idly did I stray"), 107–9, 129–30; "Remembrance" ("Cold in the Earth, and the deep snow piled above thee!"), 99, 114n.39, 172n.13;

"Shall Earth No More Inspire Thee," 141; "Stanzas" ("Often rebuked, yet always back returning"), 155–58, 160, 161, 165, 171n.11; "The Visionary" ("Silent is the House—all are laid asleep"), 129–31; *Wuthering Heights*, 129, 154, 157, 159
Browning, Elizabeth Barrett, 85, 91, 142; works: *Aurora Leigh*, 67–76, 78n.26, 79n.34, 80n.43, 87, 88–90, 94–95; "The Poet's Vow," 92–95, 97, 102; "Sounds," 133; "A Vision of Poets," 102
Browning, Robert, 89
Burbick, Joan, 45n.50
Byron, Lord (George Gordon), 106, 157

Cameron, Sharon, 6n.1, 112n.5, 120
Campbell, Colin, 42n.27
Capps, Jack L., 114n.34, 114n.41
Carton, Evan, 117–18, 125
Cavell, Stanley, 147n.6
Chase, Richard, 126
Chodorow, Nancy, 5, 59, 77n.18, 87
Cody, John, 4
Coleridge, Samuel Taylor, 92, 120; works: "The Eolian Harp," 126–29; "Frost at Midnight," 140, 141
Coleridge, Sara, 127, 150n.40

Dayan, Joan, 113n.23
Deconstruction, 1–4, 6, 30, 58, 173n.32
Derrida, Jacques, 6n.1, 137, 164